BLACKSTONE'S

LAW QUESTIONS & ANSWERS Q&A

LAW OF EVIDENCE

Questions and Answers Series

Series Editors Margaret Wilkie and Rosalind Malcolm

'A' Level Law
Company Law
Conveyancing
EC Law
Employment Law
Equity and Trusts
Family Law
Jurisprudence
Land Law
Landlord and Tenant
Law of Contract
Law of Evidence
Law of Torts

Other titles in preparation

LAW OF EVIDENCE

CHRIS CHANG
LLB, Barrister

MAUREEN SPENCER
BA (Oxon), LLM, Barrister

JOHN SPENCER
MA (Oxon), LLM, Barrister

First published in Great Britain 1996 by Blackstone Press Limited, 9-15 Aldine Street, London W12 8AW. Telephone: 0181-740 1173

ISBN: 1 85431 496 3

British Library Cataloguing in Publication Data
A CIP catalogue record for this book is available from the British Library

Typeset by Montage Studios Limited, Tonbridge, Kent
Printed by Bell & Bain Limited, Glasgow

Contents

Preface

'So what's the answer?' said Laura, a rather literal-minded girl who wrote down everything Robyn said in tutorials. 'Is it a train or a tram?'
'Both or either,' said Robyn. 'It doesn't really matter. Go on Marion.'
'Hang about,' said Vic. 'You can't have it both ways.'
Nice Work by David Lodge (Secker & Warburg, London 1988)

Like David Lodge's fictional English Literature tutor, Evidence teachers are fonder of setting questions than giving answers. But in these days of modularisation and semesterisation, not to mention larger classes, students do sometimes need ready access to the answers outside the lecture theatre or the seminar room. The authors believe there is a place for modest study aids like this book. It does not pretend to replace the standard Evidence textbooks or the great practitioners' manuals as a source of authoritative information yet will be more portable and perhaps more accessible to the student in a hurry.

We wish to thank colleagues and students at Middlesex University Business School, particularly John Weldon whose notes on answering questions were very helpful. Michael Glaser made a number of useful suggestions for which we are grateful.

Chris Chang
Maureen Spencer
John Spencer
February 1996

Table of Cases

Table of Statutes

1 Introduction

Evidence is often regarded as one of the trickier subjects studied in undergraduate law courses. It is a mixture of arcane old rules and opaque new statutes and sometimes seems to offend common sense. Technical precepts are intermingled with judicial discretion and matters of high constitutional principle. So questions can range from the complex details of the application of the rule against hearsay to issues of principle such as protection of the right against self-incrimination.

Some students find it helpful to see how other people deal with answering problems and writing essays. Question and Answer books can make the reader feel superior because he or she could have done much better, or depressed at the thought of trying to get so much information onto paper in 40 minutes under examination conditions. The answers in this book are not meant to be model answers but to help the student understand the topic and see how it should be approached. One of the skills which law students have to acquire is the art of doing well in examinations. This is not merely a matter of knowing the subject, but requires self-organisation and a disciplined approach to the task of writing the examination itself. Obviously, students should reach the examination hall with an adequate knowledge of their subject. The problem so often is putting that knowledge to proper use once they get there.

Put crudely, the examinee's objective in any examination is to accumulate in the time allowed as many marks as possible. To be manageable this task needs to be broken down into three stages: planning, execution and review.

First, planning. Make sure you arrive at the examination hall in time, with adequate equipment, including statute books if these are allowed in the hall.

When you are given the examination paper, read it, read the rubric (the instructions at the top of the paper) carefully, then take five minutes to read the paper itself right through. Turn it over to make sure there's nothing on the back you have missed. You will usually be required to answer a set number of questions (say four out of ten). You must answer the number of questions required. A surprising number of candidates fail because they answer fewer questions than required. There is very little the examiner can do even for a good candidate in this position. Most papers are marked between 40 and 70 per cent, so if four questions are required and you have produced only three brilliant answers you will have a mediocre grade. If your answers are average you will have failed. You may also be required to choose one or more questions from a particular section of the paper. At this point you should begin to pick out the questions you will answer. If, for example, you have always found presumptions a source of confusion, this is no time to try and clarify your mind by answering a question about them. Try and pick the questions to display what you know, even if that is not a great deal.

Having chosen the required number of questions try and sketch out in telegraphic note form your answer to each. In problem questions in law examinations this is very often a matter of spotting the issues, as several different areas of the subject are mixed together. If at this point you can recall the names of the cases which are authority for particular propositions in the area concerned, all the better. If you can't, pass onto the next of your chosen questions. By the end of this process, which should not take more than perhaps 20 minutes, you will have sketched out in rough form your answer to each of your chosen questions. Many of your fellow examinees will already be scribbling frantically. Don't panic. Before you go to the stage of execution make a simple calculation. Take the length of the examination in minutes (180 minutes for the classic three-hour examination). Subtract the time you have spent on the planning stage (perhaps 25 minutes) and allow five minutes review time for the end of the examination. Then divide the remainder equally between the questions you have chosen. So if the examination started at 9.00 and you were asked to answer four questions you would have 150/4 = 37 minutes to answer each question. If you start your first answer at 9.30, you should begin your next at 10.07, your third at 10.44, and your fourth at 11.21. Write those times down.

Now you can start writing your first answer. If you think your handwriting is easy to read, remember that the examiner will have dozens if not hundreds of scripts to deal with and is unlikely to look kindly on any candidate whose script needs to be decyphered. So come armed with a good pen, and write clearly.

Break your answer into paragraphs, underline the names of cases and don't write in the margins.

It is very important to remember that the examiner is interested in what you do know, not what you don't know. So if you are uncertain about a particular point, it is generally better to put down what you think is the answer, provided it is relevant to answering the question. If you are right, you will gain marks, if you are wrong you will usually not have marks taken away. Don't be tempted to exceed your time limit. You are more likely to pick up marks at the beginning of your answer than at the end. Once your self-imposed time limit is up, stop writing and go on the next question. It is poor time management to chase one or two extra marks on question three and leave yourself short of time to accumulate the marks you need on question four. If necessary start the next question in a different answer book so that you have space to come back to the previous question during your review period at the end of the examination.

When the time gets to 10.45 your concentration may start to sag. It is at this point that you will appreciate having made your sketch answer to your third question at the beginning of the examination period. Your fellow examinees who rushed to get pen to paper at the start of the examination will be flagging too, but they won't have tried to think through the issues in the question when they were fresh. Your aim will be to get as many marks for your last answer as for your first.

The approach required to answering questions will vary with the type of question. There are broadly two types you will encounter in Evidence examinations: problems and essays. Briefly, in answering problem questions, the student must first identify the areas of law in which the problem falls. Almost invariably, there will be more than one issue and it is important that you identify them at the start. Having done so, you should be able to outline the legal principles which are relevant to the issues in the problem, citing the relevant cases and statutes. Ideally, citations should include the principle on which the case was decided, the significant facts which explain the principle and the name of the case. But examiners do recognise that case names can be forgotten under the stress of examination and will probably be reasonably satisfied if the examinee can give the relevant principle and facts. The next stage is to apply these authorities to the facts. This involves discussion of the facts in the light of the relevant principles, analysis of the facts to select which are significant, and where appropriate, a comparison of the problems' facts with those of the authorities, in such a way as to support your argument. Finally, come to a practical conclusion, which need not be a definitive answer, may suggest more than one alternative and should where necessary indicate what additional factual material would be required to give a definitive response.

A different approach is required when answering essay questions. Very often these are related to current controversies in the field. As part of your revision you should spend an afternoon in the library glancing through recent issues of legal journals, e.g., *Criminal Law Review*, *New Law Journal*, *Law Quarterly Review*, *Solicitors Journal*. Make a note of topics in the field of Evidence which have drawn academic comment. In many cases, this will be where your examiner will have looked when trying to put together a question. This background reading may also help you to see what the examiner is looking for in answer to his essay question. You should analyse the question to establish whether you are asked to discuss, explain or criticise a particular area of the law. You should not attempt an essay question unless you are clear what it is asking for.

We hope this book will give some idea of what your answers in Evidence ought to look like. The authors aim to give some practical guidance on handling specific issues which should be fairly typical of those likely to come up on an undergraduate examination paper. It is not a substitute for a textbook and though efforts have been made to cover the typical syllabus it cannot claim to be exhaustive. To some extent the format is rather artificial because each topic in evidence has been treated discretely except for the mixed questions at the end. In practice, examination questions usually contain several issues taken from different parts of the syllabus and part of the examiners' aim is to test the students' skill in spotting what the issues are. That skill can be acquired only by a student who has already covered the various issues in some depth. For the same reason the answers vary somewhat in length, our aim being to give the issue the attention it merits. Thus the answers on character, which often occur as a free-standing question in examination papers, are longer than those for example on competence, which rarely occur as single issue questions. We have included a mixture of problem and essay questions as do most university examinations. You will notice, particularly in the essay questions, much lengthier quotations are given than you could possibly remember in an examination. We have included them because it is artificial for us not to check the exact wording. We would recommend that at least you try to recall comments from academic writers in your answers to essay questions although clearly you will mostly paraphrase rather than quote verbatim. Perhaps perversely examiners often award more marks for a student's recall of how an academic deals with a problem of legal analysis rather than the student's intuitive response.

We have tried in the introductory sections of each chapter to give some guidance as to the appropriate way of dealing with the types of questions likely to arise in that area. Examination technique is an important part of preparation for examinations in law and attention to it will not be wasted. But technique is ultimately only a means of demonstrating effectively the student's knowledge of the relevant law. We hope this book will help students to learn how to communicate better what they know.

2 Burden and Standard of Proof; Presumptions

INTRODUCTION

These two subjects are closely related and sometimes but not always taught together. Both are a terminological minefield and you should make sure you are thoroughly familiar with the definitions and their meanings. Behind the allocation of the burden of proof operating in both civil and criminal trials is the decision as to who should bear the risk of losing the case. That allocation is decided by common law and by statute. In criminal trials the 'presumption of innocence' means that the burden of proof will be on the prosecution, unless this is reversed by some express or implied provision. Here the law of evidence safeguards what in some other jurisdictions is a matter of individual civil rights backed up by a tenet of the constitution.

You must understand the difference between the legal and the evidential burden and the occasions where they are separately allocated. Students often have difficulty in differentiating the two in criminal trials. It is helpful to see the evidential burden primarily as an aspect of the sensible proposition that there must be a degree of evidence on asserted issues before they can be a matter for the trial. It is for the judge then to decide whether the assertion can go before the jury. Thus the prosecution has to adduce enough evidence of the guilt of the accused for the judge to be satisfied that there is a case to answer. In other words, it has the evidential burden. Here, the prosecution also has the legal burden on the same matter and this is the normal state of affairs directed at convincing the jury of the defendant's guilt to the standard of beyond reasonable doubt. The tricky areas are those where there is a divorce of the legal and evidential burden. These arise primarily in situations where the prosecution cannot be expected to put up evidence to anticipate every specific defence the accused may present. Thus in order to plead self-defence the accused will have to provide some evidence to enable the court to consider the matter. The legal burden stays with the prosecution. You must be clear that these instances differ from the occasion when statute has expressly or impliedly shifted the burden on a fact in issue. Here, both the legal and the evidential burden are shifted. The allocation of the burden of proof in civil cases is evident from the pre-trial pleadings.

It has been said that there is a clear case for rationalising the terminology in this area. For example, the legal burden is sometimes called the persuasive burden, and the evidential burden the 'burden of passing the judge'. Commentators refer also to the tactical burden although this is simply an exposition of how the parties must respond to evidence.

The standard of proof is a less complex topic. In this area, as in all areas of evidence, you must be careful to apply the appropriate rules according to whether the case is a civil or a criminal one. You will be unlikely to have questions which mix the two. In problem questions you may be asked to comment on the possible flaws in a judge's summing-up. You will then have to see if the legal burden has been allocated according to law and if the appropriate standard has been applied. Other questions may ask you to advise on burden and standard and here it is probably helpful to dissect the facts in issue into their various components and decide how the legal and evidential burdens should be distributed.

Presumptions can obviate the need for proof, or make the process easier; on occasions they are irrebuttable. The word presumption has been used in various ways. Evidence courses nowadays usually concentrate on what are known as 'rebuttable presumptions of law', i.e., those of death, legitimacy, marriage and here we deal only with them. Other presumptions, including 'irrebuttable presumptions of law', such as the age of criminal liability, belong more properly to the substantive law. Finally 'presumptions of fact' are really aspects of logical reasoning.

QUESTION 1

'It has ... been submitted that the guidelines laid down in *R* v *Hunt* are inadequate.' Stein (1991, at p. 572).

Do you agree with this comment?

Commentary

Protagonists and opponents of *R* v *Hunt* [1987] AC 352 still argue the issues in the pages of academic journals. You should not attempt this question unless you are familiar with some of these writings. You need also a detailed knowledge of the House of Lords' judgment in *Hunt* and how it differed from that of the Court of Appeal in *R* v *Edwards* [1975] QB 27. You should start with a general outline of the presumption of innocence, the yardstick against which the decision in *Hunt* is to be judged. You will clearly need to deal with the House of Lords' decision in *Woolmington* v *Director of Public Prosecutions* [1935] AC 462, and also the exceptions to the 'golden thread' which it acknowledged. For good marks to this question, you must develop a coherent analysis which summarises the views of the main protagonists, but, also gives your assessment of them. You must avoid a mere narrative of the decision.

Suggested Answer

Critics of the decision in *Hunt* usually begin by referring to the celebrated defence of the presumption of innocence in Lord Sankey's speech in *Woolmington* v *DPP* (at p. 481):

> No matter what the charge or where the trial, the principle that the prosecution must prove the guilt of the prisoner is part of the common law of England and no attempt to whittle it down can be entertained.

Set against this ringing defence of principle, the pragmatic approach in *Hunt* certainly appears at first sight to be somewhat mean-spirited. However, closer examination reveals that the *Woolmington* principle itself has never been absolute. Indeed, if it is so much part of the common law of England, it does seem strange that a trial judge and the Court of Criminal Appeal as late as the twentieth century could have made so fundamental an error as to place the burden of proving lack of mens rea on the defendant. In fact, the concept that the prosecution bears the legal burden on mens rea and actus reus was still somewhat undecided until this century. For example, the common law recognised the principle that if the defendant has possession of facts known only to him, it is for the defendant to produce the relevant evidence. McEwan (1992, p. 59) cites *R* v *Turner* (1816) 5 M & S 206 where there were ten possible justifications in the relevant statute for the defendant's possession of pheasants or hares. Only Turner could know which if any were applicable and the burden was on him to prove them. Furthermore, *Woolmington* itself cited exceptions to the principle, notably the common law defence of insanity and statutory exceptions. Before examining in more detail the guidelines set out in *Hunt* it is important to stress the rationale behind the *Woolmington* principle with which they are often contrasted. This as McEwan points out (at p. 56), 'derives not only from paternalistic concern as to the fate of accused persons, but is an application of the basic theory of the trial, that parties who wish the machinery of the law to assist them should have the obligation of proving their case.' The state should bear the legal burden if it seeks to convict someone of a crime.

How does *Hunt* change this? *Hunt* of course was preceded by *Edwards* where the Court of Appeal took the view that the defendant should have the burden of proof, not only as in *Turner* where he has peculiar knowledge, but where an offence carries with it exceptions and provisos. Thus, s. 101 of the Magistrates' Courts Act 1980 enacted a common law principle applying in trials on indictment as well as summary trials. In *Edwards* the court adopted what Stein (1991, p. 571) has called a syntactical approach, classifying defences on their syntactical status or sectional location in the list of statutory norms. Stein points out that the House of Lords in *Hunt* while upholding *Edwards* saw the issue as more complex. Attention should be paid not only to the linguistic structure of the Act but also to the mischief at which it was aimed and various practical matters which affect the burden of proof.

As regards general guidelines these were as follows. Firstly, the courts should recognise that Parliament can never lightly be taken to have intended to shift the burden of proof onto the defendant. Secondly, a factor of great importance was the ease or difficulty that parties met in discharging the probative burden. Here the courts drew on the House of Lords decision in *Nimmo* v *Alexander Cowan & Sons Ltd* [1968] AC 107, where the plaintiff employer was allocated the burden of proof on the issue of whether it was 'reasonably practicable' to observe health and safety standards. Finally, the gravity of the offence should be borne in mind.

In *Hunt* itself the House of Lords reversed the Court of Appeal and held that on the proper construction of the statute, the composition of the alleged prohibited drug was an element of the offence which the prosecution should prove. However, a number of critics, while applauding the actual decision, point out its dangerous implications. By abdicating on the matter of principle the House opened the door to serious inroads on the presumption of innocence. Mirfield (1988, p. 19) draws a distinction between the judgments of Lord Templeman on the one hand and Lords Griffiths, Ackner, Keith and Mackay on the other. All but Lord Templeman expressly supported the notion that Parliament may impliedly place the burden of proof on the accused. In cases of ambiguity in the statute, instead of relying unequivocally on the presumption of innocence, their Lordships were prepared only to see the necessity of avoiding the imposition of 'onerous burdens' on the defendant.

Bennion (1988, p. 34) argues that the exception in Hunt could only be taken to apply to offences of strict liability for 'Where the ingredients of the offence require mens rea, the onus must always remain on the prosecution to prove the evidence of this'. He suggests that this is illustrated by the House of Lords decision in *Westminster City Council* v *Croyalgrange Ltd* (1986) 83 Cr App R 155 where the House agreed that the prosecution should prove the landlord company knew a necessary licence had not been obtained by their tenants. On the other hand, Mirfield (1988) examines the Public Order Act 1986 to show how on the basis of the *Hunt* guidelines the statute could be interpreted to shift the burden of disproving the mental element of riot. He suggests (at p. 234) that Lord Templeman distinguished *Woolmington* in that it dealt with mens rea not actus reus but that Lords Griffiths and Ackner would accept 'judicial sovereignty over the burden of proof at common law, but not, for constitutional reasons, over statute'. In theory after *Hunt*, Parliament could be taken to have shifted, impliedly, the burden on the mens rea. Mirfield thinks this is unlikely in the case of riot, but possible in less 'obvious' cases, because the policy considerations set out in *Hunt* did not stress the most important one, namely that of maintaining the *Woolmington* principle.

Stein (1991) takes this approach further in analysing *R* v *Alath Construction Ltd* [1990] 1 WLR 1255, the first reported case decided under the *Hunt* guidelines. In this case the defence that the tree was dying or dead and therefore not subject to a preservation order was for the defendant to prove. This case shows how sectional separation between offences and defences could not be relied upon to obviate a shift in the burden of proof. Stein claims the Court of Appeal, relying on *Hunt*, is confusing justification where there should be no legal burden on the accused and an 'actor-related 'excuse'' where s. 101 would apply. Traditional common law defences such as duress or necessity only require an evidential burden from the accused, but, in sanctioning reversal of the burden of proof in these cases under statute, *Hunt* confirmed that both the evidential and the legal burden should shift.

The *Hunt* guidelines do have their defenders. Birch (1988, p. 221) thinks they are 'not unhelpful'. It has to be said that the courts have since the decision been wary of applying the guidelines too trenchantly. But two questions remain to be answered. Why should Parliament not be called upon to shift the burden of proof expressly if it so wishes? In fact, the Criminal Justice and Public Order Act 1994 expressly shifts the burden of proof in a number of sections, e.g., in s. 63(7) on attending raves: 'it is a defence for the accused to show that he had a reasonable excuse for failing to leave the land as soon as reasonably practicable, or as the case may be, for again entering the land'. Thus, the actual effect of the *Hunt* guidelines may be less sweeping since Parliament appears ready to shift the burden of proof by express stipulation.

Another question that arises is, why did the court in *Hunt* not adopt the recommendation of the 11th report of the Criminal Law Revision Committee 1972 (Cmnd 4991 paras 137-142), that in cases of implied statutory exceptions only the evidential burden should shift? In its favour, *Hunt* held that the defendant has only the lesser standard of proof to discharge, namely the balance of probabilities. However, the main problem remains that the *Hunt* guidelines are designed to deal with ambiguities. The result is that the law in this area of implied statutory exceptions is still uncertain and it may be difficult to anticipate how the court will interpret a specific statutory exception. In essence the matter is really not so much one of logic but concerns what is felt to be just. As Cross and Tapper (1995, p. 154) conclude: 'The truth of the matter is that most lawyers find it distasteful that a jury should ever have to be directed to convict when it thinks, after considering all of the evidence, that it is as likely as not that the accused is innocent'.

QUESTION 2

Answer both parts of the question.

(a) The (imaginary) Computer Safety Act 1996 specifies as follows:

Section 1. It is an offence for an employer to require his employees to input data into a computer, other than one with voice recognition facility, for longer than five hours a day unless he has a certificate of exemption from the Health and Safety Board.

Anne, managing director of a printing company, is prosecuted under s. 1. She pleads not guilty. Advise on burden and standard of proof.

(b) Comment on the following judicial summing-up:

Ladies and gentlemen of the jury, you have heard the defence acknowledge that the defendant struck the blow which felled Mr Jones but that she has no recollection of this at all. If she does not convince you that it is more likely than not that she did suffer a black out you must find for the prosecution.

Commentary

Both these questions deal with burden and standard of proof in criminal trials. They both raise the issue of whether the burden should shift to the defendant and if so to what standard. Part **(b)** requires you to deal with the difference between evidential and legal burden. Use of the right terminology is crucial here and you must remind yourself that the legal burden is the obligation placed on a party to prove a fact in issue, whereas the evidential burden (the 'burden of passing the judge') is that placed on a party to adduce sufficient evidence on a fact which is asserted for it to become an issue in the trial. These questions are simpler and briefer than you would expect in most Evidence examinations where burden and standard of proof is likely to appear as part of a question which raises several issues. They are included here to enable you to test your familiarity with the basic principles of the area.

Suggested Answer

(a) The offence here consists of four elements of the actus reus: (i) requiring employees to input into a computer; (ii) which does not have a voice recognition facility; (iii) for longer than five hours; (iv) without a certificate of exemption from the Health and Safety Executive. The general rule in criminal cases is that it is for the prosecution to prove all the elements of an offence beyond reasonable doubt: *Woolmington* v *DPP* [1935] AC 462. The presumption is that the burden of proof on the actus reus and the mens rea lies on the prosecution. However, this is subject to statutory exceptions either express or implied. Here the issue is whether the statute impliedly reverses the burden on parts of the actus reus.

It is not clear whether the offence here is summary or triable on indictment, though it may be that its relatively mild character marks it as a summary offence. The rule as far as summary offences are concerned is given by the Magistrates' Courts Act 1980, s. 101 and a similar rule applies to trials on indictment according to the House of Lords in *R* v *Hunt* [1987] AC 352 where it was held that s. 101 enacted a principle of the common law that statute could impliedly shift the burden of proof from prosecution to defence. The tenet that the burden of proof should lie on the prosecution is not absolute. The House of Lords were here approving the decision in *R* v *Edwards* [1975] QB 27 where the Court of Appeal held that the same principles should apply to summary trials and trials on indictment. Section 101 provides that where a defendant relies for his defence on any exception, exemption, proviso, excuse or qualification he bears the burden of proving the exception, etc. The problem is in recognizing an exception, etc. The statute here contains arguably three exceptions or provisos etc., namely the reference to the need for five or more hours of inputting, the stipulation of a computer 'other than one with voice recognition facility' and finally the exemption if there is a certificate from the Health and Safety Board.

The courts have interpreted 'exceptions', etc., in different ways. Contrasting conclusions were reached in interpreting similarly worded sections of the Highways Act 1980. Thus in *Gatland* v *Metropolitan Police Commissioner* [1968] 2 QB 279, the exception was held to apply but in *Hirst and Agu* v *Chief Constable of West Yorkshire* (1986) 85 Cr App R 143 it did not. However Birch (1988, p. 228) suggests that the difference between the two interpretations relates to whether the mental element is present. *Hirst* was a case on s. 137 which requires a person to obstruct 'wilfully' without excuse whereas *Gatland*'s was under s. 161 which is an absolute offence.

On its wording s. 1 of the Computer Safety Act appears to resemble more s. 161. As Lord Pearson said in *Nimmo* v *Alexander Cowan & Sons Ltd* [1968] AC 107 (at p. 135), 'there is no usual formula for an "excuse" ... You have to look at the substance and effect of the enactment, as well as its form in order to ascertain whether it contains an "excuse or qualification" within the meaning of the section'. In *R* v *Hunt* [1987] AC 352 the House of Lords developed the Court of Appeal's view in *R* v *Edwards* that the incidence of the burden of proof is determined by examining the wording of the enactment. It looked beyond this to policy considerations.

The first difficulty is posed by the issue whether the number of hours is an element of the offence which must be proved by the prosecution, or whether it amounts to an exception, etc. In *R* v *Hunt* the House held that the composition of the morphine was an element of the offence and it was for the prosecution to prove it. The majority went on further to argue that if the statute does not clearly indicate where the burden should lie, the court may consider other matters such as the seriousness of the offence and the ease or difficulty a party might find in discharging the burden. Certainly, it would be easier for the defendant than the prosecution to show the time spent inputting and this might be a consideration in favour of its being an exception as in *Nimmo* v *Alexander Cowan & Sons Ltd*.

The certificate of exemption, it is submitted, is analogous to the licence which the seller of liquor was required to prove in *R* v *Edwards*. Finally, with regard to the presence of a voice recognition facility, similar principles of interpretation apply. Is the make-up of the computer an element of the offence or does the phrase 'other than' constitute an exception? In *R* v *Alath Construction Ltd* [1990] 1 WLR 1255 the Court of Appeal held that, in a prosecution under the Town and Country Planning Act 1974 for felling a tree which was subject to a preservation order, the burden of proving that the tree was dying was on the defence. If the tree was in such a condition, the preservation order could not apply. The court held that this constituted an exception from liability and the defence bore the burden of proving it on the balance of probabilities. Before deciding whether the defence has a burden of proof, the court has to analyse the offence to see whether the matter in question was an element of the offence in which case the prosecution has the burden. The court has also to analyse the statute to see whether s. 101 of the Magistrates' Court Act 1980 should be applied in the specific case. The House of Lords in *Westminster City Council* v *Croyalgrange* [1986] 1 WLR 674 did not find it applicable. In that case the House was considering a statute which required operators of sex shops to be licensed. The landlord of a building being operated as a sex shop without a licence claimed in his defence that he did not know the tenant had no licence. The council argued that no mens rea was required, but their Lordships, approving the Court of Appeal, said that it was for the prosecution to show that the defendant knew there was no licence. The exemption the defence tried to rely on qualified a prohibition in a separate section of the statute and not the offence charged. On the facts in this case it is arguable that the existence of a voice recognition facility is an excuse, like the pending death of the tree, and it is therefore for Anne to prove she has one on her computer. This is not one of those cases like *Croyalgrange* which explicitly require mens rea by including a term such as 'knowingly'.

Finally, Lord Griffiths in *R* v *Hunt* said that Parliament can never lightly be taken to have intended to impose on an accused an onerous duty to prove his innocence and the courts should be very slow to draw such an inference from the language of a statute. But the offence in question here is not a serious one and it may be appropriate for the burden on this fact in issue to be placed on the defendant. If so it is both the legal and evidential burden and the standard is the balance of probabilities (*R* v *Hunt*).

There should be no doubt that the task of proving mens rea lies on the prosecution because there is nothing in the statute quoted to suggest that Parliament has impliedly affected this burden.

(b) While the prosecution must prove the defendant's guilt, there is no burden laid on the defendant to prove her innocence and it is sufficient for her to raise a doubt as to her guilt. This is the principle in *Woolmington* v *DPP* [1935] AC 462, where the House of Lords held that where the defence of accident was raised it was for the prosecution to disprove the defence and not for the defendant to prove it. The defence here is automatism and the leading case is the House of Lords decision *Bratty* v *Attorney-General for Northern Ireland* [1963] AC 386. It is clear that the defendant would not be liable if she had genuinely suffered a black-out at the time she struck the blow because she would lack mens rea. Her explanation must have sufficient substance to merit consideration by the jury. It is a matter of law for the judge to decide whether the defendant has satisfied this evidential 'burden'. The issue is whether there is evidence such as to raise any defence, excuse or explanation which could, if accepted, lead the jury to acquit. The defendant merely has to 'collect from the evidence enough material to make it possible for a reasonable jury to acquit' (per Lord Devlin in *Jayasena* v *R* [1970] AC 618, 623). The mere fact that defence counsel raises the issue unsupported by evidence is not enough to give the issue enough substance to go before the jury.

In cases of automatism the judge must first decide whether the defence has laid a proper foundation for the issue to be put before the jury. Otherwise the Crown can rely on the presumption that every man has sufficient mental capacity to be responsible for his crimes (per Lord Denning in *Bratty* v *Attorney-General*). A hypothetical possibility that the accused was acting from automatism, unsupported by medical evidence pointing to the cause of mental incapacity is not enough, as the Court of Appeal held in *R* v *Stripp* (1978) 69 Cr App R 318. It seems in the present case that the judge considered the issue fit to go before the jury, in other words that the defendant has discharged the evidential burden.

The second issue for the judge is whether the automatism is insane within the *M'Naghten* Rules, that is whether it is produced by a defect of reason amounting to a disease of the mind: *M'Naghten's Case* (1843) 10 Cl & Fin 200. If the judge does consider the automatism insane the jury must decide if the accused is guilty or not guilty by reason of insanity as the Court of Appeal held in *R* v *Burgess* [1991] 2 QB 92. Otherwise, if he considers there is evidence of non-insane automatism, it is for the prosecution to show beyond reasonable doubt that the defendant had mens rea. The Court of Appeal held in *R* v *Burns*

(1973) 58 Cr App R 364 that where the issues of insane and non-insane automatism both arise, the judge should direct that the accused has not only the evidential burden of proving non-insane automatism but the legal burden of proving insanity. If, as appears from the brief account of the facts, the issue here is non-insane automatism, the judge has wrongly required the defendant to prove her defence to the civil standard, that is to say on the balance of probabilities. The true position is that she merely had to show that the issue has sufficient substance to merit consideration by the jury. It is for the prosecution to prove her guilt. The onus on the prosecution is not discharged unless the jury were sure that guilt was established beyond reasonable doubt.

QUESTION 3

Loamshire District Council are suing Amy for money they allege was paid her in error while she was working under contract as a temporary gardener. They claim she has fraudulently retained the money. She claims she has no idea she was overpaid since her pay was paid directly into her bank account and she did not receive pay slips. She has no records relating to the period and simply denies the liability. Amy claims further that if there were any payment beyond her wages it was for a bonus the council promised to pay her. Loamshire are also claiming for a rake which they say she broke. She relies on a clause in the contract which exempts her from liability for damage for any tools providing she was not negligent.

Advise the parties on burden and standard of proof.

Commentary

Questions on the burden and standard of proof in civil cases do not raise as many controversies as those in criminal cases. The simplest approach is to realise that the burden generally lies on the party who pleads an issue. Two possibly problematic issues arise here. One is whether the standard of proof is affected because the council are alleging fraudulent retention by Amy of money not owing to her. Secondly the burden in the exemption clause and its proviso will arguably shift from one to the other as assertion meets counter-assertion.

Suggested Answer

The general principle in civil litigation is that the burden of proof lies on the asserter of a claim. It is thus for the council to prove the excessive payment under the contract. The incidence of the burden is thus here a matter of substantive law and the House of Lords held that it is usually clear from the pleadings: *Wilsher* v *Essex Area Health Authority* [1988] AC 1074. The council therefore have the legal burden of proof on the issue of the overpayment. They also have the evidential burden in the sense that they must put in some evidence to convince the court there is a case to answer.

Amy may simply deny liability but she runs the risk tactically of losing. She is, however, putting up a specific defence, namely that the overpayment was money due from a bonus. She has the legal and evidential burden of mounting this defence. The incidence of the legal burden of proof will decide the outcome of the case if the tribunal is not able to come to a decision on which to prefer. In *Rhesa Shipping Co. SA* v *Edmunds* [1985] 1 WLR 948 the House of Lords, overturning the Court of Appeal, held that the judge had not been obliged to choose between two versions merely because the defendants had chosen to put forward their explanation of events.

Thus, the plaintiff, Loamshire District Council has the task of proving its case more probable than not, not more probable than Amy's version of events.

The standard of proof is on the balance of probabilities. There is a possible further consideration in that the council are alleging that Amy held the money fraudulently. In *Hornal* v *Neuberger Products Ltd* [1957] 1 QB 247, a case involving an allegation of fraudulent misrepresentation, the Court of Appeal rejected the view that there was a higher standard necessary than balance of probability but rather puzzlingly commented per Denning LJ at p. 258 'the more serious the allegation the higher the degree of probability that is required' and per Morris LJ at p. 266 'the very elements of gravity become a part of the whole range of circumstances which have to be weighed in the scale when deciding as to the balance of probabilities'. Again in *Miles* v *Cain, The Times,* 15 December 1989, the Court of Appeal reaffirmed that in a civil action the plaintiff must prove the case on a balance of probabilities but the degree of probability must be commensurate with the seriousness of the subject matter. Thus, a high degree of probability was required to prove that a defendant in a civil action committed sexual assaults of a criminal nature. The council, in alleging fraud, will have to produce quite cogent evidence to win.

As regards the rake, again the council have the burden of proving that it was broken and that this constituted breach of contract. It is for Amy to prove it is a tool which falls within the exemption clause, although this is a matter of construction for the court: *Munro Brice and Co.* v *War Risks Association* [1918] 2 KB 78. However, it is arguable that if a plaintiff relies upon a proviso to an exemption clause the burden of proving that the facts fall within the proviso may be on the plaintiff: *The Glendarroch* [1894] P 226. Amy may argue by analogy with this reasoning that the plaintiff council will have to prove she was negligent.

QUESTION 4

Jane and Harry are legally married in 1960 in Birmingham. In 1961 Harry leaves to join a revolutionary group in Bolivia, but tells Jane he will return in a year. In fact Jane does not hear from him again and in 1963 gets a letter from the group leader saying Harry has been missing for six months following an expedition against counter-revolutionaries. Jane hears no more and in 1972 marries Oliver, an older man, in Paris. In 1973 Jane gives birth to twins Barry and John and in 1975 to Margaret. In 1995 Jane and Oliver are both killed instantly in a car crash. Shortly before he was killed Oliver told John that Margaret could not be his child because he had not had intercourse with Jane for a year before her birth. At the funeral, Alan, an old college friend of Jane and Harry's, who has been out of touch for years, tells John that he saw Harry in a cafe in La Paz in 1971 but says Harry disappeared before he could speak to him. Jane's will said that if she died after Oliver her estate should be divided between her children and a charity for distressed Bolivian revolutionaries. Oliver's will left all his property to his 'legitimate children'. When John and Margaret, after the car crash, look through old photographs in the attic they come across one showing Oliver and an unknown woman. On the back is noted 'Wedding day, 29 March 1969'.

Advise whether Margaret can claim under Oliver's will and whether all children can succeed under Jane's will.

Commentary

Presumptions do not figure in all evidence courses, so you should check your syllabus. This is conceptually quite a tricky area and you need to keep in mind the difference between presumptions in civil cases and criminal cases and the traditional classification of irrebuttable presumptions of law, rebuttable presumptions of law, and presumptions of fact. It is mainly the second with which you need to be concerned in this question. In addition, you will need to distinguish persuasive presumptions, that is those where the effect of the presumption is to put the legal burden of disproof on the party who wishes to challenge it, and evidential presumptions where the evidential burden only is placed on the party against whom it operates. In this question, the examiner is looking for a clear application of the law on presumptions to the facts, rather than discussion on the rationale of presumptions more appropriate to an essay question. You should begin by listing the events in chronological order and stating the relevant presumptions. In your approach to presumptions, you must first acknowledge that the primary facts must first be proved; if they are, the specific presumption must be drawn from them although it may be rebutted by other conflicting facts. Thus you must first see if the presumptions apply and then see if they can be rebutted.

The issues are:

1960 Jane and Harry marry — presumption of validity of marriage.
1972 Jane and Oliver marry — does presumption of Harry's death operate? What is the effect of the 1971 sighting of Harry? Is validity of marriage challenged by 1969 'wedding photograph' of Oliver and unknown woman? Does it matter marriage takes place in Paris?
1973 John and Barry born.
1975 Margaret born — presumption of legitimacy but does what Oliver told John rebut presumption of Margaret's legitimacy? Does the 'wedding photograph' affect all children's legitimacy?
1995 Jane and Oliver killed — presumption of order of death and effect on inheritance.

Suggested Answer

The order of death of Jane and Oliver is determined by their seniority (Law of Property Act 1925, s. 184, but see Administration of Estates Act 1925, s. 46(3) (added by Intestates' Estates Act 1952) and Law Reform (Succession) Act 1995). As Jane is the younger of the two, Oliver will be presumed to have died first, thus in accordance with the terms of her will her estate is divided between John, Barry and Margaret and the Bolivian charity.

Oliver's estate raises more complicated issues. John, Barry and Margaret can inherit only if they are legitimate. The validity of the marriage betwen Jane and Oliver could affect the legitimacy of all three. The validity of the marriage is threatened by two pieces of evidence. One is the evidence of Alan that Harry may have been alive after he was presumed to have died. The other is the photograph which suggests that Oliver was not free to marry Jane. The presumption of the validity of a marriage is a very strong one. There are two presumptions which may be operative here. On proof of the celebration of a marriage ceremony, that is one which is capable of producing a valid marriage, the law will presume the formal validity of the marriage, that is to say that the formalities have been complied with. The primary facts thus are the evidence of the ceremony that is valid according to local law. In *Mahadervan* v *Mahadervan* [1964] P 233 it was argued that the presumption did not apply in favour of a foreign marriage but Sir Jocelyn Simon P said (at p. 247):

> To accept it would give expression to a legal chauvinism that has no place in any rational system of private international law. Our courts in my view apply exactly the same weight of presumption in favour of a foreign marriage as of an English one, and the nationality of any later marriage brought into question is quite immaterial.

It is not significant therefore that the marriage took place in Paris.

This presumption is a persuasive one and there is a legal burden on the party seeking to rebut formal validity. The standard of proof to be met by that party is high. In *Mahadervan* Sir Jocelyn Simon P held that the presumption can only be rebutted by evidence which establishes beyond reasonable doubt that there was no marriage.

On proof of the celebration of a marriage ceremony, relying on the same primary facts, the 'essential validity' of the marriage will be assumed. This is that the parties had the necessary capacity of marrying and that their respective consents were genuine. There appears to be little doubt about the formal validity of the marriage of Jane and Oliver: the issue is its essential validity, in other words, were the parties free to marry? Again in civil proceedings the presumption is persuasive rather than an evidential presumption, but the standard of proof is lower than that in the case of the presumption of formal validity. In *Re Peete, Peete* v *Crompton* [1952] 2 All ER 599 the issue arose as to the essential validity of a formally valid marriage in 1919. There was some evidence of the existence of an earlier marriage and the presumption of validity of the 1919 marriage failed. Even so, the photograph in itself is unlikely to be sufficient evidence to undermine the presumption that Oliver was free to marry Jane.

The issue whether Jane was free to marry is more complicated. Evidently, she relied on the presumption that Harry was dead when she went through the ceremony with Oliver. The rules relating to presumption of death were set out in *Chard* v *Chard* [1956] P 259. Harry is presumed dead when four circumstances apply: there is no acceptable evidence that he has been alive for at least seven continuous years; there are persons likely to have heard of him, had he been alive; who during that period have not so heard; all due enquiries have failed to locate him. We aren't told whether Jane made inquiries about Harry after his disappearance, but assuming she did she was entitled to presume his death by 1970. Had she been properly advised she would have followed the special procedure laid down by s. 19 of the Matrimonial Causes Act 1973, petitioning for a decree dissolving the marriage and presuming the death of the spouse. This does not require that enquiries be made; takes no account of the likelihood that the petitioner would have heard of the person had they been alive and restricts the issue whether the petitioner had no reason to believe in the spouse's continued existence to events taking place in the last seven years.

If she had married Oliver without petitioning for a s. 19 decree, the marriage would not necessarily have been an act of bigamy since she could still rely on the common law presumption. Those wishing to challenge the presumption will have the evidential burden. In *Prudential Assurance Co.* v *Edmonds* (1877) 2 App Cas 487, a niece standing in a crowded street in Australia had briefly caught sight of a man she recognised as her uncle. The judge had first to decide whether or not she was mistaken. If she was, it made no difference to the presumption. If she was not, the onus was on the side claiming that he was dead to establish that he was. The House of Lords held that it was for the tribunal of fact to decide whether or not to accept the niece's evidence and that if the jury had been satisfied that she was mistaken the basic facts giving rise to the presumption were established. Here Alan is available for cross-examination and the preliminary issue is ultimately one of fact.

The next issue concerns Margaret. Does what Oliver told John affect her legitimacy and claim under Oliver's will? There is a presumption that a child born to the wife in lawful wedlock and conceived while the husband was alive is legitimate. This persuasive presumption can be rebutted by evidence which shows that it is more probable than not that the person is illegitimate and it is not necessary to prove that fact beyond reasonable doubt: Family Law Reform Act 1969, s. 26 and *S* v *S* [1972] AC 24. Oliver's remark to John (admissible under the Civil Evidence Act 1968; see **Chapter 7**) is evidence which might be capable of rebutting the presumption that Margaret is legitimate. The presumption is a persuasive one, so the legal burden of disproof falls on John and Barry, assuming it is they who are challenging Margaret's claim. However, against the remark should be set the provisional presumption (or presumption of fact) that sexual intercourse between husband and wife is likely to follow where opportunities for it occur. This is, however, a weaker presumption: *Piggott* v *Piggott* (1938) 61 CLR 378, probably destroyed here by the remark itself. John and Barry have only the tactical burden of disproving it.

QUESTION 5

Arnold's widow is suing Harnet Transport Company over his death. The plaintiff alleges that a coach in which Arnold was travelling crossed the central reservation on the motorway crashing into a car coming in the opposite direction. At the trial the plaintiff put forward no evidence about the circumstances of the accident. The defendants, however, gave evidence that a motorcycle had swerved in front of the coach causing the driver to lose control. The judge held that the burden of disproving negligence fell on the defendants and that they had not discharged the burden. He found for the plaintiff. Comment on the judge's decision and critically evaluate the law of evidence in this area.

Commentary

The main problem with a question of this sort is in recognizing the issue. It turns on rather a narrow point, namely whether the doctrine of res ipsa loquitur (literally, the thing speaks for itself) operates to reverse the burden of proof. There is not a great deal of case law on this issue but it has aroused sharp differences of opinion. You need to explain the differing views of this doctrine, namely whether it is an evidential presumption, a persuasive presumption or a presumption of fact.

Suggested Answer

The judge here has interpreted the doctrine of res ipsa loquitur to mean that the burden of proof had shifted to the defendant. This is by no means generally accepted in law. The doctrine itself turns on the presumption of negligence. Its *raison d'être* was set out by the Court of Exchequer Chamber in *Scott* v *London and St Katherine Docks Co.* (1865) 3 H & C 596, 601 per Erle CJ:

> There must be reasonable evidence of negligence. But where the thing is shewn to be under the management of the defendant or his servants, and the accident is such as in the ordinary course of things does not happen if those who have the management use proper care, it affords reasonable evidence, in the absence of explanation by the defendants, that the accident arose from want of care.

However, the effect of the presumption remains open to debate. There are conflicting views on whether it is an evidential presumption, a persuasive presumption or a presumption of fact. In *Ng Chun Pui* v *Lee Chuen Tat* [1988]

RTR 298, the Privy Council upheld the decision of the Court of Appeal of Hong Kong that the trial judge had misunderstood the doctrine of res ipsa loquitur which was no more than a legal maxim to describe a state of the evidence from which it was proper to draw an inference of negligence. The court said that it was misleading to talk of the burden of proof shifting to the defendant in a res ipsa loquitur situation because the burden of proving negligence rested throughout on the plaintiff. The case involved a road accident in which a coach driven by the second defendant and owned by the first defendant had crossed the central reservation and collided with a bus driven in the opposite direction. At the trial the plaintiffs called no oral evidence and relied on the fact of the accident or, as the judge referred to it, the doctrine of res ipsa loquitur. They relied on the inference that the coach was self-evidently not being driven with the appropriate standard of care. The defendants, however, called evidence to explain the loss of control. Because the plaintiffs had relied on res ipsa loquitur the judge wrongly held that the burden of disproving negligence lay on the defendants and they had failed to discharge it. If the defendant adduced no evidence there was nothing to rebut the inference of negligence but if he did that evidence had to be evaluated to see if it was still reasonable to draw the inference of negligence from the mere fact of the accident. Lord Griffiths said (at p. 301) that:

> resort to the burden of proof is a poor way to decide a case ... In so far as resort is had to the burden of proof, the burden remains at the end, as it was at the beginning upon the plaintiff to prove that his injury was caused by the negligence of the defendants.

If the doctrine is an evidential presumption the party against whom it operates will lose unless he adduces some evidence. But if the probability of negligence is equal to that of its not being present the defendant will succeed since the plaintiff has failed in his legal burden of proving negligence on the balance of probabilities. In *The Kite* [1933] P 154 involving a dispute over the cause of a collision of a barge with a bridge where the probabilities of the explanations were equal, the court found for the defendants.

If the doctrine, however, is a persuasive presumption negligence must be presumed if there is no evidence to the contrary. Thus the party against whom the presumption operates will lose if the probabilities are equal. This is how the Court of Appeal interpreted the presumption in *Barkway* v *South Wales Transport Co. Ltd* [1948] 2 All ER 460. The case concerned a bus which had fallen down an embankment. The court held that it was insufficient for the defendants to show the bus had left the road because of a burst tyre. This was an event which was as consistent with negligence as not. The House of Lords in *Henderson* v *Henry E Jenkins & Sons Ltd* [1970] AC 282 also held that res ipsa loquitur was a persuasive presumption. It held that the plaintiff had proved negligence. On this issue PS Atiyah (1972) thought the issue of negligence was simply not proved either way. He argued that English judges without acknowledging it were shifting the burden of proof.

Finally, some authorities, particularly Australian, hold that res ipsa loquitur is no more than a presumption of fact whereby the party against whom it operates has only the tactical burden of disproving negligence. He is not bound to lose. If the defendant adduces no evidence he runs the risk of losing but is not bound to. A finding by the tribunal of fact in his favour could be reversed on appeal.

JD Heydon (1991, p. 59) points out that conflicting authority over the effect of the presumption of res ipsa loquitur is explained by the disappearance of civil juries in England. The judge must decide whether the 'thing speaks for itself' and thus whether the plaintiff has won. Once he decides that the facts suggest negligence, naturally he requires persuasive proof to change his mind. Heydon says that one argument put for the English approach is that it is easier for the defendant to disprove negligence in modern cases such as those involving hospital machinery: 'Thus a trend towards strict liability is disguised as negligence'. He suggests perhaps the answer may be to narrow the concept of res ipsa loquitur to those cases where 'artificial weight should be given to the basic fact either to force the defendant to tell all he knows or because he is on the law of averages, more likely to be negligent than not'. Presumptions, he says, serve different purposes to fit the occasion: 'These aims cannot be achieved by a single verbally and substantively rigid rule'.

Thus, the difficulty in this case is deciding which authority to follow. Is res ipsa loquitur a rebuttable presumption of law? Does it do no more than permit but not require a finding of negligence? It seems, however, that in *Ng Chun Pui* its effect is to place only an evidential burden on the opponent. Thus, the judge's summing-up here is possibly a ground of appeal in that he appears to place the legal burden of proof on the defendants.

3 Competence and Compellability

INTRODUCTION

Witnesses are a principal source of evidence in a trial and the rules relating to their attendance indicate their importance. The starting point is that all witnesses with relevant information are assumed to be competent to give evidence and are also compellable in that the court may summon them to attend. Other interests of the witness are thus secondary to the need for the trial to have all necessary information. The competence of witnesses in criminal proceedings was historically a particularly controversial area, certain groups of people being excluded on moral or religious grounds. In addition parties to the proceedings were held to be incompetent because they had an interest in the outcome. There are now no such objections to groups of witnesses, the only reservations concerning children or persons of defective intellect, but these are looked at on a case by case basis and in practice there is by no means total exclusion. Some witnesses who are competent may, however, claim a privilege not to give evidence; thus they are not in contempt of court if they refuse to appear or if they do appear but refuse to answer certain questions. These witnesses include defendants on their own behalf, although you should bear in mind the evidential consequences of their failure to testify under s. 35 of the Criminal Justice and Public Order Act 1994.

The other main group are spouses testifying for the prosecution, a rule based on the rather quaint concept that any compulsion might lead to marital discord. However, this lack of compellability is subject to a number of important exceptions under the Police and Criminal Evidence Act 1984.

Questions on competence and compellability are easy to spot in that they will usually include a reference to a reluctant witness. You are unlikely to be asked about the position in civil cases since the rules there are quite straightforward, e.g., spouses of the parties are both competent and compellable. The position of children is a little more complex. In criminal cases under the Criminal Justice Act 1988, s. 33A(2A), introduced by the Criminal Justice and Public Order Act 1994, 'a child's evidence shall be received unless it appears to the court that the child is incapable of giving intelligible testimony'. Children are persons under fourteen years. In civil cases on the other hand the common law principles set out in *R* v *Hayes* [1977] 1 WLR 234 have been incorporated in the Children Act 1989, s. 96(1) and (2). Under this provision if any child in the court's opinion does not understand the nature of the oath, his evidence may still be heard unsworn if the court considers he understands that it is his duty to speak the truth and he has sufficient understanding to justify his evidence being heard. Spouses of the parties are both competent and compellable.

The following tables may help you remember the various permutations of the status of witnesses in criminal trials.

Table 1

	For prosecution		For defence		For co-defendant	
Witness	Competent	Comp'able	Competent	Comp'able	Competent	Comp'able
defendant where no co-defendant	No. *R* v *Rhodes* [1899] 1 QB 77	No	Yes. CEA 1898, s. 1(a)	No. CEA 1898, s. 1(a)	n/a	n/a
co-defendant pleading not guilty	No. *R* v *Grant* [1944] 2 All ER 311	No	Yes. CEA 1898, s. 1(a)	No. CEA 1898, s. 1(a)	Yes. CEA 1898, s. 1(a)	No. CEA 1898, s. 1(a)
'ex-co-def', i.e., pleading guilty, acquitted or nolle prosequi entered	Yes. *R* v *Boal* [1965] 1 QB 402	Yes	n/a	n/a	Yes. *R* v *Boal*	Yes
accomplice where proceedings are pending	Yes.	As a matter of practice (not law) only if undertaking made that proceedings will be discontinued. *R* v *Pipe* (1966) 51 Cr App R 17	n/a	n/a	Yes	Yes. *R* v *Richardson* (1967) 51 Cr App R 381

Table 2

	For prosecution		For spouse's defence		For co-defendant	
Witness	Competent	Comp'able	Competent	Comp'able	Competent	Comp'able
spouse of defendant jointly charged with him or her and pleading not guilty	No. PACE s. 80(4)	No. PACE s. 80(4)	Yes. PACE s.80(11)(b)	No. PACE s. 80(4)	Yes. PACE s. 80(1)(b)	No. PACE s. 80(4)
spouse of defendant not jointly charged	Yes. PACE s. 80(1)(b)	Only for offences in PACE s. 80(3)	Yes. PACE s. 80 (1)(b)	Yes. PACE s. 80(2)	Yes. PACE s. 80 (1)(b)	Only for offences in PACE s. 80(3)

Note 1: Criminal Evidence Act 1898 — CEA 1898
Police and Criminal Evidence Act 1984 — PACE
Note 2: former spouses to be treated as other witnesses (Police and Criminal Evidence Act 1984, s. 80(5)).

QUESTION 1

John is charged with assaulting Fred after an argument about football in a bus queue. John claims self-defence in that he says Fred was wearing knuckleduster rings and he was afraid he would be hurt. Fred denies he threatened John. The only other witness to the brawl was John's wife, Hilda. Discuss whether she is competent and compellable as a witness for John or the prosecution and critically evaluate the law of evidence in this area.

Commentary

Have in your mind a clear picture of the position of spouses under s. 80 of the Police and Criminal Evidence Act 1984 which does have rather complex wording and differentiate their position in relation to the prosecution and the defence case. You are expected here to outline the law and then comment on its rationale. It is an area that has raised several controversial issues, for example whether the relationship between spouses deserves better protection in law than others, such as that between parent and child. Be careful not to be too expansive on the historical background of the law but it is quite appropriate to set the development of the law in context.

Suggested Answer

The general rule is that any person is competent and compellable as a witness provided he or she is able to communicate coherently. Thus he or she may lawfully give evidence. It is for the court to decide issues as to the competence and compellability of witnesses as the Court of Appeal held in *R* v *Yacoob* (1981) 72 Cr App R 313. A competent witness is generally compellable. The main exceptions apply in differing degrees to spouses, children and those of unsound mind.

By virtue of s. 80(1) and (4) of the Police and Criminal Evidence Act 1984, a spouse is competent to give evidence for the prosecution in all cases unless jointly charged, so Hilda is competent for the prosecution. Subject to the same proviso, she is compellable for the defence (s. 80(2)). But by s. 80(3)(a) she is compellable for the prosecution only if Fred was under 16 at the time of the alleged assault. If she does choose to give evidence for the prosecution, provided the right of refusal has been clearly explained to her, she can be treated like any other witness, as the Court of Appeal held in *R* v *Pitt* [1983] QB 25. The prosecution has the burden of establishing the competence of a prosecution witness and the standard to be reached is beyond reasonable doubt (*Yacoob*).

Section 80(8) forbids comment by the prosecution on the failure of a defendant to call his or her spouse. This provision originally appeared in s. 1(b) of the Criminal Evidence Act 1898. Thus in *R* v *Naudeer* (1984) 80 Cr App R 9 the Court of Appeal quashed a conviction because the prosecuting counsel had told the jury it had been deliberately deprived of material evidence as the defendant had not called his wife as a witness. The case was one of shoplifting and she had been in the shop at the relevant time. The court may, however, correct the damage made by a comment. The judge may comment on the failure of a defendant to call his wife, as the Court of Appeal held in *R* v *Gallagher* [1974] 1 WLR 1204, just as he may make a comment on the failure to call any witness.

In relation to spouses their exemption from a general duty to testify for the prosecution has been a matter of some controversy. At present spouses are only compellable to testify for the prosecution if the offence in question is either a crime of violence or a threat of one to the spouse of the accused or a person under 16, or if it is a sexual offence committed against a person under 16. Before 1986, when the Police and Criminal Evidence Act 1984, came into force spouses were at common law incompetent as well as non-compellable for the prosecution. If there was a co-accused he or she was treated as being in the same position as the prosecution and similar changes in relation to the co-accused as to the prosecution were enacted in PACE. A spouse could, under the Criminal Evidence Act 1898, give evidence, however, on behalf of the accused. The rationale of the common law position was based on two factors: first the legal fiction of the single personality of husband and wife and secondly the policy consideration of preserving the institution of marriage. Thus the law did not apply to bigamously married spouses as the Court of Appeal held in *R* v *Khan* (1986) 84 Cr App R 44.

The law had also to balance another interest, that of convicting a criminal spouse and so there were many common law and statutory exceptions to the general rule of incompetence. The law was unclear however as to whether the spouse in such instances was both compellable and competent. The issue was resolved by the House of Lords in *Hoskyn* v *Metropolitan Police Commissioner* [1979] AC 474 where it was held that even in the exceptional cases the spouse was never compellable for the prosecution. Section 80 of PACE effectively overruled the House of Lords in *Hoskyn* making the wife compellable for the offences as mentioned above. Furthermore by s. 80(9) the spouse who testifies cannot refuse to disclose the content of marital communications even if they are confidential, nor refuse to answer relevant questions on when sexual intercourse took place.

The changes thus enacted go in some ways further than had been recommended by the Criminal Law Revision Committee in its 11th report (1972, Cmnd 4991). A spouse is thus compellable even in cases involving violent or sexual offences against persons under 16 who are not household members.

Generally, however, the present law has been criticised as being too restrictive and inconsistent. Thus, Zuckerman (1989, p. 291) points out that marriages are now more easily dissoluble and that it 'is difficult to imagine that granting spouses immunity from having to testify against each other in criminal proceedings makes an appreciable contribution to the general stability of marriage in our community'. There does appear to be little logical reason for protecting the marriage relationship more than that say of parent and child.

Zuckerman also suggests that the provision concerning comment on spouses' failure to testify is unsatisfactory. It applies by virtue of s. 80(8) of PACE to the spouses' failure to testify for the accused or co-accused. He points out a wife may have declined to testify in agreement with her husband so there is little threat to the marriage. It is also perhaps illogical that a co-accused's counsel can comment on a failure of a spouse to testify whereas a prosecution counsel cannot. Finally on this point the ban on prosecution comment was in line with the now repealed s. 1(b) of the CEA 1898. The prosecution may by virtue of s. 35 of the Criminal Justice and Public Order Act 1994 invite inferences to be drawn on the accused's failure to testify but not, it seems, that of his spouse, a somewhat anomalous position.

Another illogicality is that it is difficult to see why persons under 16 should be better protected as victims than, for example, old or incapacitated people.

The criminal law thus treats spouses as witnesses in an unsatisfactory way. In civil cases by contrast, spouses are treated as any other witness although the threat to the institution of marriage by compelling them to appear is arguably similar to that in criminal cases. For these reasons it is submitted that the privilege afforded to spouses as witnesses should be further restricted subject to a discretionary exemption.

QUESTION 2

Dido is charged with causing criminal damage to some gnomes in the garden of 14 Churchill Road. The prosecution case is that she was hawking flowers door to door with her daughter Janet, aged 12. Mr. and Mrs. Baldwin refused to buy from her. As she left she allegedly kicked down the gnomes in anger.

Hector, the Baldwin's 20-year-old son, who has a mental age of 10, was looking out of the window. The prosecution wish to call Janet and Hector as witnesses.

Advise whether they are competent and compellable and comment critically on the law in this area.

Commentary

This is a similar question on two other groups of witnesses who are to some extent a deviation from universal competence and compellability. The law relating to children in criminal cases is now relatively simple and amended after much research in this area. However, it has only reached this state after a number of ad hoc statutory measures. Children are now assumed to be as competent in criminal trials as any other witness. Adults may be incompetent to testify through drunkenness, or some physical or mental disability. In this as in all other cases the question of competence in any specific case remains one for the trial judge.

Suggested Answer

Janet is a competent witness and compellable for the prosecution. The fact that a witness could not be imprisoned for failure to comply is not a good reason for refusing to issue a witness summons to compel her attendance: *R* v *Greenwich Justices, ex parte Carter* [1973] Crim LR 444. As a child under 14 Janet must give evidence unsworn: Criminal Justice Act 1988, s. 33A. This section (as amended) provides that the evidence of children under 14 is to be given unsworn and that a child's evidence must be received unless it appears to the court that the child is incapable of giving intelligible testimony. The court must decide not whether she is competent on grounds of age but whether she is capable of giving intelligible evidence. It is submitted that a normal 12-year-old would be. The importance of giving truthful evidence must be explained to her by the tribunal as part of the process of putting her at her ease. If it is decided to receive her evidence it is a matter of fact for the tribunal as to how much weight to attach to it. The position of child witnesses was the subject of much controversy and research. The Pigot Committee on Video Evidence set up by the Home Office, reporting in 1989, condemned the existing position as being founded on an archaic belief that children could not be honest and coherent witnesses. The law was subsequently changed so that there is now no preliminary examination of the child's ability to give evidence. The present practice is that the child should give evidence and only be stopped if it becomes clear he or she could not give an intelligible account. The result is that there is now no minimum age below which a child cannot give evidence, although in practice judicial discretion may be exercised. In *R* v *N* (1992) 95 Cr App R 256, the Court of Appeal said that the fact that a child was too young to be prosecuted for perjury was not a reason for excluding her evidence. The present state of the law arguably brings it into line with psychological research on the veracity of children. The emphasis on judicial discretion rather than strict rule is a welcome development.

The changes in the law relating to children's evidence were the result particularly of the difficulty of achieving successful prosecutions in the case of child victims of sexual abusers. As Birch (1992, p. 269) argues, 'Children contrary to what was once thought, are not necessarily unreliable at all, and are certainly no less dangerous as witnesses than those who abuse them'. However, some commentators doubt if the law even now is fully satisfactory. Murphy (1995) writes (at p. 429), 'It is submitted that the position is now as confused as it ever was'. He suggests that the test of competence is unclear. The Criminal Justice Act 1988 (as amended by the Criminal Justice and Public Order Act 1994) requires the court to accept the evidence unless the child is incapable of giving 'intelligible testimony'. Murphy argues that this 'appears to be a less stringent test than ascertaining whether or not the child understands the duty to speak the truth. A child may be intelligible and, at the same time, appear to the court to lack that understanding'. He suggests that the requirement of s. 52(2) of the Criminal Justice Act 1991 requiring that the judge assess the child's competence as he would that of 'any other person' reverts back to the common law and the test in *R* v *Hayes* [1977] 2 All ER 288. Arguably, further legislation is needed to clarify the statute.

As regards Hector, the court will probably take a pragmatic view and allow him to testify if it considers he understands the nature of the proceedings and can speak the truth to the best of his ability. In *R* v *Bellamy* (1985) 82 Cr App R 222, the Court of Appeal held that the cases then pertaining to the swearing of children applied in the case of an alleged victim in a rape case who was 33 years old but had a mental age of 10. It was not necessary for her to appreciate the divine sanction of the oath. This decision was welcomed as a break from earlier emphasis on the difficult theological implications of understanding the oath. Expert evidence may be admitted as to the witness's mental state but it was held in *R* v *Deakin* [1994] 4 All ER 769 that it should not be taken with the jury present over the defendant's objection. If Hector is held to be incompetent as a witness, his evidence could not be admitted under s. 23 of the Criminal Justice Act 1988 (see **Chapter 7**) because a precondition of admissibility here is that there is no other objection to the admission of documentary evidence other than the one based on hearsay. In considering this section, the Court of Appeal held in *R* v *Setz-Dempsey* [1994] Crim LR 123 that the admission of documentary statements from a mentally ill witness under s. 23(1)(a) of the Criminal Justice Act 1988 was a material irregularity. The judge had erred in law in not exercising his discretion under s. 26 and inter alia should have considered the psychiatrist's evidence about the likely quality of any evidence given by the witness and also the fact that the statements could not fairly be admitted without the jury hearing the witness's evidence.

QUESTION 3

(a) Andy and Bob are charged with indecent assault on two girls aged respectively 18 and 17. Carol, Andy's wife, told the police she witnessed the assaults. She signed a statement to that effect but now refuses to testify. Both defendants deny the charges. Advise Carol whether she is competent and/or compellable to testify (i) for Andy; (ii) for Bob; (iii) for the prosecution.

(b) Joan is contesting in the Family Division of the High Court, the local authority's decision to take her daughter Amy into care. Amy is seven years old. The local authority believe she has been sexually abused by Joan. Advise on Amy's status as a witness.

Commentary

Part **(a)** of this question is another question about spouses' evidence but there is the added complication of a co-defendant. Again your starting point is s. 80 of the Police and Criminal Evidence Act 1984 and you must systematically apply the law in the three instances given. Part **(b)** is an uncomplicated question asking you to outline the law relating to the reception of children's evidence in civil cases.

Suggested Answer

(a) The general rule is that all persons are competent and all competent witnesses are compellable. Whether or not the defendant's spouse can be required to give evidence is governed by s. 80 of the Police and Criminal Evidence Act 1984.

The effect in Carol's case is that (i) she is a competent witness for Andy and can be compelled to give evidence for him since she is not jointly charged (ss. 80(2) and (4)). (ii) She is a competent witness for Bob but if not jointly charged she cannot be compelled to give evidence because though the offence is of a sexual nature it was not committed in respect of a person who was at the material time under 16 years of age (s. 80(3)(b)). (iii) She is competent for the prosecution since she is not jointly charged but cannot be compelled to give evidence for the same reason as she cannot be compelled to give evidence for Bob.

Carol should be advised that it is for her to choose whether to give evidence for the prosecution or for Bob. Her choice is not affected by her having made a witness statement. She retains the right of refusal up to the point when, with full knowledge of that right, she takes the oath in the witness box: *R* v *Pitt* [1983] QB 25. If she does give evidence she will be treated in the same way as any other witness including a hostile witness: *R* v *Nelson* [1992] Crim LR 653.

(b) Under s. 96 of the Children Act 1989, children are allowed to testify unsworn and the then existing common law test of competency was enacted to apply in civil proceedings. The test is that the child has sufficient understanding of the duty to tell the truth to justify the reception of his evidence. For the purpose of the Act 'child' means any person who has not reached the age of 18. The judge will question Amy in open court before she gives any evidence and if she does not show sufficient understanding of the solemnity of the oath and the need to tell the truth he may decide she may give evidence unsworn or not testify at all.

It is possible that some of Amy's evidence may be heard as hearsay. In any proceedings in connection with the upbringing, maintenance or welfare of a child the Children (Admissibility of Hearsay) Order 1993 allows the reception of hearsay from witnesses less than 18 years of age. In *R* v *B, ex parte P* [1991] 2 All ER 65, 72 Butler-Sloss LJ referred to the need to treat such evidence 'anxiously and consider carefully the extent to which it can properly be relied upon'.

QUESTION 4

Margaret, a partner in a hairdressing salon, is charged with conspiracy to defraud. It is alleged that at a meeting she and her partners agreed to send false VAT returns. Margaret gave no answer when asked about this meeting by the police. At the trial, she refuses to testify but claims through her counsel that she left the meeting early before the matters alleged were discussed. Advise the prosecution on how they can treat these facts.

Commentary

This question deals with a defendant's failure to respond to police questioning and also failure to testify. Failure to respond to police questioning is dealt with more fully in **Chapter 8** on confessions, but it is covered here in the specific context of its application when a defendant does not testify. A preliminary matter is the question of an alibi notice.

Suggested Answer

If this is a trial on indictment, by s. 11(1) of the Criminal Justice Act 1967, the defence may not, without leave of the court, adduce evidence in support of an alibi unless they have issued an alibi notice within seven days of the close of committal proceedings. Leave should not be refused if the accused was not told by the magistrates of the need to issue a notice. Margaret's failure to answer to the police may well allow the drawing of adverse inferences now that the right of silence has been restricted by s. 34, Criminal Justice and Public Order Act 1994. It was held in *R* v *Lewis* (1973) 57 Cr App R 830 that the judge should not comment on the accused's failure to mention an alibi when arrested but that is arguably no longer the law. If when questioned under caution, charged or informed that she might be charged, Margaret failed to mention a fact on which she subsequently relies in her defence, the court may draw such inferences as appear proper. The section applies whether or not Margaret gives evidence since it refers to a failure 'to mention any fact relied on in his defence in these proceedings'. Thus if Margaret's counsel leads on such evidence, Margaret runs the risk of adverse comment being made by the prosecution. Another condition is that the section applies if, as seems likely here, Margaret could reasonably have been expected to mention such facts when questioned by the police under caution. By s. 35 of the Criminal Justice and Public Order Act 1994, adverse inferences can also be drawn by the court from her refusal to give evidence at trial. It is not, however, contempt of court for Margaret to fail to testify in her defence.

Before the Criminal Justice and Public Order Act 1994 it was forbidden for the prosecution to comment on the accused's failure to testify although comment was allowed by the judge. The law in this regard was restated by the Court of Appeal in *R* v *Martinez-Tobon* [1994] 1 WLR 388. The judge should direct that the defendant was under no obligation to testify and that the jury should not assume he is guilty because he had not given evidence. Cross and Tapper (1995, p. 418) suggests that 'It is interesting that this guidance was provided in full knowledge of the imminent passage of s. 35'. May (1995, p. 374) however suggests that now 'the judge is free to comment as he thinks fit'. The prosecution is also permitted by s. 35 of the 1994 Act to comment on Margaret's failure to testify but the section does not specify what kind of comment is appropriate. Cross and Tapper (1995, p. 417) write, 'it may be assumed that the existing law relating to the form of comment permitted to the judge is to be extended to the prosecution'. It may be some comfort to Margaret to rely on s. 38(3) of the Criminal Justice and Public Order Act 1994:

> A person shall not have the proceedings against him transferred to the Crown Court for trial, have a case to answer or be convicted solely on an inference drawn from such a failure as is mentioned in section 34(2), section 35(3). . . .

Guidance on judicial comment where the accused does not give evidence is now to be found in the Court of Appeal's judgment in *R* v *Cowan* [1995] 3 WLR 818. In three separate cases, heard together on appeal, defendants who had not given evidence appealed against conviction on the grounds of non-compliance with sections 35 and 38(3) of the Criminal Justice and Public Order Act 1994. The court held that s. 35(4) had expressly preserved the right to silence but that while the burden of proving guilt beyond reasonable doubt lay throughout on the prosecution the court or jury might draw the inference from a defendant's failure to testify to be a further evidential factor in support of the prosecution's case. A specimen direction from the Judicial Studies Board was a sound guide and before any inferences from silence could be drawn the jury had to be satisfied that a case to answer had been established by the prosecution. In G and C's case misdirections had been made and the convictions were quashed. In C's case the judge had failed to tell the jury that they could not infer guilt solely from silence or to warn them that they could not hold his silence against him unless the only sensible explanation was that he had no answer to the case against him which could have stood up to cross-examination. In G's case there were also shortcomings in the summing up. In R's case the judge had directed the jury correctly. Thus the prosecution may invite the court to draw adverse inferences from Margaret's failure to give her explanation about her whereabouts at the investigation stage and from her failure to testify. The judge will not, however, be able to invite an inference of guilt from Margaret's silence alone.

4 Character Evidence

INTRODUCTION

This chapter is concerned with one of the most complex questions in the law of evidence, namely, those situations in which the accused may adduce evidence of his good character to suggest lack of guilt and support credibility and those in which the prosecution counsel or the counsel for the co-defendant may cross-examine him on previous discreditable behaviour. Such cross-examination however, is for the purpose of eliciting evidence to show the defendant's lack of credibility. It is not for the purpose of suggesting he is guilty of the offence for which he is now charged. Thus it is different from the purpose for which similar fact evidence is called namely, to suggest guilt (see **Chapter 5**). You must be aware of the meaning of character in this context and the general rule that evidence of bad character is inadmissible. This is an exclusionary rule fundamental to the English legal system and based on the principle that the defendant should have a fair trial based on the instant charge. As is the case with all exclusionary rules in evidence, there are exceptions to it. These occur both at common law which applies when the defendant does not give evidence and in the Criminal Evidence Act 1898 (as amended) which applies to cross-examination. Thus, you must be clear both that the rule on exclusion of character evidence only applies to the defendant and that different rules apply when the defendant gives evidence and lays himself open to cross-examination and when he elects not to testify.

This topic makes a regular appearance on examination papers on the law of evidence, both in the form of problem questions and, since it has generated a certain amount of theoretical debate, also essay questions. Whether or not you are allowed to take a statute book into the examination, you must be very familiar with the somewhat tortuous text of ss. 1(e) and (f). The following suggested answers draw your attention to some recent important cases, legislative changes and academic discussion on this topic.

QUESTION 1

Andy, Ben and Catherine are charged with theft of video machines brought to their shop for repairs by David. They all plead not guilty. Andy testifies in his own defence. He claims that Ben had asked him to help steal the machines but he had refused. Andy has several convictions for criminal damage. At the trial counsel for the prosecution and for Ben cross-examine Andy on these convictions. Ben does not give evidence but through his counsel claims he had nothing to do with the theft. He calls several witnesses to give evidence that he has done extensive charitable work for a local pensioners' club for many years. Catherine testifies at the trial and claims that David who is a prosecution witness was falsely implicating her out of resentment because she refused to have an affair with him. Catherine has a conviction for shoplifting. The prosecution cross-examine her on this. During questioning prosecution counsel refers to the fact that a shop assistant was hurt in a struggle with Catherine during the previous offence of shoplifting. In her summing-up the judge tells the jury that they may take Ben's good character evidence as relevant to his lack of credibility and his propensity to commit offences. She refers to Andy and Catherine's convictions briefly by saying they had 'a bit of trouble with the law in the past'. Ben is acquitted. Andy and Catherine are convicted.

Advise them whether they have any grounds of appeal.

Commentary

Like many questions on examination papers, this question is difficult to answer without a knowledge of the most recent cases. The astute student will be aware that academic lawyers, who set the papers, find most of their raw material in legal journals and in law reports. The final phase of revision for a law examination should include reading the most recent reported cases in that area. This can usually be done by scanning relevant articles in, for example, *New Law Journal*, *Solicitors Journal*, *Law Quarterly Review* and *Modern Law Review*. This question only asks you about appeals for two defendants so do not deal in detail with Ben's position except in so far as it affects the others. The issues are:

Andy: whether evidence of previous convictions is admissible because an imputation was made on a co-defendant, under the Criminal Evidence Act 1898; whether if they are admissible there is a discretion to exclude; whether the judge correctly directed the jury on such convictions where one defendant is of good character.

Catherine: application of the Criminal Evidence Act 1898 since she testifies; the effect of impugning a prosecution witness; whether the prosecution can cross-examine on details of the previous conviction.

Suggested Answer

The success of Andy's and Catherine's appeals rests on whether the Criminal Evidence Act 1898 and subsequent case law have been properly applied in relation to the questioning and direction on their previous convictions. Under the common law such questioning is not allowed to show evidence of disposition but only under the similar fact principle which does not apply here: *Makin* v *Attorney-General of New South Wales* [1894] AC 57. However, under the Criminal Evidence Act 1898 defendants who elect to testify may be cross-examined on their previous bad character or, as it is called, lose their shield under certain circumstances. Andy has arguably lost his shield by making an imputation against his co-defendant Ben. Section 1(f)(iii) makes a defendant liable to cross-examination on his previous convictions 'if he has given evidence against any other person charged in the same proceedings'. The meaning of 'evidence against another person' was examined by the House of Lords in *Murdoch* v *Taylor* [1965] AC 574. The case established that it means evidence which supports the prosecution case in a material respect or which undermines the defence of the co-defendant in a material respect. The intention with which the evidence is given is irrelevant.

Here, from the facts we are given, it is very likely that Andy's evidence contradicts Ben's denial of involvement. The judge is properly able to allow cross-examination on Andy's previous convictions. Though Andy has made himself vulnerable to such cross-examination because of his attack on Ben, the judge has a discretion to refuse to allow the prosecution to cross-examine Andy about his record: *Selvey* v *Director of Public Prosecutions* [1970] AC 304. That discretion is to be exercised on principles set out by the Court of Criminal Appeal in *R* v *Jenkins* (1945) 31 Cr App R 1, at p. 15. The judge should refuse leave to cross-examine where:

> the putting of such questions as to the character of the accused person may be fraught with results which immeasurably outweigh the result of questions put by the defence and which make a fair trial of the accused person almost impossible.

The fact that Andy's convictions are for criminal damage is a factor which could be taken into account in exercising the discretion since they are non-dishonesty offences and therefore do not directly bear on credibility. However, the judge is not obliged to disallow such cross-examination. In *R* v *Powell* [1985] 1 WLR 1364, the Court of Appeal acknowledged that it had too readily interfered with judicial discretion in *R* v *Watts* [1983] 3 All ER 101, and overlooked the 'tit for tat' principle enunciated in *Selvey*. If the convictions were spent by virtue of the Rehabilitation of Offenders Act 1974 the judge's permission for cross-examination would have been required.

There is, however, no discretion to prevent Ben's counsel questioning Andy on his previous offences: *Murdoch* v *Taylor* [1965] AC 574. Furthermore, the right to cross-examine is arguably only limited on grounds of relevance. Thus the Court of Appeal held in *R* v *Reid* [1989] Crim LR 719 that the trial judge had been correct to permit cross-examination of the defendant on the underlying facts of a previous conviction since he had given evidence against his co-defendant. Of course, since the purpose of the cross-examination is to show that Andy is not to be believed, it could be argued that details of a conviction for criminal damage are not logically probative: *DPP* v *Kilbourne* [1973] AC 729. Andy therefore has probably no good grounds of appeal on the issue of the admission of cross-examination on his previous convictions.

However, Andy may consider a possible ground of appeal, in that the judge may not have properly directed the jury on the evidential value of the cross-examination on previous convictions, particularly since he is being tried alongside a person of good character. The defendant has long been entitled to adduce evidence of his good character with the aim of inducing the jury to conclude that a person with that character would not commit the alleged offence. The general common law rule is that evidence of character is confined to evidence of general reputation (*R* v *Rowton* (1865) Le & Ca 520; *R* v *Redgrave* (1981) 74 Cr App R 10), though as an indulgence, such evidence is often admitted for the defendant. After 1898, when the defendant became capable of giving evidence at his trial, his good character was said to go primarily to his credibility: *R* v *Bellis* [1966] 1 WLR 234. Where a defendant of good character has given evidence, the judge is required to direct the jury about the relevance of good character to the defendant's credibility, but also to refer to the likelihood that a person of good character would act as charged. Problems arise where, as here, a person without a blot on his record (Ben) is tried alongside a defendant of bad character (Andy). By drawing the jury's attention to the fact that a person of Ben's good character is less likely than a person of bad character to have committed the offence, the judge inevitably suggests that Andy is more likely to have committed it. This is a connection between character and propensity, the very chain of reasoning the jury is not supposed to make. However, there is authority that the judge should refer to the issue whether a person of good character would commit the alleged offence, even where the co-defendant is of bad character: *R* v *Vye* [1993] 1 WLR 471. The defendant who possesses the bad character is entitled to a direction as to the limited relevance of his previous convictions. Without such a direction, the jury might assume that the previous convictions are relevant to the same issues as good character, and particularly to propensity to commit crime and, by extension, guilt. In *R* v *Cain* [1994] 1 WLR 1449 a case involving three defendants, one defendant had previous convictions, including an offence of dishonesty. The judge directed the jury as to the significance of one co-defendant's good character and said of another defendant only that he had 'had a spot of trouble with the police before'. However, the Court of Appeal dismissed the appeal of the latter on conviction. It accepted that the judge should have warned the jury to disregard the convictions as irrelevant to guilt but came to the conclusion that his dismissive language had reduced any adverse inferences which the jury might otherwise have drawn. Since a full direction would have reminded the jury that the convictions were relevant to credibility, the overall effect was not less favourable to the defendant than it would have been if a full direction had been given.

Again, the fact that Andy's convictions are for criminal damage, not an offence involving dishonesty, is unlikely to change the position, though it will probably rule out, as irrelevant, examination on the details of the offences for which he was convicted. It is therefore submitted that Andy may not have any good ground of appeal on this issue of direction on the evidential worth of his bad character.

Catherine has impugned a prosecution witness, and so has put her character in issue under s. 1(f)(ii) of the Criminal Evidence Act 1898. The major issue here is how far prosecuting counsel can question her as to the circumstances surrounding her previous offences. This issue has caused the courts a good deal of difficulty. The conviction was quashed by the Court of Appeal in *R* v *Khan* [1991] Crim LR 51, where the questioning went into too much detail about the previous conviction. In *R* v *McLeod* [1994] 1 WLR 1500, the Court of Appeal reviewed the case law on this issue and confirmed that it is undesirable for the cross-examination of a defendant under s. 1(f)(ii) of the Criminal Evidence Act 1898 regarding previous convictions to be prolonged or extensive. Prosecuting counsel should not seek to probe or emphasise similarities between the underlying facts of previous offences and that charged unless the earlier offences are admissible as similar fact evidence, as clearly in Catherine's case they are not. The prosecution seems, in Catherine's case, to have gone too far:

it is hard to see how her credibility is undermined by the details of the struggle with the shop assistant. However, as the Court of Appeal made clear in *McLeod*, defence counsel should have objected at the time to the prosecution's course of questioning and counsel's failure to do so will make it difficult for Catherine to argue on appeal that the judge wrongly exercised his discretion to allow the questioning. The Court in *McLeod* stated that in every case where the accused has been cross-examined as to his character and previous offences, the judge must in the summing-up tell the jury that the purpose of the questioning goes only to credit and the jury should not consider that it shows a propensity to commit the offence they are considering. If that was not done here, Catherine has a good ground of appeal, particularly as she is being tried as a co-defendant: *R* v *Cain*.

QUESTION 2

Thelma and Louise are jointly charged with the murder of Harry. Both plead not guilty to the charge. Their explanation is that Harry had tried to rape Louise and in the course of protecting her, Thelma had pushed him down a flight of stairs. Both had fled the scene but had later given themselves up to the police. Louise chooses not to give evidence but her counsel calls her ex-employer to give evidence that she was an excellent employee who organises the firm's social club. Her counsel also suggests in cross-examining a prosecution witness, Gary, that Harry and he had been drinking steadily for several hours on the night of the murder and that they had a struggle outside the pub afterwards. Louise has two previous convictions, one for taking and driving away a vehicle and another for assault.

Thelma elects to testify and in the course of her testimony, she explains her flight from the scene of the incident by saying that she was afraid of the police because she had cannabis in her pocket. Thelma has several other drug-related convictions and is awaiting trial on a charge of violent disorder. The police claim that Thelma had confessed to intending to kill Harry but Thelma denies making any such confession.

Discuss the evidential issues involved.

Commentary

This is a typical problem question on this topic. You will have to be familiar with the common law and statutory provisions relating to evidence of character. In approaching this question, the easiest way may be to deal with each accused in turn. With regard to Louise, you should first comment on her failure to testify and consider whether the common law or the Criminal Evidence Act 1898 apply in this situation. You would then be expected to consider the position of evidence of character at common law, more particularly the prosecution's right to introduce evidence of her bad character. Finally, with regards to Louise you should discuss whether evidence of her previous convictions is admissible by virtue of her possible imputations on the character of the prosecution witness.

As regards Thelma, you would need to consider whether she has cast imputations on the character of the prosecution witnesses and the victim thereby losing her shield under s. 1(f)(ii) of the Criminal Evidence Act 1898. You would then be expected to go on to discuss the extent to which, if any, she can be cross-examined as to the details and circumstances of the previous convictions as well as her pending charge of violent disorder. As part of this discussion, you will also have to examine the circumstances in which the court will exercise its inherent discretion to disallow cross-examination on her previous convictions. Finally, you will have to consider the meaning of the words 'tending to show' in s. 1(f) of the Criminal Evidence Act 1898.

Suggested Answer

The main issues in this case involve the question as to whether Thelma and Louise's character can be brought into evidence. With regard to Louise, the scope of permissible comment by the judge and counsel for the prosecution is covered by s. 35 of the Criminal Justice and Public Order Act 1994, whereby 'the court or jury in determining whether the accused is guilty of the offence charged, may draw such inferences as appear proper from the failure of the accused to give evidence'. This repeals s. 1(b) of the Criminal Evidence Act 1898 which disallowed comment by the prosecution on failure to testify. The judge could previously comment but the scope of such comment was limited: see *R* v *Martinez-Tobon* [1994] 1 WLR 388 and, a case subsequent to the passing of the 1994 Act, *R* v *Cowan* [1995] 3 WLR 828. Even before the passing of the 1994 Act the co-accused could comment on Louise's failure to give evidence and the judge could not prevent this: *R* v *Wickham* (1971) 55 Cr App R 199.

The accused is entitled to adduce evidence of her own good character with the aim of persuading the jury that a person with that character is unlikely to have committed the alleged offence. The rule at common law is that evidence of character is confined to evidence of general reputation and not of specific creditable acts. The leading case on this is *R* v *Rowton* (1865) Le & Ca 520 which was followed in *R* v *Redgrave* (1981) 74 Cr App R 10. In the latter case, the accused who was charged with offences relating to homosexuality, was not allowed to prove his heterosexuality by evidence of past liaisons with members of the opposite sex. The question that arises is whether the evidence of her ex-employer is evidence of her general reputation which is relevant to the case. It is likely that the court will accept that this evidence is admissible, since as May puts it (at p. 120) 'the common law rule is persistently ignored'. If this is the case, then the prosecution is entitled to cross-examine her ex-employer or call evidence of her bad reputation. As she is not giving evidence, she cannot be cross-examined on her bad character. It has been made clear by the Court of Criminal Appeal in *R* v *Winfield* [1939] 4 All ER 164 that character is indivisible. Once she has asserted her good character through her ex-employer, the prosecution can introduce the other aspects of her character. Thus, it is likely that her previous convictions for taking and driving away a vehicle and for assault can be introduced by the prosecution. It should be noted that if the previous convictions were committed by her whilst under the age of 14, these will not be admissible in evidence: s. 16(2) of the Children and Young Persons Act 1963. Further, if the previous convictions were spent convictions, then although the Rehabilitation of Offenders Act 1974 does not apply strictly to criminal proceedings, the *Practice Direction (Crime: Spent Convictions)* [1975] 1 WLR 1065 issued by Lord Widgery, makes it clear that a spent conviction should not be introduced in evidence without the authority of the judge. This authority would not be given unless the interests of justice so require it. If the previous conviction is a spent conviction, the court will have to decide whether it is in the interests of justice to allow it to be introduced.

Louise's counsel also cross-examines Gary on the fact that he and Harry were drinking steadily for several hours and had been involved in a struggle outside the pub afterwards. As she is not giving evidence, her counsel can cast imputations on the character of prosecution witnesses or the deceased without any fear of her bad character being introduced by the prosecution on these grounds. In *R* v *Butterwasser* [1948] 1 KB 4, it was decided by the Court of Criminal Appeal that at common law, evidence of the accused's bad character cannot be called for the prosecution even when the accused has attacked witnesses for the prosecution and put their character in issue, where he has not given evidence. In practice this will not make any difference if the court decides that the evidence of her ex-employer amounts to giving evidence of her good character, in which case, her bad character can be introduced under that heading.

As regards Thelma's testimony, there is nothing on the facts of the case provided to suggest that she has given any evidence of her good character.

However, it may be that her testimony amounts to casting imputations against the prosecution witnesses. Under s. 1(f) of the Criminal Evidence Act 1898, where she gives evidence at the trial, she is provided with a 'shield', whereby the prosecution may not ask her about her previous convictions or her bad character. This shield may be lost where she has cast imputations on the character of the prosecutor or the prosecution witnesses: s. 1(f)(ii) of the Criminal Evidence Act 1898.

The main question here is whether Thelma, by denying that she had confessed to intending to kill Harry, thereby contradicting the police witnesses, has cast an imputation on the character of the prosecution witnesses or whether it will be regarded as a mere denial of guilt. In *R* v *Rouse* [1904] 1 KB 184, the court held that where the accused alleged that the prosecution witness was a liar, this did not amount to an imputation. This was because it was merely a denial of guilt. Contrast this with *R* v *Rappolt* [1911] 6 Cr App R 156. The Court of Appeal in *R* v *Nelson* [1978] 68 Cr App R 12, decided that it was not an imputation to deny that he had made admissions which the prosecution witness had recounted. The reason for this was because all that the accused was doing was merely to assert his defence. However, a different approach was taken by the Court of Appeal in *R* v *Tanner* [1977] 66 Cr App R 56. In this case, the accused was held to have made imputations on the character of the prosecution witnesses where it was not possible to explain the discrepancy between the accused's and the prosecution version of the events other than by finding that either the accused or the prosecution witnesses had fabricated the evidence. This case was approved by the Court of Appeal in the case of *R* v *Britzman* [1983] 1 WLR 350, where the court laid down various guidelines as to the approach to be taken in this type of situation. The court stated, inter alia, that where there is a denial of one incident, no matter how emphatically made, it would not result in the loss of the accused's shield. It would be different if it was a denial of long interviews or observations. Further, the court stressed that there must be no possibility of mistake, misunderstanding or confusion and that allowance should be made for the strain of being in the witness box. The court also emphasised that there is no need to rely on s. 1(f)(ii) of the 1898 Act where the evidence against the accused is overwhelming. These guidelines appear to have been accepted and applied in later cases, for example, the Court of Appeal decision in *R* v *St Louis* (1984) 79 Cr App R 53.

It is thus a question of fact whether Thelma's denial of the admission is a denial of one incident or a series of incidents, due allowance being given for the stress of being in the witness stand. As this information is not provided, the question as to whether she has lost her shield by casting imputations on the prosecution witnesses is for the court to decide. If she has lost her shield, then she can be cross-examined as to her previous convictions. It would appear that she can be cross-examined about offences committed after the offence with which she is being tried: *R* v *Wood* [1920] 2 KB 179, and *R* v *Coltress* (1978) 68 Cr App R 193. However, that appears to be restricted to the situation where the subsequent offence resulted in a conviction by the time of the trial of the offence with which she is being charged. In *R* v *Smith* [1989] Crim LR 900, the Court of Appeal decided that the accused cannot be asked in cross-examination about pending charges because it may tend to undermine her right to silence in relation to those offences.

If the court rules that Thelma has lost her shield under s. 1(f)(ii) of the Criminal Evidence Act 1898, the next question that arises is whether merely the fact of the convictions can be put to her or whether she can be asked details of the earlier convictions. It is not clear on the facts to what these previous convictions relate. If the previous convictions relate to offences of violence, then unless they are ruled as similar fact evidence, the circumstances relating to those offences would not be admissible. This is because the cross-examination of the accused under s. 1(f)(ii) relates to credibility of the accused rather than to guilt. This was emphasised recently by the Court of Appeal in *R* v *Khan* [1991] Crim LR 51, and *R* v *McLeod* [1994] 1 WLR 1500.

Further, it should be noted that even if Thelma can be cross-examined on the previous convictions, the court has an inherent discretion to exclude this cross-examination: *Selvey* v *DPP* [1970] AC 304. Earlier cases such as the House of Lords decision in *Maxwell* v *DPP* [1935] AC 309, and the Court of Appeal decision in *R* v *Watts* [1983] 3 All ER 101, suggested that the court should use its discretion to exclude previous convictions which were similar in nature to the offence for which the accused is being tried. However, in *R* v *Powell* [1985] 1 WLR 1364, it was made clear by the Court of Appeal that there is no absolute rule to this effect and the court should exercise its discretion in accordance with the facts of the case. It is thus unclear whether the court will exercise its discretion to exclude these previous convictions if they were similar in nature to the offence charged.

It should be noted that s. 1(f)(ii) of the Criminal Evidence Act 1898 has been amended by s. 31 of the Criminal Justice and Public Order Act 1994, which has the effect of causing the accused to lose her shield where imputations are cast on the character of the deceased victim. The new provision, which has already drawn sharp academic criticism (see Munday, (1995), pp. 855 and 895) will complicate the defence not only of persons accused of murder but also of alleged perpetrators of other offences in which the victim has died before the trial, though the peers who were responsible for its introduction seem not to have realised its scope. Thus, if Thelma alleges that Harry tried to rape Louise, she thus runs the risk of being cross-examined on her bad character.

Concerning her explanation of her flight from the scene the evidential impact is less clear cut. In *R* v *Thompson* [1966] 1 WLR 405 the court held that introducing bad character as part of a defence did not necessarily involve loss of shield. The defendant is not hereby claiming that possession of cannabis was the totality of her bad character. On the other hand, the phrase 'tending to show' in s. 1(f) has been interpreted by the House of Lords in *Jones* v *DPP* [1962] AC 635, and the Court of Appeal in *R* v *Anderson* [1988] QB 678, as meaning tending to show to the jury for the first time. Thus, where the accused has revealed his previous convictions or the fact that he has been in trouble with the police before, cross-examination of the accused as to his record does not reveal this fact to the jury for the first time. Thus, the prosecution may be allowed to cross-examine Thelma on her previous convictions, although the restrictions as to pending charges and spent convictions apply similarly in this context.

QUESTION 3

'The courts are losing the battle to find the most satisfactory way of applying s. 1(f)(ii) [of the Criminal Evidence Act 1898]. The main gap in their defences is the rigid adherence to the view that the purpose of cross-examination under proviso (ii) is to challenge the accused's credibility ... there must now be considerable doubt whether in many cases, this purpose is being (or indeed can be) served by such cross-examination.' (Seabrooke (1987, at p. 238)).

Discuss.

Commentary

Essay questions on the Criminal Evidence Act 1898 are reasonably common in examinations on the law of evidence, since the law has generated much academic controversy and often conflicting case law. You should not attempt this question if you are not familiar with these. You are asked to comment on the approach taken by the courts to the evidential value of bad character, namely that it goes to credibility. This question requires a brief outline of the compromise achieved by s. 1(f). The Criminal Evidence Act 1898 allowed the accused to appear as a witness for the first time. Unlike other witnesses, however, he was allowed a shield in that he was protected from cross-examination on his past record unless he put his own good character in or impugned a prosecution witness. (You are not being asked in this question about the third trigger to loss of shield, namely undermining the defence of a co-accused). You should deal with the first aspect of the proviso, putting in good character, and discuss *R* v *Winfield* [1939] 4 All ER 164. Deal then with the circumstances of loss of shield by impugning a prosecution witness, the 'tit for tat' principle (*Selvey* v *DPP* [1970] AC 304; *R* v *Watts* [1983] 3 All ER 101; *R* v *Powell* [1985] 1 WLR 1364). The question requires you to discuss judicial directions on credibility and propensity and the difficulties faced where one defendant is of good character and the other has a criminal record. This raises the question of whether it is possible to differentiate credibility and propensity (the House of Lords in *R* v *Aziz* [1996] 1 AC 41, differentiated between the two on the basis that no direction as to credibility need be given when the defendant had not given evidence, and dealt with the circumstances in which a judge could refuse a direction to a defendant with no convictions; see also *R* v *Cain* [1994] 1 WLR 1449). You should then discuss generally (since there are as yet no reported cases) the recent change in law to include imputations against a deceased victim and deal finally with any academic discussion on the statutory provision. Your answer will be improved if you can show familiarity with Seabrooke's article which is quoted here and also other academics such as McEwan (1992); Zuckerman (1989); and Munday (1985).

Suggested Answer

English law only allows the jury to hear about discreditable events in the accused's past (apart of course from evidence about the instant charge or charges) in exceptional circumstances. The Criminal Evidence Act 1898, which for the first time allowed the accused to testify in his own defence, provides five of these in relation to cross-examination of the accused. These are: similar fact evidence (dealt with in s. 1(f)(i)); those occasions where the accused undermines the evidence of the co-accused (s. 1(f)(iii)); and the three referred to in this question, namely where the accused puts himself forward as a person of good character; where he impugns a prosecution witness; and since the implementation of s. 31 of the Criminal Justice and Public Order Act 1994, where the accused impugns a deceased victim (see s. 1(f)(ii) of the 1898 Act). The rationale behind the three last exceptions will be examined.

Munday (1985 at p. 79) refers to the 'commonsensical' principle behind the first limb of s. 1(f)(ii) in that there is a clear logic in the proposition that a man who claims to be of good character and therefore not the sort of person to commit the offence with which he is charged, should be cross-examined if there is evidence from his past that he is in fact the sort of man to commit that kind of offence. The cross-examination may indicate past criminal acts and suggest whether the defendant is the sort of person who is likely to tell the truth on oath. There is a paradox here in that, as Viscount Sankey pointed out in the House of Lords in *Maxwell* v *DPP* [1935] AC 309, evidence of good character is likely to be taken by the jury as evidence that the accused is a person who is unlikely to have committed the offence with which he is charged. Here the common law established before 1898 the principle that such evidence went to the issue of guilt, clearly credibility being not an issue since the defendant did not testify. The recent case of *R* v *Vye* [1993] 1 WLR 471 makes it clear that a direction as to the relevance of good character to the likelihood of the defendant having committed the offence charged, was to be given whether or not he had testified. This was to be accompanied by a direction as to the relevance of the good character to credibility as well where the defendant testifies, or alternatively, relies on pre-trial 'mixed' statements. The *Vye* direction need not be given when a defendant without previous convictions is shown beyond doubt to have been guilty of serious criminal behaviour similar to the offence charged. In these circumstances, the House of Lords held in *R* v *Aziz* [1996] 1 AC 41 it would be an insult to common sense for the judge to give the *Vye* direction. The difficulties suggested in the question of differentiating credibility and guilt are illustrated in *R* v *Cain* [1994] 1 WLR 1449. Here the issue arose of what direction was appropriate if an accused of good character is jointly tried with an accused of bad character whose previous convictions have been placed before the jury. Here the former is entitled to the *Vye* direction and the jury should be directed that the previous convictions of the other are not relevant to guilt, but are relevant to credibility. Thus, one difficulty of the application of the principle that bad character is relevant to credibility, arises when good character of a co-defendant is also presented at the trial.

Related to this is the further difficulty of appreciating the rationale of the first limb of s. 1(f)(ii). It was made clear in *R* v *Winfield* [1939] 4 All ER 164 that the purpose of the question is to match the favourable impression created by the good character evidence. Humphreys J pointed out (at p. 165) that 'there is no such thing known to our procedure as putting half your character in issue and leaving out the other half'. This leads to the somewhat anomalous position that the trial judge will allow cross-examination on previous offences even if they bear no relation to the good character evidence. McEwan (at p. 159) argues that *Winfield* is 'indefensible' in that it allows exclusion of offences close in nature to the current offence because the defendant chooses not to lose his shield, but admits offences that are totally irrelevant because he has so chosen.

She points out that the tribunal of fact is directed to assess the defendant's overall creditworthiness in the light of his bad character rather than judge if the prosecution has refuted the specific claims made. Thus, the jury is told to consider that convictions for theft are a relevant response to a claim made by a witness that the defendant was not the sort of person to assault women. The House of Lords cited *Winfield* in *Stirland* v *DPP* [1944] AC 315.

Furthermore, it is indeed questionable whether it is conceptually possible to draw a distinction between evidence going to propensity and evidence going to credibility, let alone whether the judge could convey this to the jury. Munday (p. 65) quoting Cross refers to this as 'one of those distinctions without a difference'. Partly he draws on psychology to show the fallacy of the belief that there exists some unitary entity which can be called credibility and that dishonesty in one situation suggests dishonesty in all. In any case the jury are being asked to accept that there is a recognizable distinction between the statement that the accused is of bad character and is not telling the truth and that the accused is of bad character and the sort of person who commits the instant offence.

This questionable conceptual device is even more marked in relation to the second limb of s. 1(f)(ii). Here the accused loses his shield if he impugns the character of a witness for the prosecution and, since November 1994, a dead victim. The problem of what amounts to an imputation is a difficult one but is not the subject of this question. Here, the protection against revelation of past record referred to by Munday (at p. 63 quoting Wigmore) as the 'inborn sporting instinct of Anglo Normandom' can give way to what he calls the 'crude retaliatory notion of tit for tat'. The rationale seems to be that, if the accused attacks the character of a prosecution witness, and there is no such tit for tat response, the jury will not be able to judge who is telling the truth. There are, as Munday shows, several weaknesses in this argument. First, it is not clear why it should not apply when the accused is not impugning the prosecution witness. The usual explanation is that the character evidence is too prejudicial in that it might make the jury lower the standard of proof and convict for emotional not rational reactions to the evidence. These same concerns apply whatever evidence has been given against the prosecution witness.

Secondly, an analysis of *R* v *Britzman* [1983] 1 WLR 350, the leading case on the guidelines to be applied in cases where the defendant impugns a police officer, contains a particularly odd formulation. The prosecution are told not to rely on the proviso if other evidence against the defendant is overwhelming. But why should legally admissible evidence be excluded on this strange ground? It suggests the courts are worried about this form of prejudicial evidence, reflecting as Munday (at p. 76) says 'the fragility of the conceptual framework' of the section.

Thirdly, the courts have shown a readiness to admit criminal convictions even where the imputation made was a necessary part of the defence, illustrating that the section is not only based on compensating for an intended discrediting of a prosecution witness and severely hampering the defence tactics of a defendant with a record. Thus, despite this inconsistency, the House of Lords in *Selvey* v *DPP* [1970] AC 304 held that the words of the statute should be given their ordinary and natural meaning. 'Nature and conduct of the defence' was taken to mean that which was inherent in the defence and the actual handling of the case by the defendant or his advocate.

Fourthly, the exercise of the discretion to exclude evidence under this head shows the courts have moved away from only admitting cases which reflect dishonesty, again blurring the distinction between credit and propensity. Thus in *Selvey* cross-examination was actually limited to offences of a similar type to that charged, i.e., indecency, although the effect must have been to suggest an inference of guilt since the defendant had previous convictions for similar offences. In *R* v *Powell* [1985] 1 WLR 1364, the court felt that it had interfered too lightly with the discretion in the earlier case of *R* v *Watts* [1983] 3 All ER 101 and the fact that the defendant's convictions are not for offences of dishonesty, or are for offences bearing a close resemblance to the offence charged, are factors to be taken into consideration when the court is exercising its discretion but does not oblige the court to disallow the proposed cross-examination. Thus this approach both allows similar fact in through the back door and allows non-dishonesty offences when their relationship to lack of credibility is difficult to fathom. On the similar fact point the danger of this approach is illustrated further by the recent Court of Appeal case of *R* v *McLeod* [1994] 1 WLR 1500 which took a lenient view on the extent of questioning about the surrounding circumstances of previous offences.

Finally, the changes made in the Criminal Justice and Public Order Act 1994 make the argument that the purpose of the section is to assess relative credibilities increasingly threadbare. The credibility of a dead victim can hardly be at issue.

The intellectual difficulties revealed in the statute and its application have prompted several writers to propose reform. Thus Zuckerman (1989 at p. 245) suggests that:

> [a] more effective way of combating prejudice would be to bring into the open the scope of prejudice created by evidence of past criminal record and strive to persuade juries that the principles of criminal justice, which require resisting prejudice, reflect their own perception of justice.

There is thus an argument for saying that criminal record should be routinely admitted as in continental jurisdictions and the jury should be directed to treat it as part of the defendant's curriculum vitae. This would both avoid highlighting the criminal record as happens now and also the almost accidental way a defendant can lose his shield. Zuckerman (1989 at p. 246) concludes that, 'the question of admissibility (will be) less important because the tools will be in place for counteracting prejudice'. But this position arguably underestimates the amount of prejudice juries frequently draw from convictions and also presupposes that the judiciary are able to convey such complex ethical messages to a jury of differing experiences and moral standpoints. Munday is sympathetic towards the position that all character evidence concerning the defendant should be excluded, while Seabrooke put forward the innovatory argument that only experiences in the defendant's past that are similar to the allegations he makes against the prosecution witness should be allowed. This, he argues, would ensure a real balance of retaliatory evidence. The weight of academic evidence criticizing the section does suggest that the question rightly points out how complex and intellectually muddled is the long standing attempt to differentiate credit and propensity. As Munday points out, strictly speaking, if the distinction is to be maintained as purely a logical proposition, the only previous convictions that should be admitted under s. 1(f)(ii) are those for perjury, a response the courts are unlikely to adopt.

5 Similar Fact Evidence

INTRODUCTION

The law relating to similar fact evidence has seen a radical change in the principles relating to its admissibility in recent years. Strictly speaking, to call this type of evidence similar fact is a misnomer. Whilst evidence of previous offences which are strikingly similar to the one with which the accused is being tried (hence the term 'similar fact evidence') falls within this category, it also now includes evidence of extraneous acts and disposition. In the light of recent cases such as *DPP* v *P* [1991] 2 AC 447 and *R* v *H* [1995] 2 All ER 865, the stringent requirements of striking similarity prevalent in the older cases have been eroded. It may be because of this that Murphy (1995) in the new edition of his textbook, has renamed the chapter on similar fact, 'Evidence of Extraneous Acts and Disposition'.

Some students tend to find this topic difficult. The reason is simply because, unlike the other topics, there are only a few rules or principles and the whole discussion is taken up with an analysis of the facts of various cases in order to determine how these principles have been applied. Thus, to understand fully, students will have to read the cases in full, not just the headnote or a summary, and attempt to extract from these cases the process and reasoning by which the court applied the general principles to the facts of the case. Ultimately, the admissibility of the type of evidence under discussion depends generally on concepts of relevance, probative value and the prejudicial effect of such evidence. Students who adopt this approach should find this topic manageable, and hopefully, interesting.

QUESTION 1

Jennifer, a waitress at the Brambleside Railway Café, claims that she has been indecently assaulted by Ron, a stranger, who started up a conversation with her in the café as she was about to finish her shift one evening. She alleges that they talked about train spotting and that Ron then asked her to help him carry his bag to his car in the car park. He told her that he had arthritis and thus found it difficult to carry heavy things. She agreed to help him but as they were approaching his car, Ron dragged her into the bushes and indecently assaulted her. There is no forensic evidence which links Ron to the attack. He is picked up later on a separate charge of indecent exposure but Jennifer is not confident of identifying him.

Gladys, a waitress at the Sunnyside Railway Snack Bar, is willing to give evidence that a man in an anorak chatted to her about train spotting as she was leaving work and that when they walked together to the bus stop, he showed her some obsence photographs and indecently exposed himself to her. She was not sexually assaulted. Gladys confidently identifies Ron as the offender. Jennifer and Gladys are members of the same union branch but do not know each other personally. They have, however, both sponsored a resolution recently condemning male violence to women and calling for the union to organise self-defence classes. When Ron is arrested, the police find a number of train spotting magazines in his bag.

Ron is charged with indecently assaulting Jennifer and indecent exposure to Gladys. He denies both offences claiming he was not present.

Discuss the evidential issues involved.

Commentary

There are a number of issues that have to be dealt with, the first of these being the admissibility of Gladys's evidence to support Jennifer's evidence. The *Turnbull* guidelines will have to be referred to as well as whether the evidence is admissible on the basis that it is similar fact evidence. Students will be expected to explain the test for admissibility of such evidence and whether striking similarity is a requirement: see *DPP* v *P* [1991] 2 AC 447. In answering this question, it will also be necessary to compare the two incidents and attempt to identify where the similarities are or the lack of them. The other issue that has to be dealt with is whether there is a risk of collusion between the two of them and how the judge should deal with such evidence. In answering this part of the question, students will be expected to be up to date and have read the House of Lords case of *R* v *H* [1995] 2 All ER 865.

Suggested Answer

The main issue here relates to the admissibility of Gladys's evidence in order to support Jennifer's evidence. The reason why this is necessary is because of the weakness of Jennifer's identification evidence, in that she is not confident of identifying him. As such, the case will have to be dealt with in accordance with the guidelines laid down by the Court of Appeal in *R* v *Turnbull* [1977] QB 224. Under the guidelines, where the identification evidence is poor, as in this case, the judge will have to withdraw the case from the jury and direct acquittal, unless there is some other evidence which goes to support the correctness of the decision. Thus, unless Gladys's evidence can be admitted into evidence (or there is other evidence to support Jennifer's evidence), the judge may have to withdraw the case from the jury.

The admissibility of Gladys's evidence will depend on whether it falls within the ambit of similar fact evidence. Traditionally, such evidence was only admissible where there is some striking similarity between the different situations and the probative value of that evidence outweighs its prejudicial effect, as suggested by the House of Lords in *DPP* v *Boardman* [1975] AC 421. As Lord Salmon stated in the case, the similarity would have to be so unique or striking that common sense makes it inexplicable on the basis of coincidence. However, the application of this test has not been easy and cases such as *R* v *Novac* (1976) 65 Cr App R 107 and *R* v *Johanssen* (1977) 65 Cr App R 101 illustrate this difficulty. Although the facts of these two cases were very similar, the Court of Appeal reached different conclusions as to the admissibility of similar fact evidence. The different conclusions were explained by Salmon LJ on the basis that the admissibility of the similar fact evidence is a matter of judgment dependent on the circumstances of the case: *R* v *Scarrott* [1978] QB 1016.

This area of the law was re-examined recently by the House of Lords in *DPP* v *P* [1991] 2 AC 447 where it decided that, where similar fact evidence is to be given by another alleged victim, striking similarity was not an essential element to the admissibility of such evidence. The essential requirement was that the evidence had to be of probative value, which could be derived from the fact that there is a striking similarity between the cases. The only situation where striking similarity would be an essential element of the admissibility of such evidence, is where the identity of the perpetrator of the offence is in issue.

Thus, in this case, as identity is in issue, the court will have to be satisfied that the circumstances of the two incidents are so strikingly similar as to be inexplicable on the basis of coincidence and that its probative value outweighs its prejudicial effect. As will be apparent from the last statement, the striking similarity does not have to be a similarity in the offence itself but can also be with regards to the circumstances surrounding the case: *R* v *Tricoglus* (1976) 65 Cr App R 16 and *R* v *Barrington* [1981] 1 WLR 419.

The principle laid down in *DPP* v *P* seems relatively clear in dealing with cases where the issue is whether a crime has been committed as opposed to the question as to who committed the offence. Where the identity of the accused is in issue, the position is less clear. In *R* v *McGranaghan* (1995) 1 Cr App R 559, the Court of Appeal decided that where identity was in issue, the evidence of similar facts was only admissible where there was some other evidence (apart from the similar fact evidence) to support the correctness of the identity of the accused. The Court of Appeal made it clear that evidence of similar facts is used to establish that the same individual committed both offences but not that the accused was that individual. In such a situation, unless there is some other evidence to support the correctness of the identification of Ron as the person who indecently assaulted Jennifer, Gladys's evidence would not be admissible for this purpose. However, the principle set out in *McGranaghan* has not been followed in other cases and its precise limits are unclear. In *R* v *Downey* (1995) 1 Cr App R 547, the Court of Appeal did not follow *McGranaghan* and distinguished it on the basis that in cases where the separate offences are closely intertwined, it is proper for a judge to direct a jury that if they are satisfied that the evidence establishes that the same man perpetrated the two offences, they were entitled to take into account the evidence relating to both offences when reaching their decisions in respect of the separate offences. The dicta in *Downey* were approved in *R* v *Black, The Times,* 1 March 1995. In *R* v *Barnes, The Times,* 6 July 1995, the court expressly restricted the *McGranaghan* principle to the situation where similar fact evidence was used to support a doubtful identification. It would therefore seem that notwithstanding the uncertainty as to the precise limits of *McGranaghan*, the principle is applicable to the facts of the present case. Thus in this case, Gladys's evidence cannot be used to establish the correctness of the identification of Ron as the person who committed the indecent assault on Jennifer. There must be some other evidence to support the identification of Ron as the perpetrator of the offence. If there is none, then it is possible that the judge may withdraw the case from the jury.

If there is some other evidence to support the correctness of the identification of Ron as the person who committed the offence against Jennifer, the other question that has to be considered is whether the two offences should be severed and tried separately. This would depend on the test laid out in *DPP* v *P*, namely that there must be probative value in the evidence justifying trying the two offences together. From the facts of the case, apart from the fact that both victims were waitresses working in eating establishments near railway stations and the alleged perpetrator chatted to them about train spotting, there does not appear to be any other similarity. What appears lacking is any special or unique quality in the two incidents which makes them inexplicable on the basis of coincidence. There may be little probative value in having both cases tried together. In Jennifer's case, she was persuaded to walk with the offender on the pretext of helping him carry his bag to car because of his arthritis. There did not appear to have been any indecent suggestion before the attack occurred. In Gladys's case, they were both walking to the bus stop together, when the offender showed her indecent photographs and indecently exposed himself to her. There was, however, no assault in the latter's case. It is therefore doubtful whether the the two offences can be tried together. However, that is ultimately a question for the court to decide.

If the court does decide that both offences can be tried together, another problem arises. The problem arises from the fact that both Gladys and Jennifer belong to the same union branch and they have both recently supported a resolution condemning male violence. There may be a risk that there could be a collusion between the two of them. It was made clear in *Boardman* v *DPP* that similar fact evidence will have to be excluded if there is a risk of collusion between the parties. It is clear that this would cover not only actual collusion but also cases where there was a danger or real possibility that one witness may have been influenced, consciously or unconsciously, by the other witness: *R* v *Ryder* [1993] Crim LR 601 (applying the Court of Appeal decision in *R* v *Ananthanarayan* [1994] 2 All ER 847). In *Ryder*, Taylor LCJ ruled that where there was risk of collusion, the court should hold a voire dire to determine the admissibility of the evidence. However, more recently, in *R* v *H* [1995] 2 All ER 865, the House of Lords decided, inter alia, that where the question of collusion has been raised, it is the duty of the judge to direct the jury on the importance of the issue and leave it to them to decide whether it is free from collusion. The Law Lords went on to say that only in very exceptional cases should a voire dire be held to determine this issue. Thus, the court will have to direct the jury to decide whether there is a risk of collusion between Gladys and Jennifer.

As regards the search of Ron's bag and the discovery of train spotting magazines, it could be argued that this does no more than to establish Ron's interest in train spotting, a relatively commonplace activity. Unlike cases like *Thomson* v *R* [1918] AC 221 and *R* v *Reading* [1966] 1WLR 836, where incriminating articles were found in the offenders' possession which pointed to the offenders' involvement, and were therefore admitted into evidence, these magazines are neutral as to whether he is likely to have committed the offence with which he is or will be charged. Thus whilst it could be admitted in evidence, its relevance is that it does no more than to establish his interest in train spotting.

QUESTION 2

'It is undoubtedly not competent for the prosecution to adduce evidence tending to shew that the accused has been guilty of criminal acts other than those covered by the indictment, for the purpose of leading to the conclusion that the accused is a person likely from his criminal conduct or character to have committed the offence for which he is being tried. On the other hand, the mere fact that the evidence adduced tends to shew the commission of other crimes does not render it inadmissible if it be relevant to an issue before the jury, and it may be so relevant if it bears upon the question whether the acts alleged to constitute the crime charged in the indictment were designed or accidental, or to rebut a defence which would otherwise be open to the accused'. Lord Herschell LC in *Makin* v *A-G for New South Wales* [1894] AC 57 (at p. 65).

Discuss the extent to which this still represents the law today.

Commentary

A consideration of the development of the rules relating to similar fact evidence tends to be a popular essay question. In order to answer this question well, students need to be aware of the problems with the formulation in *Makin*, the restatement or reformulation of the test of admissibility of such evidence in *Boardman*, the interpretation of this test by the later courts and the more recent House of Lords authorities on the point. Students would be expected to have read a number of articles in this area, including Colin Tapper's article entitled 'The erosion of *Boardman* v *DPP*' 1995 NLJ 1223.

Suggested Answer

In this formulation, Lord Herschell sets out a presumption of exclusion of evidence tending to show that the accused has been guilty of criminal acts other than that with which he is being tried, and then provides various examples where this presumption could be displaced. However, this formulation has been subject to a number of criticisms. The main criticism is that cases immediately after the decision took the examples as fixed categories. Illustrations of this approach can be seen in cases such as *R* v *Armstrong* [1922] 2 KB 555 and *R* v *Straffen* [1952] 2 QB 911. Much effort was expended in fitting the cases into somewhat artificial categories such as proof of identity, system or design.

As a result of the criticisms, as well as what Colin Tapper (1995) describes as the 'distaste for the difficulty of operating a rule cast in such terms', the House of Lords reformulated the rule in *DPP* v *Boardman* [1975] AC 421. Lord Wilberforce stated that:

> [t]he basic principle must be that the admission of similar fact evidence ... is exceptional and requires a strong degree of probative force. This probative force is derived, if at all, from the circumstance that the facts testified by the several witnesses bear to each other ... a striking similarity....

With this decision it was made clear that the basis of the admissibility of similar fact evidence was not dependent on whether it fell within the fixed categories but on whether there was a strong degree of probative force in the evidence. The test of admissibility, therefore, is whether the evidence of previous offence or disposition sought to be admitted is strikingly similar with the offence with which the accused is being tried and whether the probative value of this evidence outweighs its prejudicial effect. On the facts of the case, Lord Wilberforce found the case to be on the borderline of the striking similarity test.

Although the test of admissibility as set out in *Boardman* appears straightforward, the application of it by the courts has been erratic in some instances. An illustration of this can be seen in *R* v *Novac* [1976] 65 Cr App R 107 and *R* v *Johanssen* [1977] 65 Cr App R 101, where on very similar facts, the courts reached different conclusions. This apparent conflict was recognised by the Court of Appeal in *R* v *Scarrott* [1978] QB 1016, where the court made it clear that each case had to be looked at on its own facts. Scarman LJ in *Scarrott* found it difficult to explain how the inconsistency arose.

Two recent House of Lords decisions have now forced a reconsideration of the approach to be taken by the courts when dealing with this type of evidence. In *DPP* v *P* [1991] 2 AC 447, the accused was charged with four charges of rape and four charges of incest against each of his two daughters. The Court of Appeal allowed the accused's appeal against conviction on the charge of one rape and all the counts of incest in respect of his two daughters. The Court of Appeal allowed the appeal on the basis that there was a lack of striking similarity between the offences committed against each daughter. The prosecution appealed against this decision and the House of Lords allowed the appeal. The House of Lords made it clear that the striking similarity test was still a requirement where the identity of the accused was in issue. In other cases, there was no need for the evidence to be strikingly similar in order for evidence of similar fact to be admitted. In such a case, the test is one of whether the evidence has sufficient probative value to outweigh the prejudicial effect which is a question of degree in each case. In the instant case, the issue was whether there had been an offence, not who committed it.

In *R* v *H* [1995] 2 All ER 865, the accused was convicted of indecent assault and of committing gross indecency against his adopted daughter and having sexual intercourse with her when she was aged 13. He was also convicted of indecent assault on his stepdaughter. There was no suggestion that the offences were strikingly similar. The only issue was whether the evidence which was adduced in relation to one daughter could be used in relation to the other daughter.

The House of Lords decided that where there was an application to exclude alleged similar fact evidence and there is a risk of collusion between the victims, the court had to approach the question of admissibility on the basis that the similar fact evidence was true and the test in *DPP* v *P* was applicable. It would be up to the jury to decide whether the evidence was contaminated by the risk of collusion.

It is clear from these two House of Lords cases that the reformulated test for the admissibility of similar fact evidence laid down in *DPP* v *Boardman* has been further eroded. It is clear that the test proposed by *DPP* v *P* is pegged at a much lower level than the *Boardman* test and that admissibility of the similar fact evidence, in the absence of the issue of identification, is dependent solely on the probative value of the evidence without the necessity of establishing striking similarity.

The extent to which similar fact evidence is admissible where the identity of the perpetrator is in issue was considered by the Court of Appeal in *R* v *McGranaghan* (1995) 1 Cr App R 559. The Court of Appeal in that case decided that where identity was in issue, the evidence of similar facts was only admissible where there was some other evidence (apart from the similar fact evidence) to support the correctness of the identity of the accused. The Court of Appeal made it clear that evidence of similar facts is used to establish that the same individual committed both offences but not that the accused was that individual. However, in *R* v *Downey* (1995) 1 Cr App R 547, the Court of Appeal did not follow *McGranaghan* and distinguished it on the basis that in cases where the separate offences are closely intertwined, it is proper for a judge to direct a jury that if they are satisfied that the evidence establishes that the same man perpetrated the two offences, they were entitled to take into account the evidence relating to both offences when reaching their decisions in respect of the separate offences. *Downey* was approved in *R* v *Black, The Times*, 1 March 1995. Further, in *R* v *Barnes, The Times*, 6 July 1995, the court expressly restricted the *McGranaghan* principle to the situation where similar fact evidence was used to support a doubtful identification.

It would therefore seem that the courts have moved a long way from the original formulation in *Makin*, such that evidence of disposition and of extraneous acts is now also admissible whether or not they are striking similar with the offence with which the accused is being tried, in addition to the traditional, strikingly similar evidence. The key requirement is relevance to an issue in the trial. The move from *Makin* is not new. May (pp. 100–101) cites *R* v *Straffen* [1952] 2 QB 911 and *R* v *Ball* [1911] AC 47 to suggest that 'contrary to the proposition in *Makin*, evidence may be adduced for the purpose of showing that the accused is a person likely from his past conduct to have committed the offence charged. This must lead to the conclusion that *Makin* is not a wholly accurate statement of the law'.

QUESTION 3

Nicholas is charged with indecently assaulting Peter, aged 12, in a public park. The prosecution allege that he met Peter in the public park whilst rollerblading and dragged the boy into some bushes and indecently assaulted him. Nicholas denies being in the park and claims mistaken identity. Advise the prosecution on the following matters:

(a) whether Nicholas can be asked if he is a homosexual;

(b) when Nicholas was arrested, he was found in possession of various hardcore gay pornography magazines;

(c) whether evidence is admissible to show that shortly before the attack on Peter, Nicholas was stopped and cautioned by the Parks Police because he was abusive to the other park users.

Commentary

The first two parts of this question deal with the issue whether evidence of the accused's propensity by virtue of the fact that he may be homosexual and the discovery of incriminating evidence or materials on him can be admitted into evidence under the similar fact rule. Students should be aware that such evidence may now be admitted where the evidence has the requisite probative value under the test set out in the House of Lords decision in *DPP* v *P* [1991] 2 AC 447. Part **(c)** relates to the issue of whether the evidence of an earlier incident, notwithstanding that it tends to show the accused's criminal disposition, is admissible to establish his presence in the park.

Suggested Answer

(a) Here, the prosecution wishes to ask Nicholas whether he is a homosexual. However, this would depend on whether the question is relevant to the issues in the case. As Nicholas is claiming mistaken identity as his defence, the fact that he may be homosexual could be relevant to an issue. This is because it may defy coincidence that a person who had been misidentified also had homosexual tendencies.

In *Thompson* v *R* [1918] AC 221, the court allowed into evidence the finding of indecent photographs of young boys and the accused's possession of a powder puff. Lord Sumner stated that persons who committed the offence under consideration sought the habitual gratification of a particular perverted lust, which stamped them with the hallmark of a specialised and extraordinary class as much as if they carried on their bodies some physical peculiarity. The consequence of such a decision was that evidence that the accused was a homosexual was admissible into evidence to show that he committed the offence and that evidence of homosexual behaviour on previous occasions would likewise be admissible. This was taken a step further in *R* v *King* [1967] 2 QB 338 where the Court of Appeal allowed into evidence the accused's reply in cross-examination to a question as to whether he was a homosexual. This was on the basis that this was within the principle in *Thompson*. In *R* v *Horwood* [1970] 1 QB 133, the Court of Appeal made it clear that *King* was an exceptional case and that it could not be taken as authority for the proposition that in all cases where a man is charged with a homosexual offence, he may be asked either by the police or the prosecution whether he is a homosexual. Even if it is to rebut a defence of innocent association, such a question would be allowed only in exceptional cases. In *DPP* v *Boardman* [1975] AC 421, the House of Lords stressed that there was no special rule or principle applicable to sexual or homosexual offences. Although *King* and *Horwood* were decided before *Boardman*, it has been suggested that it still remains good law.

In this type of situation it is clear that it is not appropriate to apply the striking similarity test suggested by the House of Lords in *DPP* v *P* [1991] 2 AC 447 (in cases where identity is in issue). In such a situation, the law requires that the evidence has positive probative value. Here, it is suggested that the question to be asked has positive probative value in relation to Nicholas's defence of mistaken identity and would therefore appear to be permissible.

(b) The issue here is whether Nicholas's possession of these magazines can be admitted into evidence. The purpose of introducing this into evidence is to show Nicholas's propensity towards homosexuality. Traditionally, such evidence has been admissible where its probative value has outweighed its prejudicial effect. In *Thompson* v *R* [1918] AC 221, the House of Lords allowed into evidence the finding of indecent photographs of naked boys in the accused's room and his possession of a powder puff when he was arrested. Various reasons were given as to why such evidence was admissible. Lord Finlay LC stated that the possession of these items showed the same propensities as those pertaining to the man who committed the offences in question. In *R* v *Reading* [1966] 1 WLR 836, where the accused was alleged to have hijacked a lorry, he was convicted of robbery and taking a motor vehicle. The Court of Criminal Appeal allowed into evidence his possession of a walkie talkie and a police type uniform although it was not established that these had been used in the robbery. The evidence was admitted in order to rebut his alibi and his defence of mistaken identity. This case was followed in *R* v *Mustafa* (1976) 65 Cr App R 26, where the accused was convicted of obtaining goods by using a stolen credit card. Evidence of another credit card found in his home was admitted into evidence because it could be used to identify the accused as the perpetrator of the offence.

This type of evidence is admissible if it is relevant and its probative value outweighs its prejudicial effect. An argument may be that the accused is the person who committed the offence with which he is now charged because the finding of the magazines establishes that he has homosexual tendencies, and therefore it is likely that the identification of the accused as the perpetrator of the offence is correct. The inference is that the likelihood that a man wrongly identified as the perpetrator also has homosexual tendencies is slim. Thus in *R* v *Lewis* (1982) 76 Cr App R 33, evidence was admitted of interest in paedophilia to rebut a defence of 'innocent association'. As identity is in issue in this case, the finding of the magazines may be admissible because it will have probative value.

(c) The question that arises here is whether the prosecution will be allowed to introduce into evidence the caution given by the Parks Police to Nicholas, on the basis that it tended to rebut his denial of being present there at the time of the attack. It is clear that evidence of the accused's disposition on another occasion can be admitted, notwithstanding that it tended to show his criminal disposition to the jury, because of its relevance in establishing part of the prosecution's case.

In *R* v *Salisbury* (1831) 5 C & P 155, the prosecution was allowed to adduce evidence of the accused's interception of a letter which had its contents removed and bank notes stolen from another letter put in its place. The accused was charged with the larceny of the bank notes. The evidence was admissible in order to prove a link in the events which was required to prove the charge of larceny against the accused. Likewise, in *R* v *Mackie* (1973) 57 Cr App R 453, evidence was admitted to show that the accused had mistreated the victim prior to the latter's death. The accused was charged with manslaughter, when the victim, a three-year-old boy, fell to his death whilst running away from the accused. Although this evidence tended to show the accused's criminal disposition, it was admitted to prove the victim's state of mind at the time of the fall which was an important part of the prosecution's case.

Thus an analogy can be drawn with these cases. It can be argued that the evidence of the caution, although tending to show his criminal conduct, is admissible to prove or establish his presence in the park at the time of the attack on Peter, proof of which is an essential part of the prosecution's case.

6 Hearsay: The Rule and the Common Law Exceptions

INTRODUCTION

The rule against hearsay used to be described as the great rule underlying the law of evidence. However, with the intervention of statute (both current and forthcoming), the importance of this rule in civil cases will literally be non-existent. Statutes have also made inroads in criminal trials; see, for example, the Criminal Justice Act 1988. A consideration of the various statutory exceptions will be undertaken in **Chapter 7**. In this chapter, the emphasis will be on the exclusionary rule itself, the rule relating to implied assertions and the common law exceptions to the rule (those that still remain).

It is important that students are familiar with the definition of hearsay. In *R* v *Sharp* [1988] 1 WLR 7, in the House of Lords, Lord Havers adopted the definition of hearsay used by Cross (1985), namely, that it was 'an assertion other than one made by a person while giving oral evidence in the proceedings ... as evidence of any fact asserted'. However, it should be noted that Murphy (1995, at p. 172), argues that the definition of hearsay in *Sharp* is insufficiently comprehensive. He suggests that a more comprehensive defiinition should be adopted. He defines hearsay as:

> Evidence from any witness which consists of what another person stated (whether verbally, in writing, or by any other method of assertion such as a gesture) on any prior occasions, is inadmissible, if its only relevant purpose is to prove that any fact so stated by that person on that prior occasion is true.

Such a statement may, however, be admitted for any relevant purpose other than proving the truth of facts stated in it.

The Civil Evidence Act 1995 defines hearsay as 'a statement made otherwise than by a person while giving oral evidence in the proceedings which is tendered as evidence of the matter stated'.

It must be appreciated that not all out of court statements are necessarily hearsay. It will be hearsay where it is an out of court assertion (whether orally, in writing, or by any other means) **and** it is admitted to prove the truth of the facts stated therein. An out of court statement will not be hearsay, where for example, it is used to prove the state of mind or emotion of the witness. See, for example, the Privy Council decision in *Subramaniam* v *Public Prosecutor* [1956] 1 WLR 965 and *Ratten* v *R* [1972] AC 378. Other examples where the statement will not be regarded as hearsay include statements admissible as confirming other evidence, statements as evidence of identity or origin, or statements which are admitted to prove that it was made or was made in a particular way. It is also not hearsay to admit a prior statement to prove its falsity rather than the truth: *Khan* v *R* [1967] 1 AC 454.

With regard to the rule relating to implied assertions, until relatively recently, it was unclear whether such assertions fell under the hearsay rule. The decision of the House of Lords in *R* v *Kearley* [1992] 2 AC 228 now makes it clear that such assertions are within the hearsay rule and would therefore be inadmissible unless they fell within one of the exceptions to the rule. Of the common law exceptions, the important ones include statements made as part of the res gestae, dying declarations, and declarations against interest.

QUESTION 1

Heather is charged with the manslaughter of Ted. The prosecution allege that Ted and Heather, who were lovers, got into a heated argument whereupon Heather, in a fit of rage, fatally stabbed him. Consider the admissibility of the following evidence:

(a) Mark, Ted's neighbour, who claims that he heard Ted shout, 'Put that thing away, you silly woman' at about the time of the stabbing.

(b) Kit, a passer-by, who administered first aid to Ted, when he staggered out of his house covered in blood. Ted gasped, 'It was Heather who did it, I've had it. Make sure that I have a Christian burial'.

(c) Ted's mother to whom Ted confided, on the morning of the stabbing, that he was going to confront Heather about her infidelity.

Commentary

(a) This part of the question requires students to discuss whether this statement amounts to an implied assertion and as such whether it infringes the rule against hearsay. Students should be familiar with *R* v *Kearley* [1992] 2 AC 228 and the cases leading up to it, such as *Teper* v *R* [1952] AC 480 and *Ratten* v *R* [1972] AC 378. If the statement is inadmissible because of the hearsay rule, students will then have to consider whether it could be considered to be a statement made as part of the res gestae and therefore be admissible as one of the exceptions to the hearsay rule.

(b) The issue here is whether the statement made to Kit is admissible as a dying declaration or, in the alternative, a declaration against interest, in order for it to be admissible as an exception to the hearsay rule.

(c) Again, it is clear that the statement made here infringes the rule against hearsay. What needs to be considered is whether a person's declaration of his or her intention is regarded as an exception to the hearsay rule.

Suggested Answer

(a) The question to be considered is whether the hearsay rule applies to what Ted said and whether any of the exceptions to that rule apply. It could be argued that the statement made by Ted is an implied assertion, i.e., an assertion which is made from which it is possible to infer a fact. In this case, the statement by itself does not prove anything because Ted could be referring to something other than a knife. In order for the statement to be of use to the prosecution, the jury must be able to infer from the statement that Ted was referring to the knife.

Until recently, it was not clear whether implied assertions fell within the hearsay rule and were therefore inadmissible. In *Teper* v *R* [1952] AC 480, the court held that an implied assertion was inadmissible hearsay. In contrast, in *Ratten* v *R* [1972] AC 378, the Privy Council allowed into evidence telephone calls made by the victim to the telephonist at a local exchange at about the time of the murder, asking for the police. The Privy Council was of the view that there was no hearsay element in the evidence but then went on to consider the admissibility of the evidence on the basis that it was hearsay, namely that it was admissible as part of the res gestae, which is an exception to the hearsay rule.

The modern authority is now *R* v *Kearley* [1992] 2 AC 228, where the House of Lords was of the view that implied assertions fell under the hearsay rule and would be inadmissible. On the facts of that case, the implied assertions did not fall within any of the exceptions to the hearsay rule.

Thus, on the facts of this case, the statement is likely to be regarded as hearsay and would be inadmissible unless it fell within one of the exceptions to the hearsay rule. It may be possible to argue that the statements were part of the res gestae, as the statement was made so close to the events in question that it can be said to form part of the transaction. *Ratten* v *R* is an example of the application of this exception. The difficulty with this evidence relates to the question of relevance, in that the statement does no more than to show that Ted asked Heather to put down an item. There is no specific reference to the knife and so the court may rule that the evidence is irrelevant because it does not prove that Heather was holding a knife.

(b) The statement made by Ted to Kit is a hearsay statement in that it is adduced for the purpose of establishing that what it says is true. It may, however, be admissible as a dying declaration, which is a common law exception to the hearsay rule. The general rule here is that oral or written statements of a deceased person are admissible evidence of the cause of his death, at the trial for his murder or manslaughter, provided he was under a settled, hopeless expectation of death when the statement was made and provided that he would be a competent witness if called to give evidence: *R* v *Woodcock* (1789) 1 Leach 500.

The reason why this is accepted as an exception to the hearsay rule is because the imminence of death is assumed to reduce the risk of fabrication and there is unlikely to be any motivation to tell lies. It must be clear that there is a settled, hopeless expectation of death on the part of the declarant. If the declarant had a faint hope of recovery, the declaration would not be admissible: *R* v *Jenkins* (1869) LR 1 CCR 187. There is no objection to the admission of the dying declaration, even if the declarant took some time before dying, so long as when the statement was made, the declarant had no expectation to live: *R* v *Bernadotti* (1869) 11 Cox CC 316.

Thus, in order for Ted's statement to be admissible as a dying declaration, the requirements stated earlier have to be complied with. The difficulty is in establishing whether Ted had a 'settled, hopeless expectation of death', with no hope of recovery. It could be argued that when he said '... I've had it. Make sure I have a Christian burial ...', such an expectation was present. Further, there is nothing to suggest that Ted would not have been a competent witness if he had lived. The other difficulty is whether the court will be satisfied that the statement made by Ted relates to his death. The words '... Heather did it ...' might, in the circumstances, suggest that he was referring to who stabbed him, especially in view of his physical condition. On the other hand, it could be argued that the statement is ambiguous and vague, and therefore would not satisfy the requirements. The court will have to decide whether the dying declaration is admissible into evidence as an exception to the hearsay rule.

If, for any reason, Ted's statement is not admissible as a dying declaration, it could be argued that the statements were part of the res gestae, as the statement was made so close to the events in question that it can be said to form part of the transaction. *Ratten* v *R* [1972] AC 378, is an example of the application of this exception. Lord Wilberforce stated (at p. 389) that:

> ... [a]s regards statements made after the event it must be for the judge ... to satisfy himself that the statement was so clearly made in circumstances of spontaneity or involvement in the event that the possibility of concoction can be disregarded.

Thus, the test of admissibility of such statements depends on whether the statements were made in such circumstances as to make concoction or fabrication unlikely. This test was applied in later cases such as *R* v *Turnbull* (1985) 80 Cr App R 104 and approved by the House of Lords in *R* v *Andrews* [1987] AC 281. In the latter case, the facts of which are similar to the facts of the case in hand, Lord Ackner stated that the judge had to consider all the circumstances of the case in order to satisfy himself that the event was so unusual as to dominate the thoughts of the victim, so that his utterance was an instinctive reaction to the event giving no opportunity for concoction or distortion. Where a possibility of malice on the part of the declarant is raised, the judge must be satisfied that there was no possibility of concoction or distortion. Further, the judge had to take into account the possibility of error, if only the ordinary fallibility of human recollection, but that this went to the weight of the evidence not to its admissibility.

Thus, it could be argued that Ted's statement falls within the test laid out in *Ratten* which was explained and approved in *Andrews*, in that the circumstances of the case are such that there is no possibility of concoction or distortion. In the absence of the court being satisfied that there was malice on the part of Ted, it is likely that this statement could be admitted as a res gestae statement.

(c) It is arguable that what Ted told his mother on the morning of the stabbing is a hearsay statement. It indicates that Tom thought that Heather was unfaithful which is relevant to the prosecution's case of motive. Thus it would be inadmissible unless it falls within one of the exceptions to the hearsay rule. Statements made by a person concerning his or her contemporaneous state of mind or emotion are admissible as evidence of his or her state of mind or emotion as an exception to the hearsay rule. It would appear that statements as to the person's intention fall under this exception, as evidence of his or her intention at the time when the statement is made. The difficulty that arises is whether, as in the case here, the court is able to infer from the statement that the intention was carried out.

There is a lack of agreement by the courts on this issue. In *R* v *Buckley* (1873) 13 Cox CC 293, the court admitted into evidence a statement made by the victim, a police officer, to his senior officer, that he was going to watch the movements of the accused the night that he was killed. Likewise, in *R* v *Moghal* (1977) 65 Cr App R 56, a tape recording made six months earlier as to the intention of a third party, was admissible into evidence. However, the correctness of *Moghal* was doubted by the House of Lords in *R* v *Blastland* [1986] AC 41. In contrast, in *R* v *Wainwright* (1875) 13 Cox CC 171, the court refused to allow into evidence a statement made by the victim to a friend, on the afternoon of her murder, that she was on the way to the house of the accused. The court similarly refused to allow into evidence a statement as to where the victim was going just before her death, in *R* v *Pook* (noted at (1875) 13 Cox CC 171). The reasons for the court's refusal to admit such evidence is on the basis that it was merely evidence of the victim's intention, which may or may not have been carried out.

There are therefore conflicting authorities as to whether Ted's statement is admissible into evidence. This will be a question for the court to decide.

QUESTION 2

'Rather than rely on precisely defined and technically complex, and at the same time, legally inconclusive exceptions, trial judges should have the power to admit hearsay whenever it is of sufficient probative value.' Zuckerman (1989, at p. 216).

Discuss in relation to criminal trials.

Commentary

This is the type of general question on the hearsay rule that occurs frequently in evidence examinations. In answering this question, students must be clear as to the rationale for the hearsay rule. They must also recognise the criticisms of the rule, the main one being that credible and reliable evidence may be excluded as a result of the rule even though in some cases this may tend to prove the innocence of the accused. The answer should also cover the academic views on the rule and how the courts have found ways of avoiding its application.

Suggested Answer

A useful explanation of hearsay can be found in *R* v *Sharp* [1988] 1 WLR 7, where Lord Havers adopted Cross's definition of the term: '... [a]n assertion other than one made by a person while giving oral evidence in the proceedings is inadmissible as evidence of any fact asserted.' This exclusionary rule of evidence applies to both oral and written statements and includes what the witness said at an earlier occasion if the purpose of the admission of such evidence is to prove the truth of the facts stated therein. Murphy (1995 at p. 172) suggests, however, that this explanation of hearsay is insufficiently comprehensive. As an alternative he suggests that the following would be a more comprehensive definition of hearsay:

> Evidence from any witness which consists of what another person stated (whether verbally, in writing, or by any other method of assertion such as a gesture) on any prior occasions, is inadmissible, if its only relevant purpose is to prove that any fact so stated by that person on that prior occasion is true. Such a statement may, however, be admitted for any relevant purpose other than proving the truth of facts stated in it.

This definition is more helpful in that it makes it clear that a hearsay statement consists not only of what was said or written but includes gestures. It should be stressed that not all prior out of court statements would necessarily infringe the hearsay rule. The important criterion is that in order to be hearsay, the prior out of court statement is admitted for the purpose of proving the truth of the facts stated therein. See, for example *Khan* v *R* [1967] 1 AC 454, where the statement was admissible to prove the falsity of the statement, or *Subramaniam* v *Public Prosecutor* [1956] 1 WLR 965, where an out of court statement was admitted to prove the state of mind and emotion of the witness.

There are numerous reasons for this exclusionary rule. First, it has been argued that the person who made the statement may have wrongly perceived the events in question. Secondly, there is a risk that because of the fallibility of human nature, the memory of the person who heard the statement may be flawed. Thirdly, there is a risk of concoction or distortion of the events in question. Finally, the statement may have been misunderstood by the person who wrote down or heard the statement. Unlike a witness who is open to cross-examination, and the accuracy of his or her testimony can be tested, this is not normally possible with a hearsay statement. Zuckerman (1989 at p. 178) argues that this is the central reason for the exclusion of hearsay statements. He goes on to argue that there is a risk that the jury may attribute too much probative force to such evidence. Lord Bridge in *R* v *Blastland* [1986] AC 41, states that '... The danger against which this fundamental rule provides a safeguard is that untested hearsay evidence will be treated as having a probative force which it does not deserve.'

Whilst it is clear that the risk exists that such statements are unreliable because of concoction, distortion or fallibility of human nature, the extent to which the hearsay rule applies is much wider than is necessary. As a result of the rule, evidence which is both credible, reliable and of probative value may be excluded if it does not fall strictly within one of the exceptions. An example of this can be seen in *R* v *Blastland* [1986] AC 41, where the House of Lords suggested that a confession by a third party that he committed the crime with which the accused was being tried, would be inadmissible because of the hearsay rule. Arguably, that evidence may have been credible but the rules of evidence would have prevented it from being admitted. Likewise in *Myers* v *DPP* [1965] AC 1001, credible evidence was held to be inadmissible because of the hearsay rule. It should be noted that the evidence in question is now admissible under the statutory exceptions but the point is that at the time of the decision it was inadmissible. The other criticism of the rule is that it excludes evidence which may prove the innocence of the accused: *Blastland* and *Sparks* v *R* [1964] 1 All ER 727 are examples of this.

Bentham argued that hearsay evidence should be admissible unless there is oral evidence available on the same or similar point, on the basis that this was the best available evidence. He was of the view that to exclude such evidence may lead to mistaken factual conclusions. Other jurists, including Thayer, and McCormick supported Bentham's view on this. Wigmore, on the other hand, favoured the hearsay rule but this was on the condition that there should be reform of the rule.

In order not to exclude potentially reliable and credible evidence, the courts have used numerous devices in order to avoid excluding the evidence on the basis of hearsay. An example of this is the case of *R* v *Osbourne* [1973] QB 678, where the court allowed into evidence the testimony of a police officer at an identification parade that a witness picked out the accused. The court stated that this was admissible to prove the fact of identification. The element of hearsay inherent in this was ignored. A similar approach was taken in *R* v *Okorodu* [1982] Crim LR 747. Other illustrations of the courts' evasion of the hearsay rule include cases such as *R* v *Rice* [1963] 1 QB 857 (a case which is now subject to the Criminal Justice Act 1988) and *R* v *Kearley* [1992] 2 AC 228. A point to note is that, in the light of *Kearley*, it is unclear how courts will now treat cases of hearsay conduct and cases like *Woodhouse* v *Hall* (1980) 72 Cr App R 39.

Thus it is clear that the hearsay rule is disliked by both jurists and courts and the latter have been prepared in some instances to avoid its application. However, there is no consistency to this approach and the reason is simply because of the fear of letting in unreliable evidence. Zuckerman (1989 at p. 216) argues that there should be the legitimisation of the inclusionary principle in that trial judges should have the power to admit hearsay evidence which is of probative value. The effect of this, he argues, would be to get rid of the exceptions and its technical manifestations. There is much to be said for this approach, after all, the judges have been given discretionary powers in most instances, and there is no real reason why they cannot be given the discretion to rule whether the hearsay evidence is admissible because of its probative value. Further, the trend of legislative intervention in this area appears to be in favour of the admissibility of such evidence, the Criminal Justice Act 1988 being an example of that approach in relation to documentary hearsay. In conclusion, it is submitted that it is now time to reform this area of the law in general and suggestions made by Zuckerman as to the legitimisation of the inclusionary principle are worth considering.

QUESTION 3

Anna and Monisha are charged with robbery from the Hendfield Building Society. At an identification parade held a short time after the robbery, Anna was picked out as one of the robbers by Paul, the manager of the branch. As a result of a concussion received in a road traffic accident, Paul is suffering from amnesia and is unable to remember what happened at the identification parade. However, Detective Inspector Daniels was present at the identification parade and is able to testify that Paul picked out Anna during the parade. Monisha was identified by Edmund, the assistant manager who recognised her when he viewed the video tape recording of Monisha during the robbery. The recording was accidentally deleted by Edmund shortly afterwards.

A few months after the arrest of Anna and Monisha, Gertrude confessed, just before she died, to having been one of the two persons who committed the robbery.

Advise as to the admissibility of the evidence.

Commentary

This question relates to the issue as to whether Detective Inspector Daniels is able to testify to what occurred during the identification parade. The problem with his testimony is that it may be hearsay. The other issue relates to the video recording and the identification of Monisha by Edmund and whether this infringes the rule against hearsay. The final point of the question requires a discussion as to whether a confession by a third party is admissible into evidence in view of the fact that it may infringe the hearsay rule and if so, whether any of the exceptions apply.

Suggested Answer

Dealing with each issue in turn, the first evidential issue that arises is whether Detective Inspector Daniels is able to testify that he saw Paul identify Anna, as one of the robbers during the identification parade. Prima facie, it could be argued that this would infringe the rule against hearsay because '... [a]n assertion other than one made by a person while giving oral evidence in the proceedings is inadmissible as evidence of any fact asserted' (*R* v *Sharp* [1988] 1 WLR 7) and therefore would be inadmissible into evidence.

However, a number of cases have suggested that this type of evidence may not infringe the rule against hearsay. In *R* v *Osbourne* [1973] QB 678, a witness could not recall what happened at an identification parade held some seven and a half months earlier. A police officer who was present at the identification parade was permitted to testify that the witness picked out the accused. The Court of Appeal was of the view that the evidence was admissible as it sought to prove the fact of identification at the identification parade. The court did not deal satisfactorily with the point that the testimony of the police officer may be hearsay. It has been suggested that the attitude of the Court of Appeal may indicate that there is a new exception to the hearsay rule. However, Lord Morris in *Sparks* v *R* [1964] AC 964 stated that there is no rule which permits the giving of hearsay evidence merely because it relates to identity. By analogy, in *R* v *Okorodu* [1982] Crim LR 747, a photofit picture which was constructed by a witness, who subsequently failed to pick out the accused at an identification parade, was admitted into evidence. The court was of the view that this should be admitted because where identification was in issue, the jury should have all relevant information available to them. Although this case is not strictly in point with the issue at hand, a parallel can be drawn with *Osbourne* and *Virtue* in that the court appears to be prepared to admit evidence of identity even though it is technically hearsay. (*Okorodu* has now to be read in the light of *R* v *Cook* [1987] 1 All ER 1049, where the Court of Appeal stated that sketches, photofit pictures and photographs were evidence which were in a class of their own. This type of evidence did not infringe the hearsay rule.)

The decision in *Osbourne* has to be compared with *Jones* v *Metcalfe* [1967] 1 WLR 1286 and *R* v *McClean* (1967) 52 Cr App R 80. In these two cases, the issue revolved round whether a witness could refer to his conversation with another person as part of his testimony. It was held in both these cases that these were hearsay statements and therefore inadmissible. It is however, likely that the court will be prepared to allow the testimony of Detective Inspector Daniels. If details of the identification parade had been written down, the position may be covered by the Criminal Justice Act 1988. The Courts generally take a liberal approach in admitting identification evidence, see *R* v *McCay* [1990] 1 WLR 645.

As regards the evidence of Edmund who identified Monisha from the video tape recording, it is clear that the video tape itself, if it was still available, would be admissible in evidence as original evidence: *Kajala* v *Noble* (1982) 75 Cr App R 149 and *R* v *Dodson* (1984) 79 Cr App R 220. However, in this case, it would appear that the video recording has been accidentally erased by Edmund. In *Taylor* v *Chief Constable of Cheshire* [1986] 1 WLR 1479, a video recording which was alleged to show the accused in the act of committing the offence was erased before the trial. The Court decided that it was proper for the police officers who had seen the recording to give oral evidence of the contents of the tape. Thus, it would appear that on the facts of the case, Edmund could give evidence of what he saw on the tape.

The final issue that has to be considered is whether the admission by Gertrude is admissible into evidence. Since she is unable to give evidence in court, her statement when she was dying is clearly hearsay. However, it could be argued that this evidence has probative value in that it may cast doubts on the prosecution's case that it was Anna and Monisha who committed the robbery. In *R* v *Blastland* [1986] AC 41, the House of Lords suggested that a confession by a third party that he committed the crime with which the accused was being tried, would be inadmissible because of the hearsay rule. The House of Lords in this case approved the earlier decision in *R* v *Turner* [1975] 61 Cr App R 67 where it was held that a confession by a third party who was not called to give evidence was inadmissible. The reason usually given for excluding this evidence is that it is not up to the courts to create new exceptions to the hearsay rule. That is a matter for Parliament.

On the assumption that Gertrude's confession is inadmissible because of the hearsay rule, the next question is whether it could be admitted under one of the exceptions to the hearsay rule. It may be possible to argue that Gertrude's confession amounts to a declaration against her interest. In order to be admissible under this exception, five conditions have to be satisfied. First, it must be established that the declaration is against the pecuniary or proprietary interest of the declarant. It should be noted that a statement which tends to expose a person to a criminal prosecution does not appear to satisfy this requirement: *Sussex Peerage Case* (1844) 11 Cl & Fin 85. On the facts of this case, it could be argued that Gertrude's statement is inadmissible because it amounts to a declaration which exposes her to criminal prosecution. There is some debate as to whether it is right to regard such statements as being admissible nonetheless because fines can sometimes be imposed which would be against her pecuniary interest. Keane (at p. 225) is of the view that this is not enough to bring it within the exception. Arguably, if Gertrude is open to a civil claim for damages as a result of this, it could be regarded as falling within this exception. The second condition is that the statement must be against the interest of the declarant at the time it was made. Thirdly, the declarant must have known that the statement was against his interest. Fourthly, the declarant must be dead. Finally, the declarant must have personal knowledge of the facts. On the facts of this case, it would appear that apart from the first condition, the conditions are satisfied. Thus it will be for the court to decide whether Gertrude's confession is admissible under this exception.

7 Hearsay: Statutory Exceptions

INTRODUCTION

The last 30 years have seen the erosion of the rule against hearsay through a succession of statutes aimed at simplifying and rationalising the law in this area. Early inroads were made in the field of criminal law by the Criminal Evidence Act 1965, brought in after the House of Lords confirmed in *Myers* v *DPP* [1965] AC 1001 that however absurd the results of its application, further exceptions to the hearsay rule could only be made by Parliament. This was a limited measure allowing documentary records of a trade or business to be admitted as evidence where direct oral evidence of the facts recorded was not available for specified reasons. It was followed in 1968 by a much more sweeping measure in the civil law field, namely the Civil Evidence Act 1968. This created a new code covering oral and written hearsay statements as well as evidence produced by computers. The 1968 Act which applies only to hearsay statements of fact provides for a complicated notice procedure by the party seeking to adduce hearsay evidence. Another Civil Evidence Act, in 1972, extended the principles to hearsay opinion. Remember that common law exceptions are preserved by s. 9 of the Civil Evidence Act 1968 and it may be preferable to use this, for example, for confessions because the complicated notice provisions would not apply.

When the Civil Evidence Act 1995 comes into force it will repeal the hearsay provisions in the 1968 and 1972 Statutes. Section 1 of the Act states that hearsay evidence shall not be excluded because it is hearsay, which is defined as a statement made otherwise than by a person while giving oral evidence in the proceedings which is tendered as evidence of the matters stated. Though such evidence is admissible, the rules of court will provide for the giving of notice that it is to be adduced. Failure to give notice in accordance with the rules will affect the weight to be attached to the evidence and could be penalised in costs. Where a hearsay statement is adduced, the other parties can call the maker as a witness and cross-examine him. The Act spells out in section 4 the considerations which are relevant to the weighing of hearsay evidence. These are:

(a) whether it would have been reasonable and practicable for the party by whom the evidence was adduced to have produced the maker of the original statement as a witness;

(b) whether the original statement was made contemporaneously with the occurrence or existence of the matters stated;

(c) whether the evidence involves multiple hearsay;

(d) whether any person involved had any motive to conceal or misrepresent matters;

(e) whether the original statement was an edited account, or was made in collaboration with another or for a particular purpose; and

(f) whether the circumstances in which the evidence is adduced as hearsay are such as to suggest an attempt to prevent proper evaluation of its weight.

Hearsay evidence of a witness who is being called in the proceedings can only be admitted with leave of the court or to rebut a suggestion that his evidence has been fabricated. The Act also simplifies the procedure for the production of business records, providing in s. 9 that a document which is shown to form part of the records of a business or public authority may be received in evidence in civil proceedings without further proof. Its status as part of a business record must be certified by an officer of the business or public authority.

In criminal cases, major changes came in 1984 with the Police and Criminal Evidence Act 1984 ('PACE') replacing the provisions of the 1965 Act and itself in turn substituted by provisions in the Criminal Justice Act 1988. Section 69 of PACE still remains, however, providing a procedure for the admission of computer records. Remember that this section is not free standing, material has first to pass the test of s. 23 or s. 24 of the Criminal Justice Act 1988. Section 23 of the 1988 Act admits first hand documentary hearsay where the maker is not available to give evidence and there is an acceptable reason for not calling him. Section 24 of the Criminal Justice Act 1988 widens the scope of admissible multiple documentary hearsay to include documents created or received in the course of trade, business, occupation, profession or office, paid or unpaid. Be sure to consider s. 25 and s. 26 of the 1988 Act on the exercise of judicial discretion over admissibility of hearsay documents. Finally, you should be aware of the special provision for experts' reports in s. 30 of the Criminal Justice Act 1988 (covered in **Chapter 11**).

For the student, a problem in this area is distinguishing the provisions in criminal and civil cases. Thus, for example, there has to be a reason for not calling the witness in the criminal cases under s. 23 of the Criminal Justice Act 1988, whereas, although a reason for absence of the witness facilitates the notice procedure in civil cases, it is not necessarily fatal to the admission of hearsay evidence. Another major difference between the two is that in civil cases firsthand oral hearsay is admissible, but there is no parallel provision in criminal cases. Remember also that the civil law has been in some areas more stringent than the criminal law. This is partly because the criminal statutes were enacted after the corresponding civil ones and lessons were drawn from their operation. This, in short, is an area where piecemeal reform is the order of the day. It is interesting to note that under s. 17 of the Criminal Justice (Scotland) Act 1995, oral hearsay is now admissible and in recent consultation paper (no. 138) the Law Commission has recommended that hearsay evidence be admitted in criminal trials if the interests of justice require it.

QUESTION 1

Tom is charged with sexually assaulting Harriet at a residential university summer school. He denies the charge and claims that Harriet made it up because he had spurned her advances. She did not report the incident until some time after it allegedly happened. Tom claims that in fact he was away from the summer school on the day in question on a bicycle trip. However, the computer records which list the bicycle hirings have no record of his name and no one else can substantiate his alibi. The college bursar, Graham has a note on file on the day in question, based on information from Carol, a gardener at the school. She claims to have seen a couple she identified as Tom and Harriet struggling in the grounds. They had not seen her and she did not intervene but saw Harriet run off with her clothes dishevelled. Having thought about the incident she went later and reported it to Graham who made a note of it on his tape recorder and it was subsequently typed by his secretary, John. Carol is now working in Australia and has not been traced.

Discuss the admissibility of Carol's evidence and of the computer bicycle hire records.

Commentary

In this question you are asked to consider whether the items in question are hearsay and then whether they may be admitted under any of the statutory or common law exceptions. Bear in mind that you must first characterise the statements as hearsay or not on the basis of the common law definition. The bicycle records raise the preliminary matter of whether absence of a record is hearsay and you need not worry about acknowledging the uncertainty of the law in this area. In Carol's case you need to be familiar with the provisions of the Criminal Justice Act 1988 ('CJA') s. 24 and what is meant by acting in the course of trade etc. Bear in mind the discretion to exclude under ss. 25 and 26 of the CJA and the need to discuss whether the document was prepared for the purposes of a pending or contemplated criminal investigation.

Suggested Answer

The rule against hearsay states that an assertion other than one made by a person while giving oral evidence in the proceedings is inadmissible as evidence of any fact charged, as the House of Lords confirmed in *Myers* v *DPP* [1965] AC 1001. Carol could give direct oral evidence of what she had seen and this would clearly be relevant to the facts in issue since Tom's defence is alibi and fabrication. Since she is not available, the only evidence of this is what she has told Graham. The question then arises as to whether the evidence is admissible by virtue of the exceptions for documentary hearsay under the Criminal Justice Act 1988 ('CJA').

Some forms of documentary hearsay are admissible as an exception to the general hearsay rule. By s. 10(1)(c) of the Civil Evidence Act 1968 (whose definition of a document applies in criminal proceedings by virtue of the Criminal Justice Act 1988) a tape recording is a document. Graham's tape-recorded note of what Carol told him is thus to be treated as a statement in a document. The admissibility of evidence in this situation is governed by s. 24 of the CJA. This provides that under certain specified circumstances a statement in a document can be admissible as evidence of any fact of which direct oral evidence would be admissible if the document was (i) created by a person in the course of a trade, business, profession or other occupation or as an office-holder, and (ii) the information was supplied by a person (whether or not the maker of the statement) who had personal knowledge of the matters dealt with.

Whether or not the tape recording is admissible, then, depends on Carol's and Graham's status. Carol had personal knowledge of the facts as she perceived them. Graham received the information in the course of his occupation as supervisor. It should be noted that there is no requirement that the persons in the chain are acting under a duty as in civil cases. There is no requirement for the statement to be part of a 'record' as the Civil Evidence Act 1968 requires. The admission of the typed notes from Graham's recording is subject to the same principles as the tape recording. They are admissible also under s. 24 CJA because the typist was acting in the course of business.

A statement prepared for the purposes of criminal proceedings or investigation, for example a witness statement, is not admissible under s. 24 CJA unless either one of the reasons for non-appearance of the witness in s. 23(2) or (3) CJA is met, or the maker of the statement cannot reasonably be expected to have any recollection of the matters dealt with having regard to the time which has elapsed and all the circumstances (s. 24(4) CJA). It is therefore necessary to consider the purpose for which the tape recording was made. In *R* v *Bedi* (1991) 95 Cr App R 21 the prosecution had been allowed to adduce evidence of bank reports concerning lost and stolen credit cards. The judge had not considered as he should have done the purpose for which the reports were prepared. Here, the Court of Appeal held they were business documents to which s. 24(1) applied but that s. 24(4) did not. This was a matter of fact to be determined by the judge in the light of the surrounding circumstances. On the facts, it does appear unlikely that Graham made the statement for the purpose of criminal proceedings. In any case even if he did, Carol's absence probably is one of the acceptable reasons for non-appearance, following the Court of Appeal in *R* v *French* (1993) 97 Cr App R 421.

The party seeking to rely on s. 24 CJA must satisfy the court that the requirements of the section have been met. Here it is the prosecution which wishes to use the statement and the criminal standard of proof will apply. The judge must generally hear oral evidence in a voir dire. The Court of Appeal in *R* v *Minors* [1989] 1 WLR 441 held that 'the foundation requirements of s. 24 of the Act of 1988 will also not be susceptible of proof by certificate'. The court has a discretion to exclude the statement even if it is technically admissible under s. 25 CJA, s. 78 of the Police and Criminal Evidence Act 1984 ('PACE') and at common law.

The exclusionary discretion under s. 25 CJA is to be exercised in the interests of justice. If the documents had been prepared for pending criminal proceedings, s. 26 CJA would have applied, which creates a presumption of non-admissibility unless the interests of justice require it. The guidelines for the exercise of the s. 25 discretion are set out in s. 25(2). The interests of justice include the public interest in seeing the offender prosecuted. The most relevant principle to consider here includes:

> . . . any risk, having regard in particular to whether it is likely to be possible to controvert the statement if the person making it does not attend to give oral evidence in the proceedings, that its admission or exclusion will result in unfairness to the accused or, if there is more than one, to any of them.

Since Carol will not be available to be cross-examined on the identification, which is a fact in issue, it may be argued this would create unfairness to Tom.

The prosecution may wish to show the computer printout from the bicycle hirings to suggest that Tom's alibi is false. The first issue is whether it is hearsay. There is a conflict of authority on whether absence of a record constitutes hearsay. In *R* v *Patel* [1981] 3 All ER 94, the Court of Appeal, while accepting that the Home Office records which did not contain the name of the alleged illegal immigrant were hearsay, would have allowed the officer responsible for their compilation to give evidence. Murphy (1995, at p. 196) is critical of this decision. In the subsequent case of *R* v *Shone* (1982) 76 Cr App R 72 the Court of Appeal took the view that the absence of a record was non-hearsay, circumstantial evidence. Murphy concludes: 'At present, therefore, the position of evidence of this kind is unclear.' The 'non-statement' here is in documentary form generated by a computer. Cross and Tapper (at p. 703) points out that s. 24 CJA has not clarified the situation:

> In contrast to the position in some other jurisdictions no explicit provision is made in relation to statements of negative purport. It might be thought that this would cause difficulty in the light of the condition requiring personal knowledge since the negative cannot be within anyone's personal knowledge.

If the absence of Tom's name is hearsay, then s. 24 CJA should be considered (see above). In addition s. 69 of PACE has to be satisfied whether the document is hearsay or not. In *R* v *Shephard* [1993] AC 380, the House of Lords made it clear that if a document produced by computer is hearsay, it will have to comply with the provisions of s. 24 CJA and s. 69 PACE. There must be proof by a certificate or oral evidence that the computer was being used properly and working properly. 'Computer' is not defined in PACE. Before *Shephard* it had been thought that the definition in s. 5(6) of the Civil Evidence Act 1968, i.e. 'any device for storing and processing information' should be adopted. However, the Court of Appeal in *Shephard* said it seemed likely that Parliament, in the light of the recommendation of the Law Commission, had intended to leave the word undefined.

QUESTION 2

'Another controversial effect of the hearsay rule is to prevent the admission into evidence of confessions to crimes other than those made by the defendant. Although the common law appears to regard some statements against interest as inherently more reliable than other hearsay statements, there appears to be no available exception in English common law to accommodate third party confessions.' (Jenny McEwan, *Evidence and the Adversarial Process*, 1st edn, Oxford: Blackwell, 1992, at p. 203).

Commentary

Hearsay is an area which lends itself to essay questions where you will be expected to discuss the rationale and alleged absurdities of the rule. To answer such questions well you need to show your knowledge of the law and also make some references to the academic debates. There are a number of controversial aspects of the rule against hearsay. Here you are just asked to deal with one, namely the exclusion of third party confessions. Be careful you do not stray over into making a general diatribe against the rule. Focus as always on the specific question set. However, the exclusion of third party confessions of course is one aspect of the general principle that the rule applies equally to the defence as to the prosecution. The difficulty with broad questions of this sort is in imposing your own plan on the material. A suitable one here would be to discuss first of all whether the extract describes an existing state of affairs. If so (and it will presumably be so to some extent at least!) give examples of exclusion of third party confessions. Then go on to discuss why this is so. You should then discuss finally whether there is a case for reform. Your essay thus falls into three parts, not forgetting of course a well-observed conclusion.

Suggested Answer

Here, McEwan is passing comment on the common law position in relation to hearsay evidence. This exclusionary rule operates to prevent admissions by third parties. That this is undoubtedly how the courts have interpreted the law is made clear in the House of Lords decision in *R* v *Blastland* [1986] AC 41. The Court of Appeal had refused to allow confessions made by M, whom the defendant B claimed had approached the victim after him; the court felt bound by the Court of Appeal decision in *R* v *Turner* (1975) 61 Cr App R 67, and also by *Myers* v *DPP* [1965] AC 1001, where the House of Lords held that it was for Parliament to create any new exceptions to the hearsay rule. This state of affairs raises the issues referred to in the question, namely is this an accurate assessment of the law, and if it is, is it desirable?

In *Turner*, the judge was held to have rightly refused to admit evidence that a third party, not called as a witness, had admitted that he had committed the robbery, with which the defendant was charged. The court rejected the view that any of the cases cited to it were authority for the proposition that hearsay evidence admissible in a criminal case to show that a third party who has not been called as witness in the case has admitted committing the offence charged. The principle applies even if the third party is dead. Thus, in *R* v *Thomson* [1912] 3 KB 19, the Court of Appeal upheld the trial judge's exclusion of statements by a deceased woman that she had intended to carry out an illegal abortion on herself and that she had in fact done so.

In *R* v *Blastland* [1986] AC 41 the exclusion of two sets of statements was upheld by the Court of Appeal. One was a confession by the third party to the police and the other a statement by him on the night of the murder and on the following day in which his state of mind was revealed, in particular his knowledge about the murder at a time when it was not generally known. Leave was given to apply to the House of Lords only on the second statement, and, although not clearly dissenting from the Court of Appeal who held it was hearsay, the ratio of their decision was that the statement should be excluded because it was irrelevant.

The case law suggests that the exclusion has primarily been applied to confessions made by third parties who are not called as witnesses, so arguably the evidence of their guilt is weak. However, as the above case law suggests, there is nothing in the rule to indicate it should be confined to those cases. The case law then does certainly affirm the existence of the rule to which McEwan refers. However, as she points out, it is at least theoretically possible for ss. 23 and 24 CJA 1988 to apply. This allows documentary hearsay evidence to be admitted. A third party confession could be admissible, if written or not oral. As regards firsthand documentary hearsay, it may be admitted at the discretion of the court (under s. 25 CJA) provided the maker of the statement is unable to attend court as a witness for one of the reasons set out in s. 23(2), (3) CJA, namely, that he is dead or unfit to attend as a witness, that he is outside the UK and it is not reasonably practicable to secure his attendance, that he cannot be found, or that having made a statement to a police officer or an investigating officer he does not give evidence through fear or because he is kept out of the way. Furthermore, under s. 24 CJA, which covers multiple hearsay, business documents may be admitted as long as each of the intermediaries was acting in the course of trade, business etc. Thus theoretically a confession by a third person made, e.g., to a teacher could be admitted as long as it is made in the form of a statement.

Furthermore, if a statement is prepared for the purpose of criminal proceedings or investigation, one of the reasons for not calling the maker listed above must be met or the additional reason that the maker cannot reasonably be expected to have any recollection of the matters dealt with having regard to the time which has elapsed. The latter reason, however, would be unlikely to apply to a confession to a criminal offence.

Under s. 25 and s. 26 CJA the court has a discretion to exclude statements admissible under ss. 23 and 24 CJA and as regards statements arising out of criminal investigation there is a presumption of non-disclosure. In view of the decision in *R* v *Blastland* it may be difficult to satisfy particularly s. 25(2)(c) CJA, namely that the court should pay attention 'to the relevance of the evidence that it appears to supply to any issue which is likely to have to be determined in the proceedings'. However under s. 26(b)(ii) CJA, the court, in considering whether to grant leave to admit in the interests of justice, should have regard to whether 'Its admission or exclusion will result in unfairness to the accused'. To date there appear to be no reported cases where third party confessions have been admitted under ss. 23 or 24 CJA and it is arguable that the reasons for the exclusion under common law will hold. However, in the recent trial of Rosemary West, a confession by her dead husband to the offences for which she was charged was admitted as documentary hearsay.

One area of contention is whether a confession made by a co-defendant may be tendered by a defendant. In *R* v *Beckford* [1991] Crim LR 883, the Court of Appeal held that s. 76(1) PACE applied only to confessions tendered by the prosecution. *Beckford* was distinguished in *R* v *Campbell* [1993] Crim LR 448 and as Murphy (1995, p. 223) says, 'it remains a contentious issue whether such statements are admissible at common law'. In that case one co-accused was allowed to adduce in chief a confession by another despite the rule against hearsay. In *R* v *Rowson* [1986] QB 174 the Court of Appeal held that the trial judge had no discretion to prevent counsel for the co-accused from cross-examining the maker of an inadmissible confession. Such questioning is for the purpose of attacking credibility by showing inconsistency. In *Lui-Mei Lin* v *R* [1989] 88 Cr App R 296 the Privy Council held that as long as the matter is relevant the right to cross-examine is unfettered.

Are the courts applying the law correctly in relation to third party confessions? Birch (1987) looks at this decision in the light of the rule against hearsay generally. She argues (at p. 27) first of all that *Myers* 'does not exclude the possibility of tinkering with existing exceptions'. She cites the common law exception most suitable to be amended as the declaration against interest, acknowledging that this exception identified by the House of Lords in the *Sussex Peerage Case* (1844) 11 Cl & F 85 must be against the proprietary pecuniary interest of the declarant and that the declarant must have died before the trial. Birch comes, however, to the conclusion that it would be unrealistic to expect these obstacles to be overcome. She further argues that concern over letting in a third party confession by the back door led the House of Lords to uphold a 'hearsay fiddle' by calling M's indirect evidence in *R* v *Blastland* of his 'state of mind' irrelevant.

Third party confessions are excluded primarily because of the risk of a spate of false confessions. McEwan points out that the Lindbergh kidnapping in the United States resulted in over 200 confessions. Obviously many such cases can be eliminated early on because the maker has insufficient knowledge of the details of the offence. But McEwan suggests that the adversarial system is ill-equipped to test the untrustworthiness of third party confessions although an inquisitorial procedure, not relying on oral evidence, could do so more easily.

There is thus a strong argument on grounds of lack of reliability for excluding third party confessions. The weakness of this type of evidence is that of hearsay evidence generally, summarised by Tribe (1977, at p. 959) as faulty perception, erroneous memory, ambiguity and insincerity.

With regard to declarations against interest admissible as exceptions to the rule against hearsay, he points out that the sincerity problem is overcome by the assumption that a person is unlikely to make a statement adverse to himself unless it is true and ambiguity is avoided by admitting only statements that are sufficiently unambiguous that they can be found to be against the declarant's interest. He argues that defects of memory or faulty perception may apply. It could be submitted, however, that this is unlikely in the event of confession to a crime.

The question then arises, is there anything specifically at issue in third party confessions which would argue for a new exception to be made to the hearsay rule? The major objection to the present state of affairs is that although it applies to prosecution and defence, obviously it most harms the defence (except in those cases where the third party confessor is a co-defendant). Thus as Zuckerman (1989, at p. 184) points out, the rule violates the principle of protecting the innocent. He also adds (at p. 185) that it defies common sense.

Clearly confessions of defendants can be unreliable and psychologists have pointed out the many reasons for confessing other than truth. In fact, attempts to find general rationales are probably unwise. The question points to the desirability of an inclusionary discretion for hearsay evidence based on the strength and weight of evidence, not its form. The courts have taken very seriously the principle made in *Myers* that Parliament must make any radical changes on the rule against hearsay. But this principle is not universally applied in the law of evidence. Thus, in *R* v *Andrews* [1987] AC 281, the House of Lords made major changes to the common law res gestae exception to the rule against hearsay. There is a strong case to be made for a flexible, inclusionary discretion in relation to hearsay to avoid what Zuckerman (at p. 216) calls 'an amount of casuistic sophistry' in the interests of a rule which is wider than its rationale requires.

Murphy (1995) criticises the exclusion of statements by third parties exculpating the accused. He writes (at p. 242) 'It is submitted that the time may have come to re-evaluate the admissibility of such evidence'. He puts forward a possible solution:

> ... it might logically be argued that such a statement is non-hearsay, relying on the theory that the mere fact that such a statement, so manifestly contrary to the interests of the maker, has been made is some circumstantial evidence tending to suggest that the accused may not be guilty.

It is difficult to dispute Murphy's observation that one could assume that an admission by a person who had nothing to gain and much to lose was inherently reliable.

QUESTION 3

Henry is charged with causing grievous bodily harm to James. The prosecution case is that he attacked James with a knife after a row in a public house. James has been disfigured as a result of the wounding. Henry denies the attack claiming he was elsewhere at the time and that he has never met James. James was taken to hospital by ambulance. As he travelled there he gave an account of the incident to PC Green. PC Green read it back to James and he nodded his agreement, not being able to sign because of the drips in his arm. After an operation he has not regained consciousness. Tom and Gerry were eyewitnesses to the incident and both made statements to the police which they subsequently signed. However, Tom has told the police he is too afraid to tell the court about what he saw and Gerry's mother has told police he also is too scared to give evidence. Freda, a Brazilian tourist, made a statement to Henry's solicitor after the incident that she was with Henry at the cinema at the relevant time. She has now returned to Brazil.

Advise on evidence.

Commentary

You are presented in this question with several 'statements' and you are thus alerted that the Criminal Justice Act 1988 ('CJA') may apply. You need to be aware of the recent case law on the application of ss. 23 and 24 of this statute. It is not enough simply to summarise the sections. In this question you need also to be aware of how the courts have interpreted these somewhat overlapping provisions and how their requirements can be proved. A failure to refer to the Court of Appeal decision *R* v *McGillivray* (1992) 97 Cr App R 232, for example would be a weakness in an answer to this question. There is also some important case law on what is meant by 'fear' in s. 23(3) CJA. This question is an illustration of how evidential issues are closely related to procedural ones. Evidence courses vary in their emphasis on this area.

Suggested Answer

James makes a statement to a police officer but is not available as a witness at the trial because he is unconscious. Section 23(1) of the Criminal Justice Act 1988 ('CJA') provides that a statement by a person in a document is admissible in criminal proceedings as evidence of any fact of which direct oral evidence would be admissible. Thus 'firsthand' documentary hearsay evidence is admissible provided certain conditions are met. Section 23 CJA rather than s. 24 CJA is the appropriate section here, since the Court of Appeal held in *R* v *McGillivray* (1992) 97 Cr App R 232 that s. 24 CJA does not apply to a statement made by a person subsequently deceased to a police officer. The court apparently took the view that s. 24 CJA was intended to apply to ordinary business transactions but not to 'police documents' although Smith (1994) disagrees with this interpretation. The maker of the statement must be unable to attend court as a witness for one of the reasons set out in s. 23(2) CJA.

Here, s. 23(2)(a) CJA will apply since the witness unfit to attend. A further condition is that the statement must be made by a person in a document. Here James had clearly not made the statement himself. In *R* v *McGillivray* the Court of Appeal also held that an unsigned statement made by a deceased person to the police was admissible under s. 23 CJA provided that the deceased had clearly acknowledged by speech or otherwise that the statement was accurate. The victim who had been set alight made a statement to a police officer in hospital as a nurse confirmed. The court said the statement was admissible because the victim, who later died, had indicated it was accurate but he was physically unable to sign it. Here, the prosecution must lay a foundation for presenting the evidence and it is arguable that James's condition is analogous with that of the victim in *McGillivray*.

With regard to Tom, the prosecution may seek to rely on s. 23(3) CJA that 'having made a statement to a police officer or an investigating officer he does not give evidence through fear or because he is kept out of the way'. There has been some recent case law on the interpretation of this section. In *R* v *Acton Justices, ex parte McMullen* (1990) 92 Cr App R 98, the Divisional Court had to be satisfied that the witness was in fear as a consequence of the offence or of something said or done subsequently relating to it and the possibility of the witness's giving evidence. Furthermore, the same case held that it does not have to be proved that something has occurred since the commission of the offence to put the witness in fear so as to keep him out of the way.

The issue has arisen of the relationship between s. 23(3) CJA and s. 13(3) Criminal Justice Act 1925 which related to witnesses 'kept out of the way by means of the procurement of the accused or at his behalf'. As a result, decisions on s. 13(3) CJA 1925 should not automatically be applied to s. 23 CJA according to the Court of Appeal in *R* v *Moore* (1992) Crim LR 882. As May (1995, at p. 249) points out in relation to a case under the 1925 Act, in *R* v *O'Loughlin* (1987) 85 Cr App R 157, it was held at first instance that the prosecution must prove beyond reasonable doubt by admissible evidence that the witness has been kept out of the way on the defendant's behalf. In *R* v *Ashford Magistrates' Court ex parte Hilden* [1993] QB 555, the Divisional Court held that there was no obligation on a court to hear evidence that a witness is in fear but it might come to that conclusion by observing the witness in the witness box. Here, however, we are not told whether Tom appears at all. In *Hilden*, the witness was prepared to answer some questions but not others.

A problem may arise if the jury asks why a witness was not called. In *R* v *Churchill* [1993] Crim LR 285, where the judge told the jury he had decided circumstances applied in which a crucial witness who claimed to be in fear need not give evidence, the Court of Appeal said the judge should have discussed with counsel how to handle the question. The judge's 'explanation had amounted to something in the nature of a pat on the back for a witness whose testimony had been disputed but had not been tested in cross-examination'. The jury might wrongly have inferred that the failure to testify could be a matter to the discredit of the accused. In the circumstances the judge should simply have said he could not answer the question. In *Neill* v *North Antrim Magistrates' Court* [1992] 1 WLR 1220, a case arising under a similar Northern Ireland provision, namely article 3(3)(b) of the Criminal Justice (Evidence, etc.) Northern Ireland Order 1988, the House of Lords held that the fact that a witness was absent through fear had to be proved by admissible evidence. There, the evidence of the police officer as to what he had been told by the mother of the two youths about their apprehensions had been hearsay and could not be admitted under the exception to the hearsay rule that enabled the court to receive first degree hearsay as to state of mind. The House held (at p. 1229) that:

> Whatever may be the intellectual justification of the exception to the hearsay rule which enables the court to receive first degree hearsay as to state of mind ... it cannot be stretched to embrace what is essentially a third hand account of the witness' apprehensions.

Accordingly, the statements of the youths should not have been admitted in evidence. *R* v *O'Loughlin* was applied. The court held (obiter) that a statement by a witness who is afraid of appearing through fear would be admissible as a res gestae statement of present state of mind, the common law exception. Thus, the police officer may here give evidence of what Tom said directly to him but not what Gerry's mother told him, in explaining to the court why the witnesses will not give evidence.

The prosecution if they seek to rely on this section, must satisfy the court beyond reasonable doubt, that the requirements are met. It is the defence who will presumably try to rely on s. 23 CJA for Freda's statement. In satisfying the court that the requirements of the statute are met, the defence will only have to comply with the civil standard of proof as the Court of Appeal held in *R* v *Mattey, The Times*, 13 October 1994. Freda's statement was presumably endorsed by her and the appropriate reason for not calling her appears to be that she is outside the United Kingdom and it was not reasonably practicable to secure her attendance. In *R* v *Case* [1991] Crim LR 192, the trial judge had admitted witness statements by two Portuguese tourists including the victim. The Court of Appeal held that they had been wrongly admitted because the court should have been presented with other evidence on non-availability other than the contents of the statements. Thus, the defence must produce additional evidence that Freda cannot attend. The court must consider all the circumstances of the case. Following *R* v *Case*, the court may take account of the costs of Freda's travel in deciding what is reasonably practicable. In *R* v *Gonzales* [1992] Crim LR 180, the Court of Appeal held that the trial judge had been wrong in concluding that it was not reasonably practicable to secure the attendance of two booking clerks from Bogota. Further steps could have been taken such as offering to pay their fares.

For all of these statements, even if these preliminary requirements are met, the court will only admit in the light of the discretion afforded under s. 26 CJA. The effect of this section is to exclude a statement prepared for the purposes of pending or contemplated criminal proceedings or investigation, unless the court gives leave in the interests of justice. It applies to both defence and prosecution evidence; each will have to prove such interests to the appropriate standard. With regard to Tom and Gerry's statements, the fact that Henry may have to give evidence to controvert them is not in itself unfair, as the Court of Appeal held in *R* v *Moore* [1992] Crim LR 882. In each case, the court must conduct a balancing exercise between the interests of the public as represented by the prosecution and the interests of the particular defendant. In *R* v *Cole* (1990) 90 Cr App R 478, the Court of Appeal laid down guidelines for the exercise of this discretion. The court held that it was proper to have regard to the likelihood of it being possible to contradict the statement by the defendant giving evidence and calling witnesses. It may thus be unfair to admit the evidence of Tom and Gerry and not Freda's evidence because Henry may not have any other witness to back up his alibi.

One final point of interest to note is that the recent decision of the Court of Appeal in *R* v *Montgomery* [1995] 2 All ER 28 confirms that a witness who does not give evidence through fear and whose evidence is admitted in documentary form may still be sentenced for contempt of court. So Tom and Gerry may still face gaol on those grounds.

QUESTION 4

Jean is injured in an accident at work and had an operation as a result of it. A jack placed under a car she was repairing collapsed and the car fell on Jean's legs. The jack had been put in place by the foreman, Philip. Jean managed to give a verbal account of the accident to her workmate, Beryl, who gave her first aid on the day of the accident but Jean suffered total memory loss after the operation. Philip telephoned his union representative George about the incident and the representative made a note of the conversation. The substance of the note is that Philip accepted he had not secured the jack. Jean is suing her employers for negligence and the defendants are denying liability, claiming Jean was at fault. At the trial, which takes place five years after the incident, there is a dispute over the admissibility of Jean's statement to Beryl, and the statements made by Philip to George. In relation to Jean's statement counsel had put in a notice under RSC Order 38, but no notice of intention to put in George's statement was served on the defendant's advisers and the reasons for non-compliance were not disclosed to the judge. Philip is now in the United States. He is refusing to come and give evidence but George, who is concerned about safety provisions, has offered evidence to Jean.

Advise on admissibility of the above statements.

Commentary

At the time of writing, the Civil Evidence Acts 1968 and 1972 are in force though they are to be replaced by the Civil Evidence Act 1995. The question has been answered therefore by applying the rather complex notice rules still currently in force. In any case a familiarity with these provisions may still be useful because their application may bear on how the courts apply the new regime. Here you need to know about the content of the statute and the procedural requirements of RSC Order 38. The issues here are the admissibility of Jean and Philip's oral statements, the admissibility of George's written statement and whether the notice procedures have been complied with. A preliminary issue is whether these statements are in fact hearsay.

Suggested Answer

Section 1 of the Civil Evidence Act 1968 ('CEA 1968') provides that:

> In any civil proceedings a statement other than one made by a person while giving oral evidence in those proceedings shall be admissible as evidence of any fact stated therein . . .

Jean's statement is clearly relevant to the proceedings and as long as there is no other bar to admission such as competence it should be admissible by statute. It is hearsay in that it is made out of court and the purpose of adducing it is to suggest that Jean's version of events is true. Under s. 2 CEA 1968, in the case of a statement made orally, no evidence other than direct oral evidence by the person who made the statement, or any person who heard it or otherwise perceived it being made, is to be admissible for the purpose of proving it. Thus, Beryl must be available to make the statement in court.

George's note of Philip's phone call is not admissible under s. 2 CEA 1968, because, although made in a document, the document was not made by Philip. Under s. 4 CEA 1968, a document can be admitted if it is, or forms part of a record — see *H* v *Schering Chemicals Ltd* [1983] 1 WLR 143. Bingham J refused to admit the documents as a record and defined the word 'record' as meaning primary or original sources, not digests of information:

In *Savings and Investment Bank* v *Gasco Investments* [1988] Ch 422, Peter Gibson J held that the document should not amount to a selection of material submitted with comments and conclusions. In *Re D* [1986] 2 FLR 189, the court held that a solicitor's selective notes of an interview with a potential witness did not qualify as a 'record'. They were intended to be used as an aide-memoire. The admissibility of the union representative's note will therefore depend on its form.

George's note may not satisfy the restrictive definition. Selective summary of facts does not qualify as a record.

Even if the hurdle of the restrictive definition of 'is, or forms part of a record' is overcome, others still remain. Section 4 CEA 1968 requires that information is supplied by persons (whether acting under a duty or not) who had, or may reasonably be supposed to have had, personal knowledge of the matters dealt with. Philip, as someone involved in the incident, clearly qualifies here. Furthermore, the information must be given to someone 'acting under a duty'. This 'includes a reference to a person acting in the course of any trade, business, profession or other occupation in which he is engaged or employed or for the purpose of any paid or unpaid office held by him.' Arguably, a trade union representative fulfils this qualification. Alternatively, George may give oral evidence of what Philip told him under s. 2.

If ss. 2 or 4 are applied, then the failure to observe the notice procedures may prove fatal. If the notice procedure is complied with, as we are told it has been in the case of Jean's statement and it has not been challenged, in effect it is admitted. If there is a counter-notice, then the court has discretion to include it.

Section 8 CEA 1968 and the Rules of the Supreme Court ('RSC') Order 38 provide that any party intending to rely on a s. 2 statement should give notice to the other parties of such intention within 21 days of setting down for trial. The notice should contain the time, place and circumstances at or in which the statement was made, the person by whom and the person to whom the statement was made and finally the substance of the statement. Furthermore, s. 8 CEA 1968 gives acceptable reasons for not calling the witness and the notice should state the reason if the party is relying on this. The possible reasons are that the maker of the statement is dead, beyond the seas, unfit or cannot with due diligence be identified or found or cannot reasonably be expected to have any recollection of the matters in question.

Here, Jean is clearly unfit to give evidence so the s. 8 reason should be included in the notice. In that case the defendants may within seven days challenge the notice but only on grounds of the s. 8 reason. If the reason is proved to exist, the s. 2 statement may be proved as of right according to the Court of Appeal in *Piermay Shipping Co. SA* v *Chester* [1978] 1 WLR 411.

We are told the notice procedure has not been complied with in the case of George's statement.

The usual result of failure to comply with notice procedure covered by s. 8 and Rules of the Supreme Court Order 38, rr. 20-34, even where there is a valid s. 8 reason, is that the s. 2 statement is excluded. But the court has a discretion to overlook non-compliance. In *Ford* v *Lewis* [1971] 1 WLR 623 the defendant's counsel sought to put in evidence a written statement made at the time of the action by his client. At the time of the trial the defendant had become a patient in a mental hospital. The judge admitted the evidence without hearing the defendant's reason for non-compliance, although no notice had been served on the plaintiff. The defendant had not complied with the notice procedure because he aimed to take the plaintiff by surprise. The Court of Appeal said that under these circumstances, where the rules were deliberately flouted, the procedural failure could not be overlooked.

In *Morris* v *Stratford-on-Avon RDC* [1973] 1 WLR 1059, a key witness for the defendant gave inconsistent and confused evidence at trial, and counsel obtained leave to put in a statement made by the witness four years previously to the defendant's insurers. The judge's decision was here upheld by the Court of Appeal, since there was no possibility that the plaintiff was prejudiced by the admission of the evidence. It would seem that any decision to admit George's statements may be open to challenge on appeal, since the judge cannot have exercised his discretion properly without knowing the reasons for non-disclosure. However, the judge's decision might still be upheld if the reasons are within s. 8. Philip's absence is a valid s. 8 reason. The key question is the motive of the plaintiff's counsel and the possible disadvantage to the defence by its admission.

8 Confessions and the Defendant's Silence

INTRODUCTION

Confessions play a large part in evidence examination questions just as they do in trials in real life. There are many cases on this subject, but the starting point is the Police and Criminal Evidence Act 1984 ('PACE') which includes both a definition of confessions (s. 82(1)) and a statement of the circumstances which would lead to their exclusion under rule (s. 76(2)(a) and (b)). You must distinguish this rule of exclusion from exclusion by exercise of the discretion by s. 78 on grounds of lack of fairness and by s. 82(3) which preserves the common law discretion. In determining whether the confession should be excluded or not, you will be called upon to see primarily if there has been a breach of the statute or the Codes of Practice. Exclusion is not automatic, you must assess the seriousness and the effect of any breach or other police malpractice such as lies. You will therefore need to examine the facts systematically, listing possible transgressions and noting if they are deliberate or not. The courts have, in relation to s. 76(2)(a) and s. 78, stressed the importance of the state of mind of the investigating officers, whereas s. 76(2)(b) applies an objective test. The most likely statutory breach you will encounter is s. 58 on access to legal advice.

The Codes of Practice which accompany PACE, issued under s. 66, are very important in determining the admissibility of confessions, specifically code C on detention, treatment and questioning of persons by police officers and Code E on the tape-recording of interviews. The revised Code C, issued in 1995, now contains a definition of a police interview (paragraph 11.1A) which was previously only defined in a Note for Guidance. Further wide-sweeping changes were introduced in the Criminal Justice and Public Order Act 1994 (CJPOA). These have implications for confessions because they make it proper for the court to draw inferences from the defendant's silence when questioned under caution under certain circumstances. The caution has been consequently reworded as follows: 'You do not have to say anything. But it may harm your defence if you do not mention when questioned something which you later rely on in court. Anything you do say may be given in evidence.' (paragraph 10.4). You must be clear on the difference between s. 34 of the 1994 Act which allows inferences to be drawn from the accused's silence after caution but is only activated if the accused or his counsel offers evidence in due course, which could have been provided in answers to earlier questions. Sections 36 and 37 of the 1994 Act, on the other hand, deal with silence on arrest whether or not the defendant offers an explanation at trial. Thus s. 36 of the 1994 Act allows inferences to be drawn from the failure of an arrested person to account for objects, substances or marks found on his person, his clothing or his footwear in his possession or in a place where he is at the time of arrest and s. 37 from his failure to or refusal to account for his presence at a place at or about the time of his arrest. (Section 35 which governs the defendant's refusal to testify is covered in **Chapter 3**).

You need then to recognise a confession (including 'mixed confessions'), to discuss whether it has been obtained in accordance with the statute and codes and finally to see if there is an argument on the facts of the case to be made for its exclusion by rule or discretion. Thus a great part of the material on confessions deals with the question of whether they have been properly obtained.

One final point to note is that silence itself may be admissible at common law as a confession if the defendant is on 'even terms' with his interrogator.

The following Table gives a summary of the new provisions on silence in the CJPOA.

s. 34	s. 36	s. 37
Suspect must have been given general caution Code C para. 10.4		
Suspect or his counsel at trial must offer explanation which might reasonably have been given earlier (s. 34(1)).	Suspect must have been arrested and given the special warning (Code C paras 10.5A and B).	
	Suspect must be interviewed at police station unless the special conditions of Code C para. 11.1 apply, e.g., danger of interference with evidence.	
If arrested, suspect at interview should be given opportunity to confirm/deny earlier silence outside police station.	Suspect should be given opportunity at start of interview to confirm/deny earlier failure to account outside police station.	
	Suspect must fail to account for objects, substances or marks.	Suspect must fail to account for presence.
Silence cannot be used as part of primary case against suspect.	His failure to so account can be used as part of the primary case against him.	His failure to so account can be used as part of the primary case against him.
Suspect shall not be committed for trial or be convicted solely on silence, failure or refusal to account (s. 38(4))		

QUESTION 1

'. . . a person who asks for legal advice may not be interviewed or continue to be interviewed until he has received it, unless delay has been lawfully authorised as described above. The result is that in many cases a detainee, who would otherwise have answered proper questioning by the police, will be advised to remain silent . . . it seems to us that the effect of s. 58 [of the Police and Criminal Evidence Act 1984] is such that the balance of fairness between prosecution and defence cannot be maintained unless proper comment is permitted on the defendant's silence in such circumstances. It is high time that such comment should be permitted together with the necessary alteration to the words of the caution.' (*R* v *Alladice* (1988) 87 Cr App R 380 at p. 385.)

Discuss.

Commentary

The right to silence is a topical and popular question in current evidence examinations. Much opposition was expressed to the changes made in the Criminal Justice and Public Order Act 1994, six years after *R* v *Alladice*. At the time of writing there is little case law on the new provisions. You should however be familiar with the relevant provisions of the 1994 Act and with the academic and judicial controversy surrounding it. Be careful here to answer the specific question set, which is whether the availability of legal advice to the defendant gives such an advantage that comment on silence at interview is a suitable quid pro quo for the prosecution. The question is about relative advantages and disadvantages to the defendant rather than a request to recite all the arguments for and against abolition of the right to silence. You must deal with the details of the new provisions introduced in 1994 and also with the practical and principled arguments on this issue. As always in essay questions, some familiarity with the academic debates will raise your answer into the upper second if not first class grade. Finally, be careful to avoid too much editorialising in such an answer. The examiner wants an analysis of the law not a political diatribe.

Suggested Answer

The court here was expressing its exasperation with the practice of suspects refusing to answer questions at the police station. It suggested that because safeguards were provided for the suspect in the interview through the provision of legal advice, there should be some redress of the balance by allowing the suspect's silence to be made evidence at the trial. In fact Alladice's confession, made without a solicitor present, was held by the Court of Appeal to have been rightly admitted, thus the comment from Lord Lane, who delivered the judgment, did not arise from this specific example primarily. Alladice did not in fact exercise his right to silence. However, Lord Lane was expressing a more general unease felt by police, sections of the judiciary and the government. Despite recommendations over the past two decades by many bodies, most recently the Royal Commission on Criminal Justice (Cmnd 2263, 1993) that the right to silence should be retained, the government has accepted the validity of this unease. Following the legislation already brought in by statutory instrument in Northern Ireland (Criminal Evidence (Northern Ireland) Order 1988), the government introduced the Criminal Justice and Public Order Act 1994, which has limited, but not abolished, the pre-trial right of silence in several key areas. Inferences may now be drawn if the defendant relies on material in court which he did not divulge to the police while under caution (s. 34), or if he fails to account for objects, substances or marks on him at the time of arrest (s. 36), or fails appropriately to account for his presence at a particular place on arrest (s. 37). The caution and the Code of Practice have been reworded. Lord Lane's invocation has thus been more than answered. The arguments over this issue have raged among academics, politicians and the legal profession for several decades. This essay will examine the procedural changes that have taken place since 1988 and their implications for the 'balance of fairness'. It will also discuss the matters of principle involved.

The observation in the question suggests that s. 58 of the Police and Criminal Evidence Act 1984 ('PACE') gives the suspect such an advantageous position that there ought to be compensation for the prosecution. Under this section the suspect is given the right to request access to legal advice, although this may lawfully be delayed, in the case of a serious arrestable offence, by a senior officer who has reasonable grounds for believing that if the right is exercised there may be interference with evidence, injury, alerting of suspects or hindrance in the recovery of property (s. 58(8) PACE). Thus, the right itself is not absolute and furthermore there are no automatic sanctions for its breach. To that extent, the suspect was, even before the 1994 changes, under some disadvantage. However arguably in their treatment of breaches of s. 58 PACE in cases where confessions were obtained, the courts protected the defendants. In *R* v *Samuel* [1988] QB 615, the Court of Appeal in holding that the confession should be excluded said that the task of satisfying a court that there were reasonable grounds for believing the consequences set out in s. 58(8) PACE applied will prove formidable. Thus, the scope for the police to deny access to a solicitor is restricted, particularly if the police act in bad faith as the court acknowledged in *R* v *Alladice* itself.

Furthermore, since 1988 access to legal advice has been improved. For example, a provision in the revised 1995 Code C accepted representations from the Law Society that the solicitor's role at the police station is 'to protect and advance the legal rights of his clients' and 'on occasion this may require the solicitor to give advice which has the effect of his client avoiding giving evidence which strengthens the prosecution case.'

Despite these pro-defendant provisions, the Court of Appeal may in *R* v *Alladice* have expressed an unwarranted concern because the number who remained silent appears to have been small although it does in fact appear that those who had legal advice did so more readily. The great majority of suspects in police stations do not exercise their right to silence. Zander (1994, p. 147) quotes a study in 1992 which showed 26% of suspects who had legal advice exercised their right, while 10% of those who had no legal advice did so. Also an ACPO study in 1993 found that 57% of suspects who had legal advice exercised their right while 13% of those who did not have a solicitor did so. Moreover, this has to be seen in the context of the report by the Legal Aid Board, also quoted by Zander, that only some 30% of suspects have legal advice in the police station either in person or over the telephone. One might argue then that even before the 1994 changes the protection afforded to silence was weak. The very nature of interrogation appears to compel cooperation. Two possible alternative views flow from this. If the protection for the defendant was illusory, why continue with the pretence? It would perhaps be better to concentrate on providing other safeguards. On the other hand, if there was no real problem with extensive exercise of the right, why was change needed to compensate the prosecution? On the latter point, the police argued that it was the small number of hardened criminals whom they were targeting. Galligan (1988 at p. 70) quotes the former Metropolitan Police Commissioner, Peter Imbert that the protection of silence has 'done more to obscure the truth and facilitate crime than anything else in this century'.

An examination of the new provisions reveals that the changes actually brought in do not reflect completely the recommendations made in *R* v *Alladice*. The Court of Appeal there appeared to suggest that comment was appropriate on silence at the interview only. However, the new statute does not clearly preclude admitting silence outside of the police station. Thus s. 34 could, if further conditions apply, be activated on the giving of a caution, before arrest. Also Code C 11. 2A provides that at the beginning of an interview carried out in a police station, the interviewing officer, after cautioning the suspect, must put to him any significant statement or silence which occurred before the start of the interview. This is particularly significant in relation to ss. 37 and 36 of the 1994 Act which deal with silence on arrest whether or not the defendant offers an explanation at trial. There seems then fertile scope for appeal on whether the silence was properly obtained. Tain (1995) suggests that the silence here could simply be the recording of a suspect's uninvited remarks out of interview which occasionally have to be adjudicated on. 'Perhaps,' he says, 'if those remarks are queried at the time they are made and no response is forthcoming to the query, then that silence is the silence referred to.'

Murphy (1995, p. 255) says: 'The most intriguing question is whether any such inferences must be drawn only subject to the rules governing confessions'. He suggests that it could be possible to argue that the silence should be excluded on the grounds of unreliability. Thus, an inexperienced accused who is wrongly denied a solicitor or interrogated harshly may be too frightened to explain himself. Murphy points out, however, that the silence may not fit the definition of a confession in s. 82(1). In any case the question of what appropriate comment may be made about silence and when such comment should not be permitted is not clearly set out in the statute.

Another refinement of the new statutory provisions is that s. 34 of the 1994 Act is restricted in its scope. This section does not allow inferences to be drawn from silence under caution per se but only from the giving of evidence in due course which evidence could have been provided in answer form during earlier questioning under caution. The 'circumstances' referred to in the question therefore are limited to those where an explanation is given at the trial. This still begs the question, however, as to the evidential worth of silence. Silence is necessarily ambiguous and might have been prompted by reasons other than guilt. Nonetheless defenders of the change advocated in *Alladice* would argue that refusal to answer questions is now, given the procedural safeguards, an informed and voluntary decision.

Furthermore on this practical point s. 34(1)(b) of the 1994 Act allows inferences from silence when charged, not just when first interviewed. Enright (1995) says this provision is leading some solicitors to advise defendants to remain silent in interview but make a statement of their case at the charge stage. There are clear advantages for such defendants since further questioning is precluded. He suggests also that juries will be less inclined to infer guilt from silence at the interview stage where the defendant has set out his position at the charge stage.

Michael Zander (1994) points out (p. 149) 'the unknown quantity will be what streetwise solicitors advise clients'. He even suggests that the abolition of the right will make solicitors more, rather than less likely to advise the client to be silent. He suggests that if a suspect is silent on the basis of legal advice it can be put to the jury that no adverse inference should be drawn. The Royal Commission on Criminal Procedure (1993) pointed out that this was the case under comparable provisions in Scottish law.

Thus there are procedural and practical anomalies accompanying the new law which enacted the change recommended in *R* v *Alladice*. More controversial perhaps are the arguments over principles. The reference to 'balance of fairness' just four years after the introduction of the elaborate balancing act of PACE, perhaps, was somewhat impatient. Furthermore, is it necessary for s. 58 PACE to be balanced at all? In *R* v *Samuel* [1988] QB 615 the Court of Appeal referred to access to legal advice as a fundamental right. Do such rights have to be compensated for?

The so-called right to silence has a symbolic as well as a practical significance. It is closely linked to the ancient privilege against self-incrimination. This is not of course an absolute privilege: the taking of fingerprints is only one example where the suspect is required to provide evidence against himself. In certain categories of offence, such as fraud, the privilege has been entirely abolished. However, it is associated with such key concepts as the presumption of innocence and the principle that the burden of proof is on the prosecution throughout to prove guilt beyond reasonable doubt.

A specific protection for the defendant who is silent is provided by s. 38(3) of the 1994 Act which provides that:

> ... a person shall not have the proceedings against him transferred to the Crown Court for trial, have a case to answer or be convicted of an offence solely on an inference drawn from such a failure or refusal ...

The evidential worth of silence was considered in *Kevin Murray* v *Director of Public Prosecutions* [1994] 1 WLR 1. The case concerned the effect of a provision in the Criminal Evidence (Northern Ireland) Order 1988 allowing a court, in a case where the accused refused to be sworn when called on to give evidence in his own defence, to 'draw such inferences from the refusal as appear proper'. The House of Lords held that where the prosecution had established a prima facie case against the defendant the court could in an appropriate case draw the conclusion that he was guilty as charged. As Rees pointed out (1994, p. 16) this has the consequence that the standard of proof for such cases is now reduced to that of a prima facie case (based on the balance of probabilities) plus silence. In a similar Northern Ireland case the European Court of Human Rights held that the right to silence was not an absolute. In *John Murray* v *United Kingdom* (Case No. 41/1944/488/570) (1996) *The Times*, 9 February, the European Court of Human Rights determined that the right to remain silent under police questioning and the privilege against self-incrimination were generally recognised international standards which lay at the heart of the notion of fair procedure. But these immunities were not absolutes. Whether the drawing of adverse inferences from an accused's silence infringed Article 6 of the European Convention on Human Rights was a matter to be determined in the light of all the circumstances of the case, having particular regard to the situations where inferences might be drawn, the weight attached to them by the national courts in their assessment of the evidence and the degree of compulsion inherent in the situation. It could not be said that the drawing of reasonable inferences from the applicant's behaviour had the effect of shifting the burden of proof from the prosecution to the defence so as to infringe the principle of the presumption of innocence. The Court however determined on the facts that denial of access to legal advice for 48 hours did infringe the Article under the specific provisions of the 1988 order.

Zuckerman (1994, p. 117) stresses a fundamental claim to equality of treatment at the hands of officials. The principle of natural justice in the determination of charges, he says, requires the suspect to have full notice of the evidence against him and that the investigation of the charges takes place before an impartial tribunal. He should not be required to participate since he is unable to do so in a free and informed manner. This situation is not altered by the presence of his solicitor. In Zuckerman's view, the right way to deal with 'ambush' defences at trial is to institute a proper system of pre-trial pleading in which prosecution and defence set out in writing the essence of their cases. Zuckerman accepts (at p. 139) that common sense in these circumstances might allow comment on silence. He argues:

> It is a matter of the most fundamental fairness that a person who has to answer a charge should be given adequate information about that charge. Until adequate provision is made for supplying suspects with such information, the process will not only be unfair but also dangerous, because it creates considerable scope for abuse. However, the courts have ample jurisdiction to ensure that comment on silence is allowed only where the questioning of the suspect has been fair. Once the courts have evolved parameters of fairness they would benefit not only the suspects who maintain silence but all suspects questioned by the police.

Not all commentators would agree with Zuckerman that comment on the suspect's silence may, given procedural safeguards, be acceptable. Galligan (1988) puts forward a justification for protecting the right to silence, basing it on the right to individual autonomy. He draws a distinction between privacy as to consciousness and privacy as to bodily parts, such as fingerprints: 'it is only privacy with respect to consciousness which is sufficiently fundamental to attract a blanket form of legal protection.'

It is thus arguable that in an adversarial system in which the police are effectively a party, the way in which the investigation is conducted does have an impact on the legitimacy of the verdict. The conflict over the right to silence sets proponents of crime control against champions of due process. It is perhaps questionable whether the idea of 'balance' has any place where the state is confronting the individual. The parties are simply not and never can be on equal terms.

Certainly, procedurally, suspects now have many more safeguards compared with pre-PACE days. Moreover the provisions for tape-recording interviews promise additional safeguards against 'verballing' (see Code of Practice E). However, given recent examples of lack of police integrity and the psychological fact that suspects may be silent for other reasons than guilt, perhaps as Zuckerman says (at p. 139), any procedural changes may be insufficient if 'they do not address the principal causes of miscarriage of justice: police bias and witness suggestibility'.

This question in short raises wider issues than the 'balance of fairness'. In any case the search for 'balance' appears never-ending. At the time of writing the government is initiating new legislation on pre-trial disclosure of evidence.

The Court of Appeal in *R* v *Alladice* focused on the pragmatic argument of achieving accuracy in decision-making. It is submitted that there are other values, independent of rectitude, which should have a place in the criminal justice system. Trials are not just a matter of allocating liabilities or the balance of protection between prosecution and defence. As Galligan, citing Ronald Dworkin has argued, to take rights seriously is to understand that society cannot, if it wishes to be consistent, confer a right and then curtail it if there are social benefits in doing so. It is arguable that access to legal advice and the privilege against self-incrimination are both rights which should not lightly be tempered.

QUESTION 2

Darcy and Bingley are suspected of the murder of Mrs. Bennett, Darcy's mother-in-law, who has disappeared in suspicious circumstances. They are both arrested, cautioned and taken separately into custody. On the way to the police station Bingley begins to sob and says, 'I'll miss the old bat, I should never have done it'. 'What do you mean? What have you done?' said PC Collins. 'Everyone knew she was an old cow but I'll never forget her face when we put the plastic bag over her,' replied Bingley. At the police station Bingley asks for a solicitor but the police refuse on the grounds that since the body has not yet been found other family members may be alerted to help conceal it. Bingley is questioned continually for nine hours, with only one break for tea and biscuits. The police then produce a skeleton which they have borrowed from a local medical school and tell Bingley they found it buried on his estate. He mistakenly thinks it is Mrs. Bennett and says, 'Oh my God. She has been moved'.

The police claim that Darcy said, when they called at his house to arrest him, 'I'm glad you've come. I did us all a favour by finishing her off'. Darcy has, unknown to the police, a rare medical condition which requires frequent rest periods. He is denied a solicitor at the police station because the police fear the solicitor might advise him to remain silent. Anxious to get some sleep because he knows he will black out otherwise Darcy announces that he will cooperate with the questioning. He tells the investigating officer that he had killed Mrs. Bennett and was proud of it. The confession is not recorded at the time but a note of it has been prepared by police to be read out at the trial. At the trial both plead not guilty and want to retract their statements at the police station. Darcy denies making the initial statement to the police at his house.

Advise Darcy and Bingley on evidence.

Commentary

You need to be careful to cover the rather specific issues in this question and not deal too generally with the law on confessions. Both Bingley and Darcy need to be advised whether their initial statements were made in the context of interviews as defined by the revised Code of Practice. Note that Darcy is in addition denying that he made the initial statement, not saying that it was improperly extracted from him. This is a question of fact not law and should arguably be tested by the jury. You need to discuss the possible breaches of PACE and the Code for each defendant and the implications of the trick played by the police on Bingley as well as whether the earlier improperly conducted interview has tainted a subsequent one. With regard to Darcy you must consider whether his desire to end the interview and get some rest is self-induced and therefore since s. 76(2)(b) PACE has been interpreted in a restrictive way (see *R* v *Goldenberg* (1988) 88 Cr App R 285), it is not applicable here.

Suggested Answer

Bingley's arrest and the administration of the caution suggest that his treatment by the police at this point is correct. In the van he makes what could be taken to be an implied confession of responsibility for Mrs. Bennett's death, according to the definition of a confession in s. 82(1) of the Police and Criminal Evidence Act 1984 ('PACE'). The question arises as to whether it is an entirely spontaneous statement outside the context of an interview. Paragraph 11.1A of Code C defines an interview as 'the questioning of the person regarding his involvement or suspected involvement in a criminal offence or offences which, by virtue of paragraph 10.1 of Code C is required to be carried out under caution'. Such interviews should normally be conducted at a police station. In *R* v *Matthews* [1989] 91 Cr App R 43 the Court of Appeal adopted a broad approach to the definition of an interview but this has not always been followed. Thus, a conversation in a car between a defendant and police officers, where the defendant offered information and the officers only asked a few questions was not an interview: *R* v *Younis and Ahmed* [1990] Crim LR 425. Bingley has volunteered to open the discussion. The issue is the intention of the police officer in making the response, to secure either an admission or an innocent explanation. On the facts, the former seems more likely. If so, there have been breaches of the Code; the questioning was conducted away from the police station and no offer of free legal advice was made. There do not appear to be any special conditions here as set in paras 11.1 of Code C. The question then arises as to whether the statement is admissible. This is clearly not an instance of oppression under s. 76(2)(a) PACE. It is unlikely either that a submission under s. 76(2)(b) PACE would succeed since the courts appear to have confined its operation to those cases where something out of the ordinary has occurred, often in situations where the defendant is particularly vulnerable, for example in *R* v *Everett* (1988) Crim LR 826. Exclusion under s. 78 PACE is possible if the breaches are considered significant enough, as in *R* v *Canale* [1990] 2 All ER 187 or if the police acted with bad faith (see *R* v *Alladice* (1988) 87 Cr App R 380). However there must be shown to be unfairness caused thereby to the proceedings to allow such a confession. If the defendant would have confessed anyway, as in *R* v *Alladice*, s. 78 PACE is not applicable. It is arguable here that Bingley was likely to have confessed unprompted.

At the police station the police are arguably acting correctly in the reason they give for delaying access to a solicitor. Murder is a serious arrestable offence and the reason given for the delay is within the scope of permissible reasons set out in s. 58(8) PACE. However in *R* v *Samuel* [1988] QB 615, the Court of Appeal stressed that the prosecution has a formidable task in satisfying the court that there are reasonable grounds for such a belief. The questioning without a proper mealbreak is unlikely to amount to a breach of the Code justifying exclusion under s. 76 or 78 PACE. The courts have held that in order to consider excluding a confession under s. 78, breaches must be 'significant and substantial' (*R* v *Absolam* (1989) 88 Cr App R 332). In *R* v *Canale* [1990] 2 All ER 187 two police officers failed to record interviews contemporaneously because they thought it best not to do so. The Court of Appeal had said that the officers had shown a cynical disregard of the Code which they had flagrantly breached. However, although the breach here in itself may be minor it has to be seen in the context of other more serious police malpractice. On the facts it appears that the police acted with bad faith with regard to the trick over the skeleton. It may be significant that it was the defendant and not his legal adviser who was tricked. In *R* v *Mason* [1988] 1 WLR 139 deceiving the solicitor was described by the court as a 'vital factor' in leading to exclusion. Thus, a confession obtained as a result of deception will be in danger of being excluded, but the particular circumstances of the case are important. Lord Lane said in *R* v *Alladice* that if the police had acted in bad faith the court would have excluded the confession under s. 78 if not s. 76 PACE. In *R* v *Walsh* (1989) 91 Cr App R 161, the Court of Appeal looked at several breaches of the statute and code and held that bad faith on the part of the police might make substantial or significant that which would not otherwise be so.

It is submitted that Bingley's confession is likely to be excluded under s. 78 PACE. There is a further consideration in that the fact that there have been breaches of the statute and/or Code in an earlier, initial interview may so taint subsequent interviews that they may affect the reliability of even a properly conducted interview. Here, the earlier possible breaches may render the second interview unreliable, irrespective of the breaches there outlined above. In *R* v *McGovern* (1990) 92 Cr App R 228, the Court of Appeal said that the question of whether a later interview should be excluded on these grounds is a question of fact and degree.

Darcy claims not to have made the initial statement. This is a question of fact and arguably should be put to the jury as the Privy Council held in *Ajodha* v *the State* [1982] AC 204.

However, under paragraph 11.2A of the revised Code of Practice C, at the beginning of an interview carried out in a police station, the interviewing officer should put to the suspect 'any significant statement or silence' which occurred before his arrival at the police station and ask him if he confirms it. Thus Darcy's alleged statement on the doorstep should have been recorded and put to him for confirmation. If these provisions have been breached there would be grounds to challenge the admissibility of the alleged confession on a voir dire (*R* v *Sat-Bhambra* (1988) 88 Cr App R 55). It is arguable that Darcy's police station confession is potentially unreliable under s. 76(2)(b) because he made it in order to get out of the interview so that he could get some rest because of his concern over his medical condition. In *R* v *Goldenberg* (1988) 88 Cr App R 285, however, the 'something said or done' limb of the test was held not to be satisfied by the conduct of the maker of the confession. Thus, the confession of a heroin addict who confessed in order to get drugs, could not be excluded under s. 76(2)(b). However, there may be grounds for exclusion under s. 78 PACE since the police have refused access to a solicitor for an improper reason. In *R* v *McIvor* [1987] Crim LR 409, Sir Frederick Lawton sitting as a Deputy High Court judge in Sheffield Crown Court held that the police should not have refused access to legal advice on the grounds that the defendant would be advised to be silent. It is, however, not clear if s. 76 or s. 78 was applied.

QUESTION 3

Police are puzzled by a series of thefts of valuable greyhounds from a kennels and suspect the perpetrators are involved in a gambling scam. They call on Gerry and Cliff, noted professional gamblers, as part of their routine inquiries. Gerry invites them in and agrees to answer any questions although he is clearly upset because he has just heard his mother is dying in hospital with cancer. As they are talking, Gerry's 14-year-old son, Tom, comes in and says: 'I hope they arrest you for cruelty to animals, it's horrible leaving that greyhound tied up in the shed. Grandma will cry her heart out when I tell her'. Gerry breaks down in tears and says: 'What a fool I have been. I said I'd mind the brute but I didn't know it was stolen. Cliff made me take it in'. He is arrested and cautioned and taken to the police station for questioning. There the custody officer asks him if he has his own solicitor. Gerry replies that he has but since he owes him money for arranging the sale of his house he doesn't like to call him. The police do not offer a duty solicitor and proceed to question Gerry further. Gerry tells them that he doesn't know any details of the thefts but the police persist in questioning him. The police then produce photographs of Tom on animal rights demonstrations and say to Gerry, 'You know we could take this further if you don't play ball'. Gerry then confesses that he, Cliff and several others had organised the thefts. He tells them that they had been forced to kill some of the dogs and they are buried on Hackney Downs. The police visit Cliff and ask him to come down to the station to help with their inquiries. He agrees but at the station asks for a solicitor. They reply that there is no need for that at this stage. They then leave him alone for about two hours. Cliff suffers from claustrophobia and when they return is in a very distressed state. Cliff is cautioned and told he is under arrest; he begins to sob violently and admits that he had stolen the greyhounds.

Advise Gerry and Cliff.

Commentary

You must systematically list the circumstances relating to the admissibility of possible confessions by both defendants. In a question of this sort it is important not to miss any of the issues. The visit to Gerry is described as 'routine' initially, so you need to discuss if and when it becomes an 'interview', and thus the requirements of the statute and Codes of Practice apply. Is Gerry's 'mixed' statement a confession? It clearly is partly exculpatory and partly inculpatory. The information on legal advice given by the police to Gerry must be checked against the Code requirements. The confession in the police station is clearly obtained under some pressure and you must check whether s. 76 or 78 PACE can be applied to exclude it. Do not overlook the issue of the incriminating of a third party, namely Cliff and whether, even if the confession is inadmissible, the trial may still consider the discovery of real evidence which it prompted, the buried dogs. Cliff's treatment raises the question of whether the police should have treated it as an interview from the beginning since he was already under suspicion as a result of Gerry's statement. Consider finally his distressed state and the possible unreliability of the confession.

Suggested Answer

Gerry's initial statement in his house is clearly incriminating although he is also trying to excuse himself. Since it is partly adverse to the maker it falls within the definition of'confession' in s. 82(1) of the Police and Criminal Evidence Act 1984 ('PACE'). If it is admitted the whole statement may be evidence of the truth of its contents, as the House of Lords held in *R* v *Sharp* [1988] 1 WLR 7. There is clearly no evidence of oppression here and therefore s. 76(2)(a) PACE is not applicable. However, it is necessary to consider the possible application of other sections of PACE and the Code of Practice. We are told the police are engaged in 'routine' inquiries, that is they are not conducting an interview, which is questioning of a person regarding his involvement in an offence, but rather questioning to obtain information. The state of mind of the police is the key question, but, on the facts as they are given, it seems the exchange was not an interview. The words uttered by Tom may amount to something said or done which was likely in the circumstances existing at the time to render unreliable any confession Gerry might have made. The Court of Appeal held that it is not necessary for the words or action to come from the police (*R* v *Harvey* [1988] Crim LR 241). There are two limbs to the test, first circumstances existing at the time and here Gerry's emotional state concerning his mother's condition may be applicable. See also *R* v *McGovern* (1990) 92 Cr App R 228. Secondly, as regards anything said or done, can Tom's words be sufficient? The main question is to find a causal connection between the words and the confession such as to make any confession in such circumstances unreliable. On the facts, there does not appear to be anything in Tom's remark which would have made any confession unreliable, unless it could be argued that Gerry confessed in order to stop Tom's tirade and painful remarks about his dying mother.

At the station, Gerry appears to have been properly cautioned but there may be inadequacies in the information given about access to legal advice which may, inter alia, render his confession inadmissible. Under s. 58 PACE and paragraph 11.2 of Code C, immediately prior to the commencement of any interview at a police station or other authorised place of detention, the interviewing officer must remind the suspect of his entitlement to free legal advice. It appears that, when Gerry is asked whether he has a solicitor and he replies that he is worried about owing him money, Gerry is not told of his entitlement to free legal advice. However, access to legal advice may be lawfully delayed for up to 36 hours in the case of serious arrestable offences (s. 116 PACE). A serious arrestable offence includes one which involves serious financial loss or gain so this may well apply in the case of the greyhounds. Thus, the failure in Gerry's case may well be permissible as long as the police can convince the court that they reasonably feared one of the contingencies referred to in s. 58(8) PACE would arise. In any case, a wrongly authorised delay in obtaining legal advice, does not render the confession automatically excluded under either s. 76 or 78 PACE. In *R* v *Alladice* (1988) 87 Cr App R 380, the court stressed that influential factors in excluding under s. 78 PACE were whether or not the police acted in bad faith and whether the presence of a solicitor would have made any difference, particularly to a seasoned offender.

However, there are arguably other pressing grounds to exclude the confession here under s. 76 PACE. Has this confession been obtained by oppression? Once the defence raises the issue and it is accepted by the judge as a possibility, the burden is on the prosecution to prove beyond reasonable doubt that it has not been so obtained. Does the implied threat to Tom amount to oppression of Gerry? Oppression is only partly defined in s. 76(8) PACE as including 'torture, inhuman or degrading treatment and the use or threat of violence whether or not amounting to torture'. Showing the photograph and the threat to 'take things further' probably does not fall within this partial statutory definition. However, in the leading case of *R* v *Fulling* [1987] QB 426 the Court of Appeal adopted the dictionary definition of 'exercise of authority or power in a burdensome, harsh or wrongful manner; unjust or cruel treatment of subjects, inferiors, etc., or the imposition of unreasonable or unjust burdens'.

In the court's opinion, it was difficult to envisage any circumstances in which oppression would not entail some impropriety on the part of the police. It is clear that Gerry here is being placed under psychological pressure as a result of the threat. The main requirement is misuse of power or authority. Thus, in *R* v *Paris* (1992) 97 Cr App R 99 the Court of Appeal held that it was oppressive within the meaning of s. 76(2)(a) PACE for police officers to shout at a suspect and tell him what they wanted to hear after he had denied the offence 300 times so it is arguable that the treatment of Gerry amounts to oppression. Also s. 76(2)(b) PACE may be applicable in that in such circumstances any confession made by the defendant would be likely to be unreliable. This test is an objective one. Section 78 PACE is widely applied to confession evidence (*R* v *Mason* [1988] 1 WLR 139) and the combination of factors, particularly police bad faith over the threat, could lead to exclusion here. Even if the confession is excluded the court may still allow evidence of finding the greyhounds, although clearly their evidential worth will be less considering that it may not be possible to admit its source (s. 76(4) PACE). One final point is that even if the confession is admitted it will not be evidence against Cliff and should be edited at the trial.

With regard to Cliff's position, it is arguable that the police were wrong not to treat their initial exchange with him as an interview under the definition in Code of Practice C paragraph 11.1A. There were already reasonable grounds to suspect him because of Gerry's confession. He should therefore have been cautioned and told of his right to free legal advice, although it is arguable that this is a serious arrestable offence and access to a solicitor could be delayed on appropriate grounds. There is perhaps, a breach of the Code also in leaving him for two hours, since under paragraph 1.1 of Code C, persons in custody should be dealt with expeditiously. As someone not under arrest Cliff was free to leave but clearly had not appreciated this. There are possible grounds for unreliability given the 'something said or done' could be leaving him for two hours and the circumstances of his claustrophobia. For exclusion on grounds of s. 76(2)(b) PACE, there is no need for police impropriety. In *R* v *Crampton* (1990) 92 Cr App R 369 according to the court it was a matter for those present at the interview to decide whether a drug addict was fit to be questioned in the sense that his answers could be relied upon to be true. The series of breaches could also, especially if bad faith was found, amount to exclusion on grounds of unfairness under s. 78 of PACE.

QUESTION 4

Arnold and Brenda are summonsed on charges of criminal damage of a wine shop in Boxfield High Street. The incident occurred at 3.00 a. m. where the window was smashed and the alarm sounded. Arnold was stopped shortly afterwards in the next street where police suspicions are aroused because he is not wearing shoes. He is arrested and questioned in the street. He refuses to say why he was in the area at that time because he had been visiting his girlfriend and did not want his wife to find out. He also refuses to explain why he is not wearing shoes. He offers no evidence at his trial. An abandoned pair of glass-strewn sandals, which the police believe are Arnold's, are found near the scene of the burglary. Brenda works at the wine shop and when she turns up for work next day and sees the debris, she asks the manager, 'What happened here?'. He replies, 'I think you know all about this don't you? Your friends and you helped yourselves'. Brenda says nothing.

Advise on the evidence.

Commentary

The defendants here have acted in different ways in the face of questioning about their involvement in the offence. You will need to examine whether their reactions and behaviour amount to confessions, if so what is their evidential worth and if there are grounds to exclude them by rule of law or exercise of discretion. Arnold's behaviour raises several issues under the Criminal Justice and Public Order Act 1994, ss. 34, 35, 36, 37 and 38. Brenda's situation involves a discussion of the law relating to silence in the face of questioning by the shop manager. You need therefore to discuss her behaviour in relation to common law provisions on silence. You are only given information about questioning outside the police station so do not speculate about other possible interviews.

Suggested Answer

The question involves an examination of the overlapping provisions of ss. 34–38 of the Criminal Justice and Public Order Act 1994 which cover circumstances where a court may invite the drawing of inferences from an accused's silence. Section 34 applies after caution and up to charge, that is both before and after arrest. However it only allows the court to draw inferences from silence if the defendant fails then to mention facts which he could reasonably have been expected to mention when questioned and which he relies on at trial for his defence. Since Arnold we are told offers no explanation at trial this section does not apply.

Sections 36 and 37 apply only on arrest and in addition the constable should give the caution and additional caution under Code C paragraph 10.5B which offers more information about the constable's questioning. Under s. 36, Arnold may find that his failure to account for his lack of shoes is put at the trial even if he does not offer an explanation there, but he may argue that the section applies to the failure to account for the presence not absence of objects, substances or marks. Similarly s. 37 covers failure to explain his presence at a particular place and also may apply even if no explanation is offered at trial. However for ss. 36 and 37 to apply, Arnold should have been cautioned and questioned at an interview conducted in accordance with Code C of PACE. He should also have been given the additional special warning (Code C paras 10.5A and B).

Code of Practice C issued under the Police and Criminal Evidence Act 1984 ('PACE') requires a police officer to caution the suspect before questioning him once there are grounds to suspect him of an offence. The caution now has been reworded and the suspect is warned of the possible consequences of his failure to mention relevant facts. It is unclear from the facts whether the police have reasonable suspicion of Arnold's involvement. His proximity to the scene of the crime and the lack of shoes do, however, appear to be significant. The issue is whether the questioning amounts to an interview. If it does then the statute and Code of Practice apply. The revised Code defines an interview as the questioning of a person regarding his involvement in an offence, but that questioning to obtain information or in the ordinary course of duty does not constitute an interview. This does leave some doubt, however, as to when questioning to obtain information turns into questioning about involvement in an offence. The case law is primarily based on the admissibility of confessions, but is arguably relevant also to the suspect's silence. *R* v *Park* [1994] Crim LR 285 upholds the principle that 'at the scene' interviews are not admissible. In that case, it was held that exploratory questions at a roadside could give rise in due course to a well-founded suspicion that an offence had been committed. So what started out as an inquiry could become an interview. However, the Court of Appeal upheld the judge's decision not to apply s. 78 PACE to exclude that part of the evidence: 'even if the roadside conversation should now be regarded as an interview ... it was, as prosecuting counsel said, only just an interview ...'.

In the instant case the police already know of the offence and so there might be more grounds for considering their questions to Arnold an interview. Arnold will thus be advised that even if he has been cautioned it is possible that the prosecution cannot make use of his silence in the street, because he should not have been questioned away from the police station. It is however appropriate that 'emergency' provisions should be considered. He may be interviewed away from the police station if the consequent delay would be likely (a) to lead to interference with or harm to evidence connected with an offence or interference with or physical harm to other people; (b) to lead to the alerting of other people suspected of having committed an offence but not yet arrested for it; or (c) to hinder the recovery of property obtained in consequence of the commission of an offence. It does not appear on the facts that any of these do apply to Arnold.

Finally Arnold's failure to testify may lead to inferences being drawn by the court (see s. 35 CJPOA and *R* v *Cowan* [1995] 3 WLR 818.

What constitutes a proper inference for the court or jury in any particular case is a matter of fact. However, Arnold may gain some comfort from s. 38(3) of the 1994 Act which provides that 'A person shall not have the proceedings against him transferred to the Crown Court for trial, have a case to answer or be convicted of an offence solely on an inference drawn from such a failure or refusal'. Here there does appear to be other circumstantial evidence such as the finding of the shoes.

Brenda faces the possibility of her silences being admitted by common law or statute. First of all, is her failure to respond to the manager's allegation admissible? Under s. 82(1) PACE a confession includes any statement wholly or partly adverse to the person who made it, whether made to a person in authority or not and whether made in words or otherwise. The first question then is whether her silence is a statement made otherwise than in words. It is by no means clear that silence would fit such a definition. The common law rule is that a statement made in the presence of the accused is not evidence against him except in so far as he accepts what has been said (*R* v *Christie* [1914] AC 545). It may be that a reply or indignant rejection of the accusation could reasonably be expected from Brenda and thus her failure to do that may be an implied acceptance of the truth of the accusation. Thus in *Parkes* v *R* [1977] 64 Cr App R 25, the defendant's silence when accused by a mother of stabbing her daughter was held by the Privy Council to have been properly admitted as evidence going to guilt. The courts have applied this principle to situations where the parties are on even terms. Brenda's accuser is her manager and she may have been quiet from considerations other than guilt. If her failure to reply is admitted, the jury should be directed to consider first whether the silence indicates acceptance of the accusation and secondly whether guilt could reasonably be inferred from what she had accepted. A failure to leave both these issues to the jury led to the quashing of a conviction by the Court of Appeal in *R* v *Chandler* [1976] 1 WLR 585. Section 34 of the Criminal Justice and Public Order Act 1994 does not apply to Brenda because it is only relevant in relation to silence when being questioned by the police or others charged with investigating offences. The shop manager does not fit this definition.

9 Improperly Obtained Evidence

INTRODUCTION

Confessions apart English law has been notoriously unwilling to acknowledge the case for excluding evidence which is obtained in a way which involves the police acting improperly or even illegally. However there is now a growing body of cases on a specific aspect of this, namely entrapment, whereby the police are arguably influencing the actual commission of the offence. Several cases have recently considered whether evidence obtained thereby should be excluded under s. 78 of the Police and Criminal Evidence Act 1984 (PACE). You will need knowledge of the common law position on this issue exemplified in *R* v *Sang* [1980] AC 402, a case which raised many academic hackles. There the House of Lords appeared to confine the discretion to exclude, on grounds of impropriety, to cases of confessions or those akin to confessions. The issue was seen to be based on the privilege against self-incrimination. Lord Diplock (at p. 436) explained it as follows:

> That is why there is no discretion to exclude evidence discovered as a result of an illegal search but there is discretion to exclude evidence which the accused has been induced to produce voluntarily if the method of inducement was unfair.

However in principle, if not in practice, the courts now appear willing to apply s. 78 to improperly obtained evidence other than confessions specifically that obtained by undercover police operations involving entrapment.

QUESTION 1

The police are concerned about a spate of burglaries from clothes shops on the Che Guevara estate where the perpetrators have not been caught. Inspector Hilary, a plainclothes policewoman, strikes up a conversation with a group of women suspects in the estate's launderette but does not say who she is. She expresses an interest in the attractive silk shirts they are washing. Alice, one of the women, agrees to get some for Hilary. They arrange to meet the next day and the shirts are exchanged for money. They turn out to have been stolen from Designer Modes, one of the shops on the estate. Alice is then arrested for dealing in stolen goods. Meanwhile PC Henry, also in plain clothes, had gained entry to the estate's youth club, run by the church, by claiming to be a council electrician. He places a listening device in the men's toilets and makes a tape recording of Tom and Gerry congratulating one another on successfully carrying out a burglary at Designer Modes.

Advise on the admissibility of the tape and on the case against Alice.

Commentary

The police in this case are engaged in undercover operations. The question turns therefore on the possibility of excluding evidence on the grounds that it has been obtained improperly. You must state the general rule of English law that the impropriety of the method of obtaining evidence generally bears no relevance to its admissibility, except in relation to confessions. The principle that there is no such rule of exclusion was set out by the Privy Council in *Kuruma* v *R* [1955] AC 197. However, although there is no rule of exclusion, there is a discretion to exclude if the admission of such evidence would be unfair. With regard to the common law discretion, the House of Lords in *R* v *Sang* [1980] AC 402 seemed to suggest that discretion to exclude evidence because it was illegally or improperly obtained only applied to confession evidence (or evidence analogous to confessions) unless its probative value was less than its prejudicial effect. *Sang* also held that there was a substantive rule that entrapment is no defence and that this could not be undermined by the use of an evidential discretion. Thus Alice, who is likely to argue she was tricked into committing the offence, cannot rely on the common law discretion. This common law discretion was limited in *R* v *Sang* to evidence obtained after the commission of the offence, so the common law is not applicable in the case of Alice if she argues entrapment. Cases of entrapment or the activities of an agent provocateur refer to those situations where the accused is either enticed or encouraged to commit an offence and is subsequently charged. However, section 78 PACE has, in theory at least, now been acknowledged as of possible application in entrapment cases, although the courts have been slow to identify actual agent provocateurs. With regard to the listening operation, here an apparent confession was recorded and you need to consider the application of the Code of Practice C in determining its admissibility.

Suggested Answer

Tom, Gerry and Alice may try to argue that the evidence against them should be excluded because it has been obtained improperly. Inspector Hilary did not reveal she was a police officer but appeared as a genuine purchaser and PC Henry was a trespasser when he gained the evidence of the confession. The general rule is that, as Crompton J put it obiter in *R* v *Leathem* [1861] 8 Cox CC 498, 'it matters not how you get it, if you steal it even, it would be admissible in evidence'. The test of admissibility is whether the evidence is relevant. Lord Fraser said in *Fox* v *Chief Constable of Gwent* [1985] 3 All ER 392, 397, 'the duty of the court is to decide whether the appellant has committed the offence with which he is charged and not to discipline the police for exceeding their powers'. However, although there is no rule of exclusion, it is open to the court as an exercise of discretion to exclude improperly obtained evidence if its admission would be unfair. In *R* v *Sang* [1980] AC 402 its exercise was limited to evidence obtained after the offence was committed. Thus the common law may apply to Tom and Gerry because they confessed after the event, but not to Alice. In practice, however, the common law discretion has given way to the application of s. 78 of the Police and Criminal Evidence Act 1984 ('PACE') which gives a statutory discretion to exclude evidence which would adversely affect the fairness of the proceedings. Thus the court has to consider the interests of the prosecution as well as the defence.

With regard to the tape recording, PC Henry was a trespasser when he installed the listening device and so the evidence has been obtained by unlawful means. Again, there is nothing in the statute to suggest that the court should discipline the police. Statutory exclusion of confessions on the grounds of potential unreliability is confined to those made 'in consequence of anything said or done' during the interrogation. This does not apply here. However, the court may apply the discretion under s. 78 PACE. The courts will, in regard to confessions, look on bad faith on the part of the police as grounds for exercising the discretion (*R* v *Alladice* (1988) 87 Cr App R 380), but the test is whether a trial containing evidence obtained as a result of a particular deceit would be fair. The approach is decided on a case by case basis. Thus, in *R* v *H* [1987] Crim LR 47 evidence of secretly tape-recorded conversations between the complainant and the suspect in a rape case was excluded, whereas in *R* v *Jelen* (1989) 90 Cr App R 456, the Court of Appeal upheld the admission of tape recordings made in secret of two defendants in conversation. The Court of Appeal drew a distinction between the two cases, in that, in the latter, the police were at an early stage of their inquiries and the defendant had not been interviewed. A more recent example is *R* v *Khan* [1995] QB 27, where the police, following Home Office guidelines, placed an undercover listening device on the outside wall of a private house of a suspected heroin dealer. The police had caused criminal damage and were trespassing. The admissions so recorded were admitted. The Court of Appeal accepted as a factor in that case that the offence was one of great gravity. Tom and Gerry's offence of shop burglary is arguably less serious. The test for admissibility lies in balancing the undermining of the defendant's privacy with the public interest in the prosecution of criminals. It is submitted that if Tom and Gerry were not suspects and had not been interrogated before, it is likely their admissions will be allowed.

Alice may possibly argue that she would not have committed the offence if she had not been asked for the shirts by Hilary. In *R* v *Sang*, the House of Lords said entrapment is no defence and that this rule cannot be changed by exercise of discretion on admissibility of evidence. However, in recent years, the courts have shown a willingness at least to consider the exercise of s. 78 PACE in using its discretion to exclude evidence obtained by entrapment.

In *R* v *Edwards* [1991] Crim LR 45 undercover officers agreed to buy drugs from the defendants who were charged with conspiracy to supply but not specifically to supply the officers. The Court of Appeal held that there was no discretion to exclude the evidence because the officers were not agents provocateurs of a particular offence. As Smith (1995, at p. 193) comments: 'The court's opinion seemed to be that there was no discretion unless the officers were agents provocateurs — standing Lord Diplock's statement of the law in *Sang* on its head.' However, he says *R* v *Edwards* seems to have been ignored in later cases.

In *R* v *Smurthwaite* [1994] 1 All ER 898, the Court of Appeal accepted that s. 78 PACE had introduced some discretion to exclude evidence in such situations. It laid down guidelines to judges when exercising their discretion whether to admit the evidence of undercover police officers. The fact that the evidence had been obtained by entrapment does not of itself require the judge to exclude it unless it would have the adverse effect described in s. 78 PACE. However, factors to be taken into account were: was the officer enticing the defendant to commit a crime he would not otherwise have committed? what was the nature of the entrapment? does the evidence consist of admissions to a completed offence or the actual commission of an offence? how active or passive was the officer's role in obtaining the evidence? was there an unassailable record of what occurred or was it strongly corroborated? Reference was made to *R* v *Christou* [1992] QB 979 where the Court of Appeal said it was improper for police officers to adopt a disguise to enable them to ask questions without having to observe the Code, although they had not done so there in setting up a fake jewellery shop to take suspected stolen goods. The questions arose inevitably in the course of the exchange of goods.

In Alice's case, these criteria are relevant. In their light it would appear that evidence of the transaction of the shirts is probably admissible but not of any accompanying confession. Alice appears to have volunteered to get a shirt for Hilary without further prompting, so that the element of entrapment is relatively minor. This appears to be one of those situations where the Inspector, Hilary, has been able to insert herself into a situation where the offence is already underway. She appears as willing to accept goods which might reasonably be expected to be stolen. Alice is presumably already in possession of the goods, so it is not a situation where, but for Hilary's intervention, the offence might not have been committed. Furthermore, the evidence relates to the actual commission of the offence, rather than to an admission to an already completed offence.

It thus seems likely that Alice had a crime in mind or was already knowingly in possession of the stolen shirts before Hilary appeared. Alice's chances of having the evidence excluded are very slim. Despite the acceptance in principle in *Smurthwaite* that evidence obtained by undercover operations before the commission of an offence could be excluded, in recent cases, the courts have not so acted. Alice has been deceived into producing evidence against herself but as the Court of Appeal said in *R* v *Christou* 'The trick was not applied to the appellants; they voluntarily applied themselves to the trick'.

QUESTION 2

In *R* v *Sang* [1980] AC 402 Lord Diplock held that 'Save with regard to admissions and generally with regard to evidence obtained from the accused after commission of the offence, [the judge] has no discretion to refuse to admit relevant admissible evidence on the ground that it was obtained by improper or unfair means'.

Critically evaluate whether such a discretion is recognised today.

Commentary

A careful reading of this question will underline that you are not being asked to discuss the application of the discretion to exclude evidence generally because it has been obtained improperly or unfairly. You must concentrate on the specific question of evidence obtained before the commission of an offence, that is by entrapment or by agents provocateurs. Do not therefore make the mistake of dealing with illegal searches or improperly obtained confessions. Bear in mind the term 'agent provocateur' is not defined in law although the Royal Commission on Police Powers 1928 (Cmnd 3297) is sometimes quoted. It is 'a person who entices another to commit an express breach of the law which he would not otherwise have committed and then proceeds to inform against him in respect of such an offence'. The question is really about how far s. 78 PACE has changed the common law position in *R* v *Sang* and whether evidence of entrapment is potentially inadmissible. *Sang* appeared to exclude the possibility of this at all. Such evidence will usually be that of police or their informers. Bear in mind you are writing an essay on the law of evidence so do not stray into a polemic about 'supergrasses'.

Suggested Answer

In *R* v *Sang* the House of Lords addressed the issue of whether there is a defence of entrapment in English criminal law. It held that such a defence did not exist and thus it followed that there was no discretion to exclude evidence of the commission of a crime on the grounds that the defendant was tricked into committing it. It was argued that to allow such a discretion would be to change the substantive law by the law of evidence. Thus, the House differentiated between trickery which led to the commission of an offence, and trickery in obtaining either real evidence or a confession after it had been committed. The question here asks for a consideration of whether the courts still take a position of refusing to exclude evidence of entrapment. Geoffrey Robertson (1993, p. 805) argues that s. 78 PACE has effectively reversed the decision in Sang. The court is now required to consider excluding prosecution evidence by exercise of the discretion on the grounds of unfairness and there is no specification that such evidence is limited to that after the commission of the offence.

However, the courts have been slow to exclude improperly obtained evidence under s. 78 PACE other than confession evidence. In *R* v *Harwood* [1989] Crim LR 285, the Court of Appeal held that it could not exclude evidence of an offence on the ground that it was instigated by an agent provocateur. The court said that the rule of law that an offence induced by an agent provocateur was not a defence to the charge was a substantive rule of law. Section 78 PACE could not be applied to abrogate this.

However, subsequent cases showed a less cautious approach. Thus in *R* v *Gill and Ranuana* [1989] Crim LR 358 the trial judge considered applying s. 78 PACE when considering allegations of entrapment. In the event he admitted the evidence finding that there was no evidence that the alleged agent provocateur had in fact acted as one. The Court of Appeal upheld this approach. It stated that the informant who had introduced the police officers, posing as IRA members ready to carry out a contract murder, was not an agent provocateur. The idea had not been that of the police and there was no 'improper behaviour' by the police.

As Sharpe (1994 at p. 796) points out, 'there is arguably an abuse of process and resultant unfairness in upholding a conviction arising through incitement whoever initiates the conspiracy'. In *R* v *Edwards* [1991] Crim LR 45 it was argued that the police undercover agents had been agents provocateurs and that their evidence should have been excluded. On the conflict between *R* v *Harwood* and *R* v *Gill and Ranuana*, the Court said there was no evidence to demonstrate that the officers involved in the instant appeal were in truth agents provocateurs so it was unnecessary for it to resolve it. In *R* v *Edwards* undercover officers had approached the defendant and agreed to buy from him a quantity of prohibited drugs. The defendants were charged with conspiracy to supply persons unknown. Smith (1995, p. 192) points out:

> The defence argument was the converse of *Sang* — that the evidence should be excluded under s. 78 PACE because the officers were agents provocateurs... The court's opinion seemed to be that there was no discretion unless the officers were agents provocateurs — standing Lord Diplock's statement of the law in *Sang* on its head.

Thus by both taking a restrictive definition of agent provocateur and by considering the case to be one of a general conspiracy rather than a specific offence involving undercover officers, the Court of Appeal decided on the facts that there was no improper incitement. The police action in setting up ruses in *R* v *Christou* [1992] QB 979 again led the Court of Appeal to consider the application of s. 78 PACE. Lord Taylor considered the trick of a shop set up by the police apparently prepared to deal in stolen jewellery did not involve unfairness although this implied that some tricks could. A similar approach was adopted in *Williams* v *DPP* [1993] 3 All ER 365, where the defendants had stolen cartons of dummy cigarettes left by police in an open van. The Divisional Court held that the evidence of the thefts was admissible.

A more robust attitude was taken by the Court of Appeal in *R* v *Bryce* [1992] 4 All ER 567. Evidence of conversations between the defendant and undercover police officers should have been excluded because they concerned the fact in issue of guilty knowledge of a stolen car. Furthermore, unlike the situation in *Christou* there was no contemporary record such as tape and film recording. Choo and Mellors (1995) criticise this decision because it based exclusion on grounds of reliability rather than extrinsic policy considerations.

In *R* v *Smurthwaite* [1994] 1 All ER 898 the Court of Appeal attempted to lay down more clearly defined guidelines applying s. 78 PACE to entrapment cases. The fact that the evidence has been obtained by entrapment does not of itself require the judge to exclude it unless it would have the adverse effect dealt referred to s. 78 PACE. Thus the nature of the entrapment would affect the application of the discretion.

Later cases have further defined the guidelines. In *R* v *Latif and Shahzad* [1994] Crim LR 750, the defendants claimed that they had been encouraged in the illegal importation of heroin by an agent of the British government. The Court of Appeal dismissed the appeal and referred as a factor to the seriousness of the offence charged.

The law does now acknowledge that entrapment can theoretically lead to non-admission of evidence of the commission of an offence, though in practice reluctant to exclude such evidence which does not also include a confession where the safeguards of statute and the Code of Practice should have been applied. Robertson (1993) questions whether this is a satisfactory state of affairs and looks at the more severe attitude to exclusion in Australia. Zuckerman ((1989) at p. 357) points out that 'the theory of immorality is still very rudimentary and much more has to be done'. A more energetic exclusionary policy than the courts have shown so far will have, he says, to concern itself with 'violations of moral standards, as well as those of express legal prohibitions, and the superior courts will have to develop criteria to identify those police measures that are considered morally unacceptable.' In the Federal jurisdiction of the United States there exists a substantive defence of entrapment, although as Choo and Mellors (1995) point out there has been difficulty over the application of the 'but for' test, namely whether the offence would have been committed without the entrapment. The question arises, does the test apply to this particular offence that the defendant must not otherwise have committed, or is it an offence of the particular type, in which case how broad is the concept of offences of a particular type? They find the English position unacceptable. They say entrapment should be isolated for special consideration given 'that it amounts, by definition, to the creation by the state of crime which would not otherwise have been committed'. Unacceptable entrapment should not merely be grounds for discretionary exclusion of evidence, but should lead automatically to a stay of proceedings as an abuse of the process of the court. They and other commentators call for the introduction of legislation or code of practice to regulate undercover police operations. Undoubtedly, however, the possibility is now left open for entrapment evidence to be excluded under s. 78 PACE, thus curtailing the *Sang* restriction of the common law discretion referred to in the question. Clearly undercover operations are sometimes necessary if conventional police methods fail but arguably better regulation is needed over the admission of evidence obtained thereby.

10 Corroboration and Identification

INTRODUCTION

The scope of the law on corroboration has been substantially reduced by recent legislative and judicial reforms. There still remain the various categories of situations where corroborating or supporting evidence is required as a matter of law, i.e., where there can be no conviction in the absence of corroborating evidence. These are imposed by statute and examples include cases of treason under s. 1 of the Treason Act 1795, perjury under s. 13 of the Perjury Act 1911, and speeding under s. 89 of the Road Traffic Regulation Act 1984. Questions are rarely asked about these sections in Evidence examinations. More important for your purposes is a category of what Murphy (at p. 508) calls the 'quasi-corroborative rule', where additional evidence (not necessarily of the same type of evidence which is necessary for corroboration) is required before an accused person can, inter alia, be convicted or have a case to answer to. This relates to the limitation on the accused's right of silence under ss. 34 to 37 of the Criminal Justice and Public Order Act 1994. However s. 38(3) of the 1994 Act makes it clear that the accused cannot have a case to answer, be committed for trial, or be convicted merely on the basis of this inference. This suggests that additional evidence is required before this can occur.

Perjury apart, the common law system has no general requirement for corroboration. A single piece of evidence is usually enough to convict. Prior to 1988, however, there were three categories of cases where although corroboration was not required as a matter of law, a corroboration warning was necessary. Failure to give such a warning was a valid ground of appeal. However, conviction was still possible without corroborative evidence. As long as the warning was given, the jury could convict in the absence of corroborative evidence. The three categories of cases were: evidence given by children of tender years on oath; evidence given by complainants in sexual cases; evidence given by accomplices on the prosecution's behalf. These provisions were criticised as being increasingly complex and technical.

The need for a corroboration warning for the first category was finally fully abolished by s. 34(2) of the Criminal Justice Act 1988. The last two categories where a corroboration warning was required were abolished by s. 32(1) of the Criminal Justice and Public Order Act 1994. There will still be cases where a corroboration warning may be required as a matter of discretion, for example, where the evidence of a witness is suspect for some reason specific to the case. If that is the case, the next question that arises is the type of additional evidence that can constitute corroboration. The classic definition of corroboration is that given by the Court of Appeal in *R* v *Baskerville* [1916] 2 KB 658. Lord Reading CJ (at p. 667) expressed the requirements as follows:

> . . . evidence in corroboration must be independent testimony which affects the accused by connecting or tending to connect him with the crime. In other words, it must be evidence which implicates him, that is which confirms in some material particular not only the evidence that the crime has been committed, but also that the prisoner committed it.

There were thus five limbs to the definition: the evidence had to be relevant, admissible, credible, independent of the witness to be corroborated and implicate the defendant in the commission of the offence.

The effect of the reforms of the Criminal Justice and Public Order Act 1994 is to abolish the common law requirement for corroboration warnings in criminal trials. The recent case of *R* v *Makanjuola* [1995] 1 WLR 1348 considers the application of the new law. Because, however, of the newness of the law and the continuing debate over whether confessions should require corroboration or a corroboration warning, you should still have an overview of the main features of the earlier law.

As regards identification evidence, students will have to be familiar with the *Turnbull* guidelines or what Murphy has called 'the quasi-corroborative suspect witness direction'. Further, students may be expected to be familiar with Code D of the Codes of Practice of the Police and Criminal Evidence Act 1984, including the various annexes to it and how the identification evidence can be excluded if the Code is not followed.

QUESTION 1

'By the end of 1994 no further reform of the law relating to corroboration in criminal trials was necessary.'

Discuss.

Commentary

The recent controversy over reform of the law on corroboration makes it a possible essay question in examinations. This question is a relatively straightforward one asking you to assess the impact of changes in the law relating to corroboration by courts and by Parliament and to assess whether further changes may be needed. The general thrust of your essay will be that even before the statutory changes, of the increasing relaxation of the formerly rigid rules by the courts even before the statutory changes, in cases like *R* v *Hills* (1987) 86 Cr App R 26 and *R* v *Chance* [1988] QB 932, not forgetting of course the Court of Appeal decision in *R* v *Turnbull* [1977] QB 224 where 'guidelines' short of a full corroboration warning were applied. There is a great deal of ground to deal with if you are to achieve a comprehensive coverage and so you need to plan your essay carefully. A possible outline is:

(a) Latest change in law. Criminal Justice and Public Order Act 1994 abolished remaining two categories of corroboration warning; culmination, however, of a number of recent statutory and judicial relaxations. Essay will review these, consider if relaxations are needed and look also if new cases of corroboration or warning are required.

(b) It is necessary to bear in mind that there were no new categories of cases which required a corroboration warning as a matter of law: *R* v *Turnbull* and *R* v *Beck* [1982] 1 WLR 461. Consider also the case of *R* v *Chance* and its application in rape cases. Part of the answer should include the definition of corroboration and the effect of *R* v *Hills* (1987) 86 Cr App R 26 on the issue of cumulative corroboration. Further, consideration should be given to whether any uncertainty remains in this area for example, whether the definition of corroboration still stands and whether there is a need for a corroboration warning in cases of confessions or where identification evidence is weak (see the Law Commission Report on Corroboration of Evidence in Criminal Trials (1991, Cmnd 1620)).

(c) The conclusion to the answer should include some comment on whether the changes are to be welcomed. New law concentrates on the quality of evidence not nature of witness, replaces over-technical complex law full of inconsistencies and anomalies.

Suggested Answer

The most recent changes made in the law relating to corroboration, were those enacted in s. 32 of the Criminal Justice and Public Order Act 1994 which were as a result of a culmination of a decade of relaxation of this area of rigid rules. This statute abolished the need for a formal warning for complainants in sexual cases and for co-defendants testifying for the prosecution. The abolition of the third category where a corroboration warning was required, namely that of child witnesses, was completed by s. 34(2) of the Criminal Justice Act 1988. These statutory changes took place in a period of judicial activism in this area which had relaxed the law. The question calls for an examination of the necessity of these changes and whether further ones are needed.

The Law Commission report *Corroboration of Evidence in Criminal Trials* (1991 Cmnd 1620) (adopted by the Royal Commission on Criminal Justice; see Cmnd 2263, 1993) had described the law in this area as 'arcane, technical and difficult to convey'. It led to unnecessary formalism and unjustified categorisation of witnesses. Particular criticism was directed at the mandatory requirement of a corroboration warning for complainants in sexual cases, irrespective of the particular witness. Witnesses, it was contended, should be treated on their merits. The courts could of course always convict in the absence of corroboration but a failure to give the warning was likely to lead to the conviction being overturned on appeal. Of course the statutory requirements of corroboration have not been affected by the abolition of the common law rules and there is little controversy on their application.

While the three main categories of cases requiring corroboration warning have been abolished by the 1988 and 1994 Acts, there is some doubt as to whether there is a residual class of cases where some form of warning should be given because the testimony of the witness may be suspect or tainted for some reason. This could be because he or she may have a grudge against the defendant, or is malicious, or has some other purpose of his or her own to serve. It should be noted that there were some suggestions in some cases that where the evidence of a witness was suspect for a reason other than because he or she fell within the three categories discussed earlier, a discretionary warning was appropriate. This existed even prior to 1988 and it is unclear whether the 1988 or 1994 Acts have removed it.

It has been submitted that where a witness has a substantial interest of his or her own to serve, there is a risk that false evidence might be given, and the full corroboration warning should be made. The courts have stated that where there is no basis for suggesting that a witness is a participant or in any way involved in the crime which is the subject matter of the trial, there was no obligation to give the full corroboration warning. However, the courts did add that where there is evidence to suggest that the evidence of the witness is tainted for some reason, the judge should advise the jury to treat the evidence with more or less caution depending on the circumstances of the case.

In *R* v *Bagshaw* [1984] 1 WLR 477, the Court of Appeal stated that patients who were detained in a special hospital after conviction for an offence, who were witnesses at the trial of nurses who were charged with assaulting them, although not falling within the established categories where a corroboration warning had to be given, satisfied the criteria which justified the requirement of a full warning. The court went on to say that nothing short of the full warning would suffice. In *R* v *Spencer* [1987] AC 128, *R* v *Bagshaw* was overruled. The House of Lords decided that where the prosecution relied on the evidence of a witness who because of his mental condition and criminal background may give suspect evidence, the judge should warn the jury that it is dangerous to convict on the uncorroborated evidence of the witness. However, the House of Lords stressed that the judge need not give the full corroboration warning required in the established categories. It was important that the jury be made aware of the dangers of convicting on the uncorroborated evidence of the witness but the extent of the warning would depend on the facts and circumstances of the case.

Another example of judicial acceptance of the need to temper the technical rules was *R* v *Chance* [1988] QB 932 where the Court of Appeal decided that where the only issue is one of identity in a rape case, only a Turnbull warning is required. In *R* v *Turnbull* [1977] QB 224 itself of course the Court of Appeal set 'guidelines' for identification cases rather than setting a requirement for a formal corroboration warning.

A major criticism of the corroboration rules had been the complex definition of corroboration, as set out by the Court of Appeal in the leading case of *R* v *Baskerville* [1916] 2 KB 658. As Bronitt (1991) pointed out, it concentrates on the quantity of testimony rather than its quality. By requiring 'independent evidence implicating the accused' rather than independent evidence that confirms the suspect witness is telling the truth, the definition concentrates on guilt rather than the witness's credibility. In *R* v *Hills* (1987) 86 Cr App R 26 the Court of Appeal held that cumulative corroboration was possible as a matter of principle, even though individually no one piece of evidence might fit the technical definition. The court thus took a welcome pragmatic view.

One question which remains, however, is whether the definition of corroboration is still needed. In the cases where the courts exercise discretion to issue a need for caution, will they rely on the technical definition of corroboration? The Law Commission report anticipated not. Murphy (at p. 509) argues that even if the facts of the case require some form of corroboration warning, it would only be applied on a case to case basis having regard to the characteristics of witnesses and evidence. Further he maintains that it is unlikely that the courts will require the full corroboration warning in the light of the abolition of the fixed categories requiring such a warning in the 1988 and 1994 Acts and the view of the court in *R* v *Spencer*. In *R* v *Makanjuola* [1995] 1 WLR 1348, the Court of Appeal adopted this approach, rejecting the need for a 'full old style direction' in cases where the trial judge decided that some form of warning may be necessary. Lord Taylor CJ said (at p. 1351): '[i]t was, in our judgment, partly to escape from this tortuous exercise which juries must have found more bewildering than illuminating, that Parliament enacted section 32'.

The above comments have covered the generally welcomed erosion of the technical rules of corroboration. However, in one area it might be arguable that a new category needs to be created. The Royal Commission on Criminal Justice (1993, Cmnd 2263), in spite of many calls for a requirement of corroboration of confessions, recommended only that it should be lawful for a jury to convict solely on the evidence of a confession, but the jury should be warned of the great care needed before doing so. Parliament has not enacted such a provision, although in Scotland it is required, but as confirmation of the essential facts of the case against the accused, not to confirm suspect testimony. The evidence thus operates for the benefit of the accused.

Furthermore, not all commentators are convinced that the position in relation to identification evidence is satisfactory. This is a notoriously unreliable area. The Devlin Committee on Evidence of Identification in Criminal Cases (1976) found that misidentification is common and thus a possible source of miscarriage of justice. Even honest and independent witnesses may be mistaken. The committee was in favour of a rule subject to some exceptions that convictions should not rest solely on visual identification, even if more than one witness made it. Neither Parliament nor the courts have accepted this recommendation. The '*Turnbull* guidelines' remain then as an exhortation and, as the Court of Appeal demonstrated in *R* v *Hunjan* (1978) 68 Cr App R 99, if a warning is found to be insufficient, the conviction could be quashed on appeal. As Zuckerman (1989 at p. 178) points out, the danger with this course is that confident and honest witnesses may be mistaken and 'no amount of care can discern a mistake'. Here, however, he suggests it is not more technical corroboration which is required, but improved techniques of identification and an insistence that the prosecution does not adduce low quality evidence.

The new regime on corroboration is on the whole a welcome relaxation of an overly complex system which many commentators agreed served to confuse juries. The new flexibility of allowing judges to deal with cases on an individual basis is attractive although it is of some concern that it may be more difficult to give equality of treatment to each defendant. There will also be fewer cases referred to appeal since the courts are less enthusiastic about intervening where the discretion has been exercised. The changes as Zuckerman (1989 at p. 175) are part of the process whereby 'our courts are losing faith in the powers of corroboration rules and are diverting their energy to a logical analysis of evidence'.

QUESTION 2

Sam and Alan are charged with the attempted rape of Amy, whilst she was intoxicated. The evidence against them was that Amy met Sam and Alan in the local wine bar and they started chatting together. After a short while Amy became intoxicated and went outside to an alleyway for a breath of fresh air. The alleyway was very dark at the time. Two men approached her and attempted to rape her. She thought she recognised one of them as being Sam but she is unsure because of the lighting conditions in the alleyway at the time. As a result of her struggles and screams, the two men stopped and ran away. An eyewitness, Mandy saw them running away and saw the face of one of them very clearly underneath a street light. Mandy gave a description to the police and helped in constructing a photofit picture of the man she saw. Giles, a police constable recognised the photofit picture as being that of Alan, whom he had previously arrested for criminal damage. Amy was unable to pick out Sam from an identification parade held at the police station later that week. Mandy has since died as a result of a road traffic accident. Sam and Alan both deny the offence.

Evaluate the difficulties which the prosecution will face with the evidence.

Commentary

This question requires a discussion of the rules relating to the treatment of identification evidence in court. As regards the victim's evidence, it is clear that because of her state of intoxication and the bad lighting conditions, a Turnbull direction will have to be given. The discussion will have to centre round whether the judge is likely to withdraw the case against Sam from the jury especially since Amy was unable to pick out Sam from the identification parade. The other issue revolves around the issue of the photofit picture and how the court should treat this evidence. Another difficulty that will be encountered is with regards to the identification of Alan by Giles. The basis of Giles's recognition of Alan and whether that is admissible in evidence will have to be considered. There is also the point in relation to corroboration in this case in that it needs to be made clear that no corroboration warning is required as a result of the Criminal Justice and Public Order Act 1994.

Suggested Answer

The problems faced by the prosecution counsel start with the identification of Sam by the victim, Amy. In effect, her identification evidence is weak both because of her intoxicated condition and the bad lighting conditions. This is further excerbated by her failure to pick out Sam during the identification parade held later that week. In *R* v *Turnbull* [1977] QB 224, the Court of Appeal laid down guidelines for the treatment of identification evidence where the case depends wholly or substantially on the correctness of the identifications. The guidelines state, inter alia, that the judge should warn the jury of the special need for caution, before convicting the accused in reliance on the correctness of the identification evidence. The judge should draw the jury's attention to the possibility that an error was made and should invite them to examine closely the circumstances in which the observation took place. The guidelines go on to provide that the jury should also examine closely the conditions under which and the length of time for which the observation took place. Factors such as whether the witness knew the accused, or whether there was any particular reason for the witness to remember the accused, or how soon after the event did the witness give a description to the police should also be considered. The guidelines makes it clear that the judge should remind the jury of any weaknesses in the identification evidence and that where the identification evidence is weak, the judge should withdraw the case from the jury unless there is any other evidence which will support the identification evidence.

It has been made clear by the Court of Appeal in *R* v *Oakwell* [1978] 1 WLR 32, that the *Turnbull* guidelines are not to be interpreted inflexibly. It is thus clear that on the facts of the present case, the judge will need to draw the jury's attention to the weaknesses present in Amy's identification evidence, namely that it was dark, that she was intoxicated, the fact that she may have remembered him because of the time spent talking to him in the wine bar and that she had failed to pick Sam out of the identification parade. It is assumed for the present purposes that the identification parade was conducted properly and in accordance with Code D of the Codes of Practice made pursuant to s. 66 of the Police and Criminal Evidence Act 1984.

On the facts of the present case, there does not appear to be any other evidence which will support the correctness of Sam's identification. Mandy does not appear to have seen Sam but only Alan. As such, in view of the *Turnbull* guidelines, it is likely that the judge will withdraw the case against Sam and direct the jury to acquit him. If, however, there was another eye witness who saw Sam running away, albeit in a fleeting glimpse type situation, whilst the judge may leave the evidence to the jury, he would need to give the *Turnbull* warning and direct them specifically that even a number of honest persons can be wrong: *R* v *Weeder* (1980) 71 Cr App R 228 and *R* v *Breslin* (1984) 80 Cr App R 226.

The other difficulty that the prosecution may have with the evidence is Mandy's testimony. If Mandy was still alive and gave testimony in court, her testimony would be subject to the Turnbull direction, as it could be argued that her evidence falls within the fleeting glance situation which the *Turnbull* guidelines were intended to cover. However, now that she is dead the question is whether the photofit is admissible into evidence. In *R* v *Smith* [1976] Crim LR 511, a photofit picture was held not to offend the rule against hearsay. However, the Court of Appeal in *R* v *Cook* [1987] 1 All ER 1049, went a step further. The Court of Appeal decided that photofit pictures were in a class of evidence of their own. Neither the rule against hearsay nor the rule against previous consistent statements had any application to such evidence. The photofit pictures are, according to the Court of Appeal, manifestations of the seeing eye, translations of vision onto paper through the medium of a police officer's skill of drawing or composing which a witness does not possess. Keane argues that the Court of Appeal's approach in drawing an analogy between a photofit or sketch and a photograph is surprising in view of the acknowledged differences between them. Nonetheless, the decision in *Cook* has been followed by the Court of Appeal in *R* v *Constantinou* (1989) 91 Cr App R 74. Thus, on the facts of this case, it is clear that the photofit picture would be admissible in evidence notwithstanding that Mandy is not able to give evidence.

However, in view of the fact that Mandy's identification originally was as a result of a fleeting glance situation, it seems probable that the judge will have to give the *Turnbull* direction with respect to this evidence and may have to withdraw the case from the jury unless there is some other evidence to support.

The third problem with the evidence is with regards to Giles's identification of Alan. Whilst it is likely that he can say that he identified Alan from the photofit picture, he is not allowed to say why he knew Alan. It is not permissible to tell the jury that the reason why Giles recognised Alan was because he had previously arrested Alan for criminal damage. The only exception to that is where the evidence comes within the similar fact evidence (*DPP* v *Boardman* [1974] 3 All ER 887 and *DPP* v *P* [1991] 2 AC 447), or it is admissible by virtue of s. 1(f)(ii) of the Criminal Evidence Act 1898. As this does not appear likely, the evidence of the previous arrest of Alan by Giles is not admissible in evidence.

It should be noted that a corroboration warning is no longer necessary even though this is a case involving a sexual offence: s. 32(1), Criminal Justice and Public Order Act 1994.

Thus, on the facts of the present case, it is likely that the case against Sam will be withdrawn from the jury and the *Turnbull* direction will, at the very least, have to be given with respect to the identification of Alan. It is not altogether clear whether the case against Alan will be withdrawn or not. This would depend on whether there was any other evidence available to support it.

11 Opinion Evidence

INTRODUCTION

This topic is one of those peripheral issues where it is difficult to predict with any certainty whether it will form the subject matter of an examination question. If it does come out in an evidence examination, it could be set as part of a question mixed with some other areas or possibly as an essay topic. The latter may be unexciting but provided the correct approach is taken, is relatively straightforward. Students should be aware that s. 1 of the Civil Evidence Act 1972 which deals with hearsay opinion evidence will be repealed when the Civil Evidence Act 1995 comes into force.

In answering a question in this area, you must be familiar with the differences between expert and non-expert opinion evidence. Be clear on when and in what circumstances both types of evidence are admissible and the questions that can be asked of the expert whilst giving evidence. The specific approach that should be taken after that depends on whether the question relates to civil or criminal trials.

QUESTION 1

'As a general rule, opinion evidence is inadmissible; a witness may only speak of facts which he personally perceived, not of inferences drawn from those facts.' (Keane, *The Modern Law of Evidence*, 3rd edn, (Butterworths, London 1994.)

Discuss and comment with reference to criminal trials.

Commentary

This is a relatively straightforward question which requires an analysis of the law relating to the admissibility of expert opinion evidence in criminal trials. It would be necessary to consider who will be regarded by the court to be an expert and when the expert opinion evidence is admissible. It is also important to consider whether the expert can give his opinion on the ultimate issue in the trial.

Suggested Answer

The general rule is as stated by Keane, is that a witness can only testify with respect to those matters which he or she actually observed or perceived. The witness is not entitled to give his or her own opinion on the matter. It is for the jury in a criminal trial to draw inferences from the evidence as the trier of fact, not the witness.

The exception to this general rule is in the case of expert witnesses. With regards to those matters for which the judge or jury may require assistance, the opinion of experts on those matters may be admissible. Examples of where the judge and jury may require assistance include scientific, medical and forensic evidence. The weight to be given to such evidence is a matter for the jury. It is apparent that this type of evidence is admissible because the jury would not be able to draw the appropriate inferences and form proper opinions from the facts requiring expert opinion: *Buckley* v *Rice Thomas* (1554) Plowd 118.

Before an expert witness can give opinion evidence relating to any particular issue, it is for the judge to decide whether that particular witness is an expert. This would be dependent on whether the witness had undergone a course of study giving the requisite expertise in that area or whether his experience is such as to make him an expert. It is not essential that in all cases the expert possess formal qualifications. In *R* v *Silverlock* [1894] 2 QB 766, opinion evidence from a solicitor was admitted, by the Court for Crown Cases Reserved, with respect to handwriting even though he did not possess any formal qualification in it but merely studied it as a hobby.

However, expert opinion evidence is not admissible per se in all criminal trials. Where the issue is one for which the jury is able to decide and does not require the assistance of experts, no opinion evidence from experts is admissible. The reason is because such evidence is usually unnecessary and irrelevant. In *R* v *Chard* (1971) 56 Cr App R 268, evidence from an expert with regards to the alleged inability of the accused to form the necessary mens rea of the offence was disallowed by the Court of Appeal. The Court emphasised that where there was no issue of mental instability or illness, it is inappropriate to allow evidence from a medical witness as to the state of the accused's mind. Likewise in *R* v *Turner* [1975] QB 834, where the accused's defence was one of provocation, the Court of Appeal excluded evidence from a psychiatrist because there was no issue as regarded his mental state. The issue of provocation was one for which the jury could decide. Lawton LJ stated in that case that the fact that an expert witness possessed impressive scientific qualifications did not necessarily make his opinion on matters of human nature any more helpful. These were matters for which the jury was competent to decide.

The restriction on the admissibility of expert evidence on matters for which the jury requires no assistance includes a restriction on expert evidence on the credibility of a witness or the accused save in exceptional circumstances: *Lowery* v *R* [1974] AC 85. Although, in *Lowery*, such evidence was admitted, Murphy (at p. 308) regards this decision as applying only to the specific facts of the case rather than establishing any general principle. This approach appears to be correct in the light of *R* v *Rimmer* [1983] Crim LR 250, where the trial judge refused to allow the evidence of an expert on the basis that this related only to the credibility of the accused.

At one time there was also the rule that expert opinion evidence was inadmissible on the ultimate issue in the case. This was because the expert would be usurping the function of the jury: *M'Naghten's Case* (1843) 10 Cl & F 200. However, it is clear that whilst the rule is still around, in practice expert evidence on the ultimate issue is allowed. In *DPP* v *A & BC Chewing Gum Ltd* [1968] 1 QB 159, 164, Lord Parker CJ in the Divisional Court stated that:

> Those who practise in the criminal courts see every day cases of experts being called on the question of diminished responsibility, and although technically the final question 'Do you think he was suffering from

diminished responsibility?' is strictly inadmissible, it is allowed time and time again without objection.

It is therefore clear that expert evidence is allowed on the ultimate issue in practice so long as, as Keane (at p. 407) puts it, 'the diction employed is not noticeably the same as that which will be used when the matter is subsequently considered by the court.'

The difficulty with expert opinion evidence is that sometimes the expert relies on the work or word of other individuals and therefore may infringe the rule against hearsay. In *R* v *Bradshaw* (1985) 82 Cr App R 79, the Court of Appeal decided that the evidence of the psychiatrist on the condition of the accused was inadmissible as this had been entirely based on what the accused had told him. It was decided that this was hearsay and therefore inadmissible. In contrast, in *R* v *Abadom* [1983] 1 WLR 126, the Court of Appeal held that the expert opinion evidence was admissible although the expert had relied on statistics supplied by the Home Office Central Research Establishment. The court decided that the expert was entitled to rely on this research in forming his opinion and that this did not violate the rule against hearsay.

Although at one time there was no statutory provision covering the admissibility of expert reports in criminal cases, s. 30 of the Criminal Justice Act 1988 has now changed that. By virtue of s. 30(1) of the 1988 Act, an expert report is to be admissible as evidence in criminal proceedings whether or not the person making it attends to give oral evidence in those proceedings. However, by s. 30(2) , where the expert does not testify in court, the written report would be admissible only with leave of the court. In deciding whether to grant leave, the court is directed to consider the various matters listed out in s. 30(3), including the risk that the admission of the written report will result in unfairness to the accused.

Therefore, it can be said that in general, opinion evidence is not usually available but that in situations where such evidence was admissible the courts have put in place various safeguards to ensure that it is admitted only in appropriate circumstances.

QUESTION 2

Sarah is suing the Henfield Health Authority for damages for pain and suffering and loss of earnings as a result of negligent treatment she received as a patient in the Henfield Hospital. She alleges that the surgeon who operated on her was negligent in that what was supposed to be a simple surgical procedure resulted in partial paralysis of her left side. Her solicitors have sought the opinion of Dr Williams who produced a written report concluding that in his opinion, the surgeon had in fact been negligent.

Advise Sarah as to how this evidence will be presented.

Commentary

This question requires a consideration of the application of the Civil Evidence Acts 1968 and 1972. More particularly, students will be expected to explain that the effect of the 1972 Act is to extend the 1968 Act to include opinion evidence (with the exception of s. 5 of the 1968 Act). A working knowledge of the procedural rules governing disclosure of expert reports as well as the cases relating to medical negligence will need to be shown. The law relating to expert evidence will be altered when the Civil Evidence Act 1995 comes into effect. The Act repeals Part I of the Civil Evidence Act 1967 and ss. 2(1), (2) and (3)(b) of the Civil Evidence Act 1972 and provides for the making of new rules governing the admissibility of expert opinion evidence.

Suggested Answer

The written report produced by Dr Williams may be used subject to the Civil Evidence Act 1972. By s. 2, a party who wishes to adduce evidence of opinion must comply with the notice procedure laid down pursuant to s. 8 of the Civil Evidence Act 1968 and contained in Order 38 rr. 21 to 31 of the Rules of the Supreme Court ('RSC'). The effect of the 1972 Act is to extend the provisions of Part 1 (with the exception of s. 5) of the 1968 Act to include statements of opinion: s. 1(1) of the Civil Evidence Act 1972. Thus, where the report to be admitted into evidence consists of a written report, s. 4 of the 1968 Act will apply but by virtue of s. 1(2) of the 1972 Act, the requirement of personal knowledge on the part of the supplier of the information has been removed. Before considering how the evidence should actually be presented, it is pertinent to note a few matters.

First, it should be noted that the expert opinion evidence is admissible even though it may give an opinion on the ultimate issue. On the facts of the present case, it is clear that Dr Williams, by concluding that the surgeon was negligent, is giving his opinion as to the ultimate issue of the case. The difficulty faced in criminal trials on this issue is not therefore present here. This is because s. 3(1) of the 1968 Act provides that where any person is called as a witness, his opinion on any relevant matter (which by subsection (3) includes an issue in the proceedings in question), on which he is qualified to give expert evidence, is to be admissible in evidence.

The second point to note is that it will be necessary to establish that Dr Williams has the requisite expertise in the area in order to give his opinion on this matter. That will be for the judge to decide prior to his testimony.

The final preliminary point to note is that Dr Williams is entitled to rely on the work of others in reaching his conclusion. This was made clear in *R* v *Abadom* [1983] 1 WLR 126 (although a criminal case, the principle would likewise be applicable here), where the Court of Appeal held that the expert opinion evidence was admissible although the expert had relied on statistics supplied by the Home Office Central Research Establishment. The court decided that the expert was entitled to rely on this research in forming his opinion and that this did not violate the rule against hearsay.

As regards the presentation of this evidence, it should be noted that in civil trials it is normally necessary to disclose the report before the trial. The procedure relating to the presentation and disclosure of the report is contained in Order 38 rr. 36 to 44 made under s. 2 of the 1972 Act. Order 38 r. 36(1) provides that no expert evidence may be adduced at the trial of any cause or matter unless the party seeking to introduce this evidence has applied to the court to determine whether a direction should be given under rule 37 or 41 and has complied with the directions given by the court, or complied with the automatic directions taking effect under Order 25 r. 8. Thus it is clear that unless disclosure has been complied with, the expert evidence cannot be adduced without either leave of the court or the agreement of all the parties.

It should be noted that even if it is intended to call Dr Williams to give oral testimony in court, Order 38 r. 37 requires that the substance of the evidence be disclosed in the form of a written report within such period as the court may specify, unless there are special reasons for not doing so, although in *Rahman* v *Kirklees Area Health Authority* [1980] 1 WLR 1244, the court decided that medical negligence cases were in a special category and therefore exempt from the general rule of disclosure. However, in *Wilsher* v *Essex Area Health Authority* [1987] QB 730, the Court of Appeal was dissatisfied with the delay that resulted from the non-disclosure of expert reports in medical negligence cases. The Court of Appeal in *Naylor* v *Preston Area Health Authority* [1987] 1 WLR 958 disapproved of *Rahman* and stated that medical negligence cases did not fall under a special category and there was a duty of disclosure of expert reports. At the time of these decisions, rule 37 was undergoing amendment and it has been suggested that the amended rule 37 should be assumed to have incorporated the effect of these decisions. Thus Dr Williams's evidence will have to be disclosed in any event to the other party and the written report prepared by him will be sufficient to comply with that requirement.

Where Dr Williams is called to give evidence in court, Order 38 r. 43 provides that the report may be put into evidence at the beginning of his examination-in-chief or at such other time as the court may direct.

It should be noted that the effect of disclosure is such that any party may put any expert report, which was disclosed to him by any other party, into evidence: Order 38 r. 42. The effect of this is that once disclosed, the report cannot be excluded or kept out if the other party wants to put it into evidence.

12 Issues in the Course of Trial

INTRODUCTION

This topic generally deals with the type of questions that can or cannot be asked in examination-in-chief or cross-examination. It should be borne in mind that in some instances, the courts adopt a different approach depending on whether it is a civil or criminal trial. One important aspect of this topic is the weight to be put on testimony which has been proven to be inconsistent with the previous statement of the witness, i.e., whether it is evidence of the facts stated therein or whether the inconsistent testimony is to be disregarded. It is in this regard that the nature of the trial is important. Generally, the inconsistent testimony is disregarded in criminal trials, whilst it is evidence of the facts stated therein in the case of civil trials. Another important aspect of this topic deals with the questions that can be asked about the complainant's sexual history in the case of a trial involving a sexual offence. For example, can the complainant be asked whether she is or was a prostitute? This will be considered in the light of s. 2 of the Sexual Offences (Amendment) Act 1976.

QUESTION 1

Daniel, a police constable, in response to a call on his radio, went to investigate an alleged burglary at Henfield Road. As he drove up to the scene of the crime, he saw Henry dressed in a T-shirt and running shorts and carrying a holdall on his back, running in the opposite direction. Daniel chased after him but soon lost him. Daniel made a note of what he had seen in his notebook. Later, Henry went voluntarily to the police station and was interviewed. He said that the reason that he was in the area at the material time was because he had been out jogging, as he was training for the London Marathon and that the holdall contained bricks to weigh him down. Henry is charged with burglary. Advise on the following evidential matters:

(a) Can Daniel refresh his memory from his notebook outside court before giving evidence?

(b) Daniel gives evidence for the prosecution without referring to the notebook. Can the defence cross-examine him as to the contents of the notebook?

(c) Can Daniel refresh his memory from his notebook in court?

(d) What use can the defence make of Henry's statement at the police station?

Commentary

This is a straightforward question concerning the witness refreshing his or her memory both inside and outside the court room and the use that the opposing counsel may make of the statements or documents used by the witness to refresh his or her memory. Part **(d)** concerns the issue of the accused's reaction on being confronted with incriminating facts.

Suggested Answer

(a) On the facts of the case, it would appear that Daniel will be called as a witness for the prosecution. The question that arises is whether he can refresh his memory from his notebook outside the court before giving evidence. It should be noted that it is common for witnesses to look at written statements which they have made, in order to refresh their memory, before testifying on the witness stand. This practice was recognised by the Court of Appeal in *R* v

Richardson [1971] 2 QB 484. In any event, even if there was a rule prohibiting such action, the rule would be unenforceable.

In *Richardson*, four prosecution witnesses were given their statements prior to their testimony. The statements were not sufficiently contemporaneous for them to be used to refresh their memory in court. The accused argued on appeal, that as the statements were not contemporaneous for the purpose of the rule on refreshing memory in court, their evidence should not have been admitted. The Court of Appeal rejected this argument and approved the dicta in *Lau Pak Ngam* v *R* [1966] Crim LR 443. In that case, the Supreme Court of Hong Kong stated that if witnesses were deprived of the opportunity of checking their recollection beforehand by reference to statements or notes made near to the time of the events in question, testimony in the witness box would be no more than a test of memory rather than of truthfulness. Further, refusal of access to the statements would create difficulties for honest witnesses, but would not hamper dishonest ones. The approach of the court in *Richardson* was later applied in the case of *Worley* v *Bentley* [1976] 2 All ER 449.

Subsequently, the court made it clear in *R* v *Da Silva* [1990] 1 All ER 29, that the judge has a discretion to allow a witness to withdraw from the witness stand in order to refresh his memory from a statement made near or at the time of the events in question. The judge has this discretion even where the statement is not contemporaneous with the events. Before he exercises his discretion, the judge must be satisfied that the witness cannot recall the events in question because of lapse of time, that the witness had made a statement near the time of the event representing his recollection of them, that he had not read the statement before testifying and that he wishes to read the statement before he continues to give evidence.

Thus, it would appear proper for Daniel to refresh his memory from his notebook outside the court before testifying on oath. Even if it is unclear that Daniel made the note of the events contemporaneously with the events in question, this would not necessarily be fatal.

(b) The next issue is whether the defence can cross examine Daniel as to the contents of the notebook. The Court of Appeal in *R* v *Westwell* [1976] 2 All ER 812 decided that if the prosecution counsel is aware that his witness has refreshed his or her memory outside the court, it was 'desirable but not essential' that the defence should be informed of this fact. Failure to do so would not be a ground for acquittal. Once the defence is aware that Daniel has refreshed his memory from his notebook outside the court, they are entitled to inspect the notebook, and cross examine Daniel on the relevant matters contained in it. This was so held by the Divisional Court in *Owen* v *Edwards* (1983) 77 Cr App R 191.

However, the court in *Owen* v *Edwards* made it clear that if the defence counsel cross examines a witness on material in the notebook or statement, which has not been used by the witness to refresh his memory, they run the risk of the notebook or statement being put in evidence. The court applied by analogy the rule applicable where the witness refreshes his or her memory in court.

Thus, provided the defence cross examines Daniel on the part of the notebook which he has used to refresh his memory, the notebook will not be put in evidence. If the defence was to go beyond that, the notebook may be put in evidence. However, it should be noted that the notebook will be admitted only as evidence of the consistency or inconsistency of Daniel's evidence going to his credit. It is not evidence of the truth of the facts stated therein: *R* v *Virgo* (1978) 67 Cr App R 323.

(c) Daniel may be entitled to refresh his memory by referring to his notebook in court provided three conditions are satisfied. First, the document must have been made contemporaneously with the occurrence of the events about which the witness is testifying. The document, or as is the case here, the record in the notebook, should have been made at the first practicable opportunity at a time when the events were still fresh in Daniel's mind. Ultimately, this is a question of fact in each case: *R* v *Langton* (1876) 2 QBD 296. A gap of 27 days between the events in issue and the making of the statement was too long in *R* v *Woodcock* [1963] Crim LR 273, whilst a delay of 22 days was permitted by the Court of Appeal in *R* v *Fotheringham* [1975] Crim LR 710.

Secondly, the notebook should be handed to the defence counsel or the court so that it may be inspected and the witness cross examined on its contents. The defence counsel can request that the jury be shown the notebook if it is necessary for the determination of an issue: *R* v *Bass* [1953] 1 QB 680. Finally, the document should be the original. However, if the original has been lost, it seems that a verified or accurate copy can be used. (There is also a fourth condition, namely that the document was supervised by or read back to the witness, but that does not apply here.)

On the facts of this case, it is unclear when Daniel made a note of the events in question in his notebook. The facts seems to suggest that the note was made contemporaneously with the events in question. If he did do so, then he may be entitled to refresh his memory in court. If there was a gap between the event in question and the time he made the note in his notebook, then the court, in the exercise of its discretion, will have to decide whether the note was made sufficiently contemporaneously with the events in order for it to be within the rule. If Daniel is allowed to refresh his memory by referring to the notebook in court, the defence counsel may inspect the notebook and cross examine him on the contents. Where the defence cross examines Daniel on parts of the notebook which were not used to refresh his memory, then the notebook may be put into evidence by the prosecution. Further, the notebook is only evidence of the consistency or inconsistency of Daniel's testimony and is not evidence of the facts stated therein: *R* v *Virgo*.

(d) The general rule is that a witness may not give evidence, during examination-in-chief, of a previous consistent statement. The reason for the rule is that it can be easily manufactured, it adds nothing to the witness's testimony and is usually self-serving: *Corke* v *Corke and Cook* [1958] P 93 and *R* v *Roberts* [1942] 1 All ER 187. Although there are a number of exceptions to the general rule, the only one which may apply here is where the accused has made a statement on being accused of the crime. Where the accused makes an admission on being accused of the crime, this is admissible in evidence of the facts stated therein. Where the accused denies the charge, the statement, whilst it may be admissible in some circumstances, for instance to show the accused's reaction when taxed with incriminating facts, is admissible only to show consistency of the accused's testimony and goes only to credit. It is not evidence of the facts stated therein: *R* v *Storey* (1968) 52 Cr App R 334 and *R* v *Pearce* (1979) 69 Cr App R 365.

Thus, it is likely that the court may allow Henry to give evidence of his prior statement which he made in the police station, as evidence of his reaction when confronted at the police station. The statement is not evidence of the facts stated in it.

QUESTION 2

Jennice is suing Frank for damages for pain and suffering as a result of injuries arising out of a road traffic accident. Jennice alleges that as she was crossing Middlefield Road, Frank hit her with his car causing a fracture of her left leg. She states that Frank was driving his car at an excessive speed and without due care and attention. Frank's defence is that Jennice lurched out onto the road suddenly and he was unable to avoid her. He admits that the accident took place and the injuries suffered by Jennice. Advise Frank on the following evidential matters:

(a) Dr Lee gives evidence on Jennice's behalf that when he examined her in the casualty department where she was brought after the accident, there were no signs of recent intoxication. Can he be cross examined on the fact that he had told Lisa, a nurse at the hospital the next day, that Jennice appeared to be drunk when she was brought into the hospital? Can evidence in rebuttal be called if Dr Lee denies the conversation?

(b) Herbert, an eyewitness to the accident, has given evidence that he saw Frank driving erratically immediately prior to the accident. Can he be cross examined that he was convicted of perjury seven years ago?

(c) Before the trial, Paul, the manager of Toasters, a wine bar, has given a written statement to Frank's solicitor. In the statement, Paul said that he served Jennice three to four Singapore Slings, a cocktail, an hour before the accident. When testifying for the defence, he states that Jennice came into the wine bar to use the ladies room and did not have anything to drink. What use can be made of his written statement?

Commentary

(a) The issue here is whether a witness can be cross examined as to a previous inconsistent statement and the evidential value to be put on such a statement.

(b) This part of the question involves the issue as to the admissibility of the previous convictions of a witness and the effect that it has on his testimony.

(c) This relates to the question as to what the defence can do where the witness called by him does not come up to proof and the value of the testimony or the previous statement made by the witness.

Suggested Answer

(a) The issue here is whether Dr Lee's conversation with Lisa which is inconsistent with his present testimony can be admitted into evidence. This is governed by s. 4 of the Criminal Procedure Act 1865. Despite its title, it is applicable to civil actions. This states that if a witness is asked during cross examination about a prior statement (whether oral or written) made by him which is inconsistent with his present testimony, and does not admit that he had made such a previous inconsistent statement, the cross examining party may adduce evidence of that inconsistent statement. Before the inconsistent statement can be adduced into evidence, the procedure laid out in s. 4 has to be complied with, namely, the circumstances in which the previous inconsistent statement was made must be put to the witness and he must then be asked whether he had made such a statement.

Thus, in this case, if Dr Lee denies making such a statement, evidence of the prior inconsistent statement can be adduced. This may take the form of calling Lisa as a rebuttal witness. If, on the other hand, Dr Lee admits making the statement, then the normal practice would be to ask him whether he still wishes to stand by his previous testimony. In most instances, when faced with such a situation, it is unlikely that the witness will stand by his previous testimony.

The next question is the value to be placed on the previous inconsistent statement. On the facts of this case, the previous inconsistent statement will help the defence's case that Jennice lurched suddenly onto the road, possibly because she was intoxicated. This will be the case if the previous statement is admissible as evidence of the facts stated in it. Although in criminal cases the previous inconsistent statement cancels out the present testimony of the witness, in civil cases this is governed by s. 3(1)(a) of the Civil Evidence Act 1968. This provides that a prior inconsistent statement which is admissible into evidence, is admissible as evidence of the facts stated therein and is not merely evidence of the consistency or inconsistency of the witness. Thus the statement by Dr Lee to Lisa would be admissible as evidence of the fact that Jennice was intoxicated when she received treatment in the hospital.

(b) Frank should be advised that under s. 6 of the Criminal Procedure Act 1865, a witness may be questioned as to whether he or she has been convicted of any felony or misdemeanour, and if he or she denies it or does not admit that fact, or refuses to answer the question, evidence can be adduced to prove such a conviction. It should be noted that, despite its title, this provision is applicable to civil actions as well. However, the application of this section in civil cases is restricted by s. 4(1) of the Rehabilitation of Offenders Act 1974. This prohibits cross examination of a witness regarding his or her previous convictions where the conviction is a spent conviction as defined by the Act. The court does, however, under the Act, retain a discretion to allow the cross examination of a witness regarding his or her previous conviction, notwithstanding that it may be a spent conviction, where it is not possible for justice otherwise to be done.

Thus, whether Herbert can be questioned about his conviction for perjury would depend on whether it is a spent conviction under the 1974 Act and whether, if it was a spent conviction, the court would be prepared to allow the cross examination about it on the basis that justice could not otherwise be done. That is a question for the court to decide. However, bearing in mind that the conviction is for perjury, even if it is spent, it is possible that the court may allow the cross examination of Herbert regarding it.

It should also be noted that the cross examination of a witness about his or her previous conviction under s. 6 of the Criminal Procedure Act 1865 does not depend on whether the previous conviction is relevant to guilt or to credit: *Clifford* v *Clifford* [1961] 1 WLR 1274. If Herbert does deny the previous conviction, this can be proved by a certificate from the court of conviction under s. 73 of the Police and Criminal Evidence Act 1984.

(c) In this situation, Frank should be advised that his witness, Paul, is not coming up to proof. The general rule is that a party may not impeach his own witness. This means that Frank cannot call evidence from another source to show that Paul is lying, forgetful or mistaken. He can, of course, call other witnesses who may be able to testify as to what Jennice drank at the wine bar, if there were any.

There are, however, exceptions to this general rule. In order for the exceptions to apply, it is necessary to determine whether Paul is merely an unfavourable witness or a hostile one. In the former case, the witness is one who is not coming up to proof whether because they are mistaken, foolish or forgetful. In such a case, the witness cannot be attacked as to his credit or challenged as to his previous inconsistent statement. However, if the witness is regarded as a hostile witness, at common law the previous inconsistent statement can be put to him and leading questions to test his memory and perception may be asked. A witness is regarded as hostile when he is not desirous of telling the truth at the instance of the party calling him.

In view of the fact that his previous statement to the solicitor is clear and unambiguous, it is possible that Paul may be treated as a hostile witness. However, this is a matter for the judge to decide. The procedure in such a situation is for counsel to make an application to the judge, to treat the witness as hostile. The judge can decide whether the witness is hostile by looking at the prior statement, the witness's demeanour and attitude.

If the judge decides that Paul is a hostile witness, then he may be asked leading questions and may be cross examined by the defence as to his previous inconsistent statement. He cannot, however, be asked questions about his character or previous convictions. Under s. 3 of the Criminal Procedure Act 1865 (which applies only in cases of hostile witnesses; see *Greenough* v *Eccles* (1859) 5 CBNS 786, a case on the identically worded s. 22 of the Common Law Procedure Act 1854), before the defence can prove that Paul made a previous inconsistent statement, he must be reminded of the circumstances of the previous statement sufficient to designate the particular occasion and must be asked whether or not he has made such a statement.

If Paul refuses to admit making such a statement, s. 3 of the 1865 Act allows the party calling the witness, the defence in this case, to prove that such a statement was made by the witness. Once that happens, by virtue of s. 3(1) of the Civil Evidence Act 1968, the previous statement is admissible as evidence of the facts stated therein. It should be noted that, in criminal cases, the position would be different: *R* v *Golder* [1960] 1 WLR 1169.

If Paul admits making the statement and admits to the truth of it, the statement becomes admissible as evidence of the facts stated therein.

QUESTION 3

John is charged with the attempted rape of Patricia. He denies the offence and claims that he was chatting innocently to the girl about her dog. He claims that she invented the attempted rape. As counsel for the prosecution, advise:

(a) on the likely admissibility of evidence from Patricia's flatmate that Patricia came home sobbing and when asked what was the matter said she had been 'interfered with'.

(b) if evidence can be given of John's immediate reaction when arrested that he had never seen the girl before. Later he admits to having been with her innocently.

(c) whether the defence can be prevented from asking Patricia about her previous sexual relationships with other men. It would seem that Pat has had an active sex life since the age of 16.

Commentary

This question involves the types of questions that the prosecution and the defence can ask either in examination-in-chief or in cross examination in a rape trial. In part **(a)**, it will be necessary to discuss the general rule with respect to the admissibility of prior consistent statements and the exception to that rule in cases involving sexual offences. In the next part of the question, the discussion is centred around the question as to whether evidence can be given of John's immediate reaction and his subsequent admission. Students, especially for part **(c)**, would have to be familiar with s. 2 of the Sexual Offences (Amendment) Act 1976 and the cases on it.

Suggested Answer

(a) The general rule is that a witness may not be asked in examination-in-chief whether he or she had made a prior statement, either oral or written, consistent with his or her testimony. The reason for the rule is that it can be easily manufactured, it adds nothing to the witness's testimony and is usually self-serving: *Corke* v *Corke and Cook* [1958] P 93 and *R* v *Roberts* [1942] 1 All ER 187. There are a number of exceptions to this general rule. It may therefore be possible for evidence to be given of Patricia's statement to her flatmate under one of these exceptions.

In cases involving sexual offences, evidence of a recent complaint by the victim may be given even though this may be a self-serving statement: *R* v *Osborne* [1905] 1 KB 551. It was suggested by Holmes J in *Commonwealth* v *Cleary* (1898) 172 Mass 175, the reason this exception is permitted is because of the '... survival of the ancient requirement that a woman should make hue and cry as a preliminary to an appeal of rape'.

In order for the complaint to be admissible, it must have been made voluntarily (i.e., it should not have been elicited by questions of a leading and intimidating nature) and at the first reasonable opportunity that offers itself. Whether these conditions are satisfied is a question of fact depending on the circumstances of the case. A week's delay between the commission of the offence and the complaint was not fatal in *R* v *Hedges* (1909) 3 Cr App R 262. The requirement that the complaint has to be made voluntarily does not rule out the complaint being procured by questioning, but only where the questions are of a leading and intimidating manner. Thus questions such as 'why are you crying?' would be permitted but not 'did A sexually assault you?'. In *R* v *Osborne*, a complaint by a girl of 13 of an indecent assault to a friend was permitted where she was asked 'why are you going home?'.

On the facts of the present case, prima facie, it would appear that Patricia's complaint to her flatmate would be admissible, provided that it was made at the first reasonable opportunity that offers itself. There is nothing in the facts to suggest otherwise. However, the question that arises is, what use can the tribunal of fact make of the recent complaint? In *R* v *Lillyman* [1896] 2 QB 167, the court made it clear that the complaint is not evidence of the facts stated therein, nor is it corroboration but it is evidence of the consistency of the victim's evidence and therefore his or her credibility and where consent is in issue, absence of it. Where the victim does not give evidence and consent is not in issue then the evidence of recent complaint is not admissible: *R* v *Wallwork* (1958) 42 Cr App R 153.

(b) The issue here is whether evidence can be given of John's immediate reaction and his subsequent admission. The prosecution will wish to use this evidence to attack John's credibility. The prosecution may be able to adduce these statements into evidence. The whole statement must generally go before the jury and what weight they attribute to it is a matter solely for their discretion. The jury will, however, have to be directed that the self-serving part of the statement, is not evidence of the truth of the facts stated in it : *R* v *Storey* (1968) 52 Cr App R 334.

In *R* v *Donaldson* (1976) 64 Cr App R 59, in the Court of Appeal, James LJ stated (at p. 65) that:

> When the Crown adduce evidence in the form of a statement by the defendant which is not relied on as an admission of the offence charged, such a statement is evidence in the trial in that it is evidence that the defendant made the statement and of his reaction which is part of the general picture which the jury have to consider, but it is not evidence of the facts stated therein.

The distinction between self-serving parts of the statement and admissions contained in it and the weight to be attributed to it is often lost on juries. As such, the Court of Appeal took a more pragmatic approach on this issue in *R* v *Duncan* (1981) 73 Cr App R 359 where it was said that the whole statement was to go to the jury and that they should be told to consider the whole statement and decide where the truth lies. However, the Court went on to say that, where approppriate, the jury should be told that the incriminating parts are likely to be true whereas excuses are unlikely to have the same weight. This approach was approved by the House of Lords in *R* v *Sharp* [1988] 1 WLR 7.

Thus, it is likely that the prosecution will be able to adduce the statements made by the accused into evidence and the judge will have to direct the jury that they will have to consider the whole statement and decide where the truth lies.

(c) In cases involving rape, questions to the victim concerning the previous consensual sexual relationship with the accused are relevant to the issue of consent and as such she may be asked questions about it and if she makes a denial, evidence can be called to rebut this denial: *R* v *Riley* (1887) 18 QBD 481. However, the victim's sexual relationships with other people are generally not relevant to consent, but only to her credibility. So, whilst questions may be asked about her previous sexual relationships, her answers are final and the defence cannot call evidence to rebut her denial: *R* v *Holmes* (1871) LR 1 CCR 334.

The ability of the defence to ask the victim questions of her sexual history is now limited by s. 2 of the Sexual Offences (Amendment) Act 1976. This section essentially provides that at a trial for a 'rape offence', the victim may only be cross examined about her experience with other men other than the accused with leave of the judge. Such leave is only to be given where the judge is satisfied that it would be unfair to the accused to refuse it. A rape offence is defined by s. 7(2) of the Act to include: rape, attempted rape, conspiracy to rape, incitement to rape, aiding, abetting, counselling or procuring rape and burglary with intent to rape. Thus it would appear that the facts of the case fall within the ambit of s. 2 and so, before the defence can ask the victim questions concerning her previous sexual relationships, leave of the court has to be obtained.

The issue which the court will have to address is whether a refusal to allow such questions would be unfair to the accused. The Court of Appeal in *R* v *Viola* [1982] 3 All ER 73, approving the decision of May J in *R* v *Lawrence* [1977] Crim LR 492, stated that the test was whether the cross examination was relevant to the defence's case and whether it was more likely than not that the cross examination might reasonably lead the jury to take a different view of the victim's testimony. Thus, if the court is satisfied of these factors, it may allow the defence to cross examine the victim as to her sexual relationships with other men. Ultimately, it is a question of the judge's judgment which depends on the facts of each case and the defence relied upon by the accused: *R* v *Barton* (1986) 85 Cr App R 5 and *R* v *Brown* (1988) 89 Cr App R 97.

Thus, on the facts of this case, where the defence appears to be one of a denial, and not that of consent or belief that she was consenting to sexual intercourse, the defence may be denied leave to cross examine the victim about her sexual relationships with other men. This is because the purpose of the cross examination would be merely to blacken her character and would not be relevant to any issue in the trial. The position would be different if his defence was otherwise.

QUESTION 4

Critically evaluate the extent to which s. 2 of the Sexual Offences (Amendment) Act 1976 has achieved its aims.

Commentary

There are not many types of essay questions that can be set on this subject. One possible question on this subject relates to the effect of s. 2 of the Sexual Offences (Amendment) Act 1976. Before attempting this question, students would be expected to be familiar with the background relating to the Act especially the Heilbron Committee Report of the Advisory Group on the Law of Rape (Cmnd 6352, 1975). It is important that students are able to demonstrate to the examiner a clear understanding of the Act and the courts' approach to this section.

Suggested Answer

Section 2 of the Sexual Offences (Amendment) Act 1976, was introduced as a result of the recommendations of the Heilbron Committee which considered the issue of rape trials in 1975 (Report of the Advisory Group on the Law of Rape, Cmnd 6352, 1975). In its report, the Heilbron Committee was critical of the use of the sexual history evidence at common law, which allowed the victim to be cross examined on her previous sexual relationships and evidence called to contradict her, where it is alleged that the victim was a prostitute or was a person who was 'notorious for want of sexual chastity' or who had had prior consensual sexual relationships with the accused.

The Heilbron Committee came to the conclusion that limitations had to be put on this aspect of the trial process because otherwise the effect would be to put the victim, rather than the accused, on trial. They recommended that such evidence be admitted only in cases where there was a striking similarity between the previous sexual relationships or conduct and the facts of the present case. Whilst Parliament did attempt to incorporate these recommendations into the 1976 Act, they failed to adhere to the formula of 'striking similarity'. Instead, Parliament substituted that with the requirement of unfairness to the accused. Section 2 of the Sexual Offences (Amendment) Act 1976 provides that at a trial for a 'rape offence', the victim may only be cross examined about her experience with men other than the accused, with leave of the judge. Such leave is only to be given where the judge is satisfied that it would be unfair to the accused to refuse it. A rape offence is defined by s. 7(2) of the Act to include: rape, attempted rape, conspiracy to rape, incitement to rape, aiding, abetting, counselling or procuring rape and burglary with intent to rape.

The question is whether the courts have followed the recommendations of the Heilbron Committee by strictly interpreting s. 2. In *R* v *Lawrence* [1977] Crim L R 492, May J stated that the test as to whether the refusal to allow the defence the opportunity to cross examine about her sexual history would be unfair to the accused, is whether it might reasonably lead the jury, properly directed, to take a different view of the complainant's evidence from that which they might take if the question or a series of questions was or were not allowed. This approach was approved and followed by the Court of Appeal in *R* v *Viola* (1982) 75 Crim App R 125 where the court stated that the questions as to the victim's sexual history will be allowed where they are relevant to an issue in the trial, for example on the issue of consent. The reason for this is because the jury should not be deprived of hearing some evidence which may cause them to view the victim's evidence differently. Temkin ([1993] Crim LR 3) criticises this later decision on the grounds that it allowed questions of the previous sexual conduct of the victim because this was relevant to the issue of consent. She argues that in the light of the comments of the Heilbron Committee that such sexual history is scarcely relevant, and the sexual *mores* of today, the Court of Appeal is attributing too much relevance and undue significance to such evidence. It may be useful to consider a number of other cases on s. 2 to see if the criticism by Temkin is justified.

Before proceeding further, it should be noted that Lord Lane CJ in *Viola* went on to say that the judge's decision whether to allow cross examination under s. 2 was an exercise of his judgment, not his discretion, and as such the appellate court could substitute the decision of the judge at first instance. On the facts of *Viola*, the court was prepared to substitute the judge's decision and to allow the cross examination of the victim regarding her sexual history. However, in *R* v *Barton* (1987) 85 Crim App R 5, the Court of Appeal stated that the decision whether to allow cross examination under s. 2 is an exercise of the judge's discretion, and on the facts of the case, it found that the first instance court had not abused the discretion. Thus, on this point alone, the courts seem to be in some disagreement whether the decision to allow cross examination of the victim's sexual history is one of judgment or discretion.

In *R* v *SMS* [1992] Crim LR 310, a case concerning the rape of a 14-year-old girl by an accused who had only one hand and a false eye, the Court of Appeal decided that leave to cross examine the victim should have been allowed because this was relevant to the issue of consent. This was because the jury may have believed that she was a virgin and come to the conclusion that she would not have wanted to lose her virginity in circumstances such as those that were present in the case. A similar approach was taken by the court in *R* v *Said* [1992] Crim LR 433.

It would appear that the courts will have regard to the nature of the defence in deciding whether or not to allow the cross examination under s. 2. In *R* v *Barton* (1986) 85 Cr App R 5, where the defence, inter alia, was that the accused believed that the victim consented to the sexual intercourse, the Court of Appeal refused to allow leave to cross examine the victim regarding her sexual history. It stated that the mere fact the defence was one of belief in consent did not oblige the court to allow such cross examination. It should be noted that in the case of belief in consent, the court may be more prepared to allow cross examination regarding the victim's sexual history (as compared with where the defence is one of actual consent), provided the facts of the case justify it. On the facts of *Barton*, there was no evidence that the victim's alleged promiscuity had a bearing on the accused's belief that the victim was consenting to the sexual intercourse and further, it was raised for the first time on appeal.

In *R* v *Brown* (1988) 89 Cr App R 97, where the accused alleged that the victim consented to the sexual intercourse, leave to cross examine under s. 2 was refused. The Court of Appeal stated that leave to cross examine the victim about her sexual history is easier to justify where the defence is one of belief that the victim consented to the sexual intercourse. The Court went on to say that, even where the defence is one of actual consent, leave to cross examine could still be granted in appropriate circumstances. The court would have to be satisfied that on the particular facts of the case, the cross examination as to the victim's sexual history was such as to persuade the jury that the victim did consent, notwithstanding her evidence to the contrary.

It is clear from these cases that there is a lack of consistency in the court's approach to s. 2. As such, Temkin may be right when she says that the courts are attributing too much relevance to the victim's sexual history especially in the context of the sexual *mores* of today. What is also clear is that the recommendations of the Heilbron Committee have not been followed. As a result there is the danger that the jury may be side-tracked by issues which arguably have limited relevance to the matters before them.

13 Privilege and Public Policy

INTRODUCTION

You will have realised by now that a great deal of the law of evidence deals with the exclusion of material from court. Thus, the rule against hearsay excludes evidence primarily because of the fear of adducing inferior albeit relevant evidence. This chapter deals with evidence which is excluded for wider public interest considerations. A party or witness or even a non-participant in the proceedings may refuse to disclose information, papers or answer questions even though such material may have a high degree of relevance and reliability.

Exclusion on the basis of privilege should be distinguished from that based on a broader public policy justification, generally called public interest immunity. There are several privileges to consider, though you may take comfort from Murphy's observation (at p. 355) that they are 'few and limited'. They are: the privilege against self-incrimination, legal professional privilege, 'without prejudice' statements and a limited privilege for journalists' sources. Not all of these are taught in all evidence courses. The existence of the privilege means that a person is not in contempt of court for refusing to disclose information coming under this head and no adverse inferences may be drawn. These species of private privilege only exist if they are claimed by the party or witness seeking to rely on them. They may be waived accidentally or purposely by the party but not by the court. The latter will, however, consider whether the privilege exists and the appropriate extent of it. The courts accept that abrogation of these privileges can only be made by statute but nonetheless there is considerable scope for judicial definition of limits.

Exclusion of evidence on grounds of public interest immunity arises where the court, not the parties or witnesses, accepts a duty of non-disclosure for the public good. Primarily, the issue is one of non-disclosure of documents rather than oral testimony. The original objection to the disclosure may be made by the court itself or by any person or body including government departments even though not taking part in the proceedings. The court will itself scrutinise the claim. There is some conflict of authority on whether the immunity can be waived though the prevailing view seems to be that this depends on the nature of the document. Those whose disclosure would endanger national security, for example, probably fall outside the category of those that can be waived, whereas those protecting confidentiality in order to promote candour, could fall inside. The whole issue of public interest immunity in relation to criminal trials was reviewed by the report of the Scott Inquiry.

QUESTION 1

Hart and Mind are suing Wellman Computer Services over a failure to deliver services under a contract. Two employees of Wellman, Dark and Horse, are called as witnesses but are refusing to answer some questions about their possible involvement in invoicing for work that was not in fact carried out. The managing director of Wellman, Hardacre, is also refusing to allow certain documents to be used in evidence because he is worried about disclosing discrepancies in information he has given to the Inland Revenue. Dark had asked the company lawyer for advice over his predicament. A note of the discussion was found by a secretary of the company, Peter, who is in fact Hart's fiancé. Peter has included a copy of the note in some papers sent to Hart, who is proposing to make use of information it contains about evasion of Wellman's contractual liabilities.

Advise the parties.

Commentary

It might not be immediately apparent to you that this is a question about the privilege against self-incrimination. However, the clue is given by the reference in the question to refusal to answer questions. Bear in mind also that the privilege extends to disclosure of documents. So you need to discuss both the reluctance of Dark and Horse to answer questions and the refusal of Hardacre to disclose documents. A good student will recognise the similarity of the scenario to that in the recent case of *AT&T Istel* v *Tully* [1993] AC 45.

Bear in mind that the privilege is related to the 'right to silence', but the discussion of the latter in evidence cases is usually confined to its application to defendants (see **Chapter 8**). There are an increasing number of statutory exceptions to the privilege, such as the Theft Act 1968, s. 31(1), Criminal Damage Act 1971, s. 9, Children Act 1989, s. 98, and Supreme Court Act 1981, s. 72. In addition there have been a number of statutes abrogating the privilege in relation to the investigation of serious commercial fraud (see *R* v *Saunders* (1995) *The Times*, 28 November). It is unlikely you would be expected to have a detailed knowledge of these provisions. The second part of the question deals with another head of privilege, namely legal professional privilege between lawyer and client covering legal advice. You need to trace carefully the stages whereby privilege may be threatened but then reclaimed.

Suggested Answer

These are civil proceedings and both Dark and Horse and their managing director are seeking to exercise a privilege against self-incrimination. The privilege has been widely criticised and the judiciary have recently been concerned to limit its scope as much as possible. But though the privilege has been abolished by Parliament in certain specific circumstances, none of the exceptions appears to apply here.

The privilege which they seek to exercise is the second of the six aspects identified by Lord Mustill giving the House of Lords judgment in *R* v *Director of Serious Fraud Office, ex parte Smith* [1993] AC 1, 30: 'A general immunity, possessed by all persons and bodies, from being compelled on pain of punishment to answer questions the answers to which may incriminate them'. The justification for the existence of the privilege, according to Lord Templeman in *AT&T Istel Ltd* v *Tully* [1992] AC 45, is first that it discourages the ill-treatment of a suspect and secondly that it discourages the production of dubious confessions.

The scope of the privilege was set out by the Court of Appeal in *Blunt* v *Park Lane Hotel* [1942] 2 KB 253, 257 per Goddard LJ:

> The rule is that no one is bound to answer any question if the answer thereto would, in the opinion of the judge, have a tendency to expose the deponent to any criminal charge, penalty or forfeiture which the judge regards as reasonably likely to be preferred or sued for.

Its scope was limited in civil proceedings by the Civil Evidence Act 1968, which provides by s. 14(1) that:

> The right of a person in any legal proceedings other than criminal proceedings to refuse to answer any question or produce any document or thing if to do so would tend to expose that person to proceedings for an offence or for the recovery of a penalty — (a) shall apply only as regards criminal offences under the law of any part of the United Kingdom and penalties provided for by such law.

It is for Dark and Horse to persuade the judge that the privilege should apply because their answers might expose them to criminal proceedings. Thus in *Rank Film Distribution Ltd* v *Video Information Centre* [1982] AC 380, the

House of Lords upheld the claim for privilege because there was a real danger of a criminal charge of conspiracy to defraud against the defendant.

A consideration which will be relevant to Hardacre is how far the application of the privilege may restrict the recovery of their money or property by Hart and Mind. The House of Lords in *AT&T Istel Ltd* v *Tully* [1993] AC 45 established that there is no reason to allow a defendant in civil proceedings to rely on it, thus depriving a plaintiff of his rights, where the defendant's own protection can be secured in other ways. As Lord Templeman said (at p. 53):

> It is difficult to see any reason why in civil proceedings the privilege against self-incrimination should be exercisable so as to enable a litigant to refuse relevant and even vital documents which are in his possession or power and which speak for themselves.

He went on to say,

> I regard the privilege against self-incrimination exercisable in civil proceedings as an archaic and unjustifiable survival from the past when the court directs the production of relevant documents and requires the defendant to specify his dealings with the plaintiff's property or money.

Referring to the defendant, Lord Templeman said:

> ... Mr Tully would be entitled to rely on [the privilege against self-incrimination] if but only if and so far as compliance with the order of Buckley J would provide evidence against him in a criminal trial. There is no reason why the privilege should be blatantly exploited to deprive the plaintiffs of their civil right and remedies if the privilege is not necessary to protect Mr Tully.

In that case a plaintiff was making a claim for damages and repayment of money obtained by fraud. At the same time a police investigation was set up. The plaintiffs were granted orders requiring the defendants to disclose all dealings concerning the money. The order contained a condition that it would not be used in the prosecution of a criminal offence. The order was later varied and the plaintiff appealed against the variation. The House of Lords varied the order after the Crown Prosecution Service gave an informal assurance that it would not seek to use the divulged material. Thus, if here the judge were assured that the material disclosed by the managing director would not be relied on by the Inland Revenue in criminal proceedings, there might be no obstacle to the disclosure of the documents sought from Hardacre by the plaintiffs.

The courts are taking an increasingly trenchant attitude to the privilege. Thus, in *R* v *Director of Serious Fraud Office, ex parte Smith* [1993] AC 1, the House of Lords said that although there was a strong presumption against interpreting a statute as taking away the right of silence of an accused person, it was the plain intention of the Criminal Justice Act that the powers of investigation should continue even after charge.

The third issue in the problem involves the note of the discussion between Dark and the company lawyer. Legal professional privilege attaches to certain communications between lawyer and client provided the purpose of the consultation is not the furtherance of crime. Though it is a common law privilege, its scope is authoritatively said to be summarised by s. 10 of the Police and Criminal Evidence Act 1984. The House of Lords so held in *R* v *Central Criminal Court, ex parte Francis & Francis* [1989] AC 346. Dark is seeking immunity for communications with the lawyer for the purpose of giving or receiving advice. The fact that the lawyer is employed by the company does not exclude his communications from the scope of the privilege. However, copies of the communications are not privileged: *Calcraft* v *Guest* [1898] 1 QB 759. But until they are actually before the court, Dark is likely to be granted an injunction to restrain the use of the documents, which were clearly obtained in breach of confidence as the Court of Appeal held in *Lord Ashburton* v *Pape* [1913] 2 Ch 469. It is not necessary for the documents to have come into Hart's hands by wrongdoing. It appears that an injunction would be likely to be available even if the documents had come into Hart's hands through the inadvertence of Dark or his solicitors: *Goddard* v *Nationwide Building Society* [1987] QB 670.

QUESTION 2

Brenda is charged with unlawful possession of pornographic photographs discovered after a legally conducted police raid on her flat. Her defence is that they were sent through the post to her, unsolicited and she, although disgusted and puzzled, had put them on one side and had forgotten to destroy them. She noted that they purported to be from an organisation called the Partners Exchange. She recalls that her neighbour Archie who had made several sexual advances to her had mentioned that he belonged to the Partners Exchange which he said arranged 'interesting introductions'. Having spurned his advances she thought no more of the matter but now she suspects that Archie, who was known to the police as a drug user, may have sent the mail and then informed on her.

Advise Brenda.

Commentary

English law has long protected the anonymity of informants in matters relating to public prosecutions, or civil proceedings arising from them. There is clearly a public interest in protecting such sources because the information might otherwise dry up. There is a presumption of non-disclosure and it is for the accused to show there is good reason, arising from the defence case, to breach it. In these instances the court must, as in all cases involving public interest immunity, balance the rights of the accused against any countervailing public interest in protection of sources. In this question, as in all practical questions, you should state the basic rule, citing if you can authority to back up your point. Then you look at possible exceptions to the principle of protection and consider the question of fact in this case, namely would disclosure help the defendant's case?

Suggested Answer

A long-established rule prevents witnesses being asked, or answering, questions about the names of informers or the nature of the information given. The rationale of the rule was explained by Lord Reid in *Conway* v *Rimmer* [1968] AC 910, 953: 'The police are carrying on an unending war with criminals many of whom are today highly intelligent. So it is essential there should be no disclosure of anything which might give any useful information to those who organise criminal activities'. However, *R* v *Ward* [1993] 1 WLR 619 placed the prosecution under an obligation to disclose to the defence all the material on which the prosecution is based. In *R* v *Horseferry Road Magistrates' Court, ex parte Bennett (No. 2)* [1994] 1 All ER 289 the Divisional Court set out the procedure the Crown should follow for voluntary disclosure of documents in criminal cases. It is for the courts to decide what should not be disclosed. The prosecution must thus assert a claim to public interest immunity if evidence of the identity of informers is to be excluded.

Where the revelation of the existence of an informer would otherwise require the abandonment of the prosecution, application can be made *ex parte* by the Crown without notice to the defence: *R* v *Davis* [1993] 1 WLR 613. The court will normally exclude evidence of an informer's identity, but where the judge is of the opinion that disclosure is necessary to establish the accused's innocence, it is a rule of law that the judge must allow the question to be asked and require an answer: *Marks* v *Beyfus* (1890) 25 QBD 494. It is for the accused to show that there is good reason to expect that disclosure is necessary to establish his innocence. This should normally be done before the trial in proceedings to set aside a witness summons or subpoena for the appropriate Crown witness: *R* v *Hennessy* (1978) 68 Cr App R 419. In *R* v *Agar* (1989) 90 Cr App R 318 it was held on appeal that disclosure of the name of an informer in a drugs case was necessary where the defendant claimed to have been set up by the informer and the police acting together.

Here, Brenda is claiming that Archie framed her and not just that he informed. In *R* v *Slowcombe* [1991] Crim LR 198, where the identity of the informer would have contributed little or nothing to the issue before the jury, disclosure was refused. If Brenda is able to put up some evidence that Archie did set the police onto her, the jury may well conclude that her story may be true, so her counsel should be permitted to ask the police whether Archie was the informant. The association with the Partners Exchange may well be relevant evidence and lead to an inference of Archie's involvement. If Archie was not the informer, the police would not be required to name the informer, however, and the jury would be asked to believe Brenda's case without that knowledge.

QUESTION 3

James is facing proceedings in the Family Division to have his children taken into care. He wishes to place in evidence a videotape made by Barsetshire Council Family Unit of a family therapy session including James's and other families which he maintains illustrates his healthy attitude to his children. The council is resisting disclosure on grounds of public interest immunity. Advise James. Would your advice be any different if he was facing criminal proceedings arising from the same facts?

Commentary

This is quite a straightforward question about public interest immunity. You need to show that you are aware that it can apply to bodies other than central government. As Lord Hailsham remarked in *D* v *NSPCC* [1978] AC 171, 'the categories of public interest are not closed and must alter from time to time whether by restriction or extension as social conditions and social legislation develop.' (at p. 230). You should also explain the different approaches of the courts according to whether the proceedings are civil or criminal.

Suggested Answer

Certain types of evidence, though relevant, are not admissible because their disclosure is held to infringe a public interest. The so-called public interest immunity differs from other types of privilege. The judge of his own motion can exclude the evidence if he thinks the public interest so demands. The principle involved was laid down in *Conway* v *Rimmer* [1968] AC 910. Public interest immunity can apply where the party concerned is not a central government department, as the House of Lords held in *D* v *NSPCC* [1978] AC 171, reversing the Court of Appeal:

There is little doubt that the video of James's family therapy session is capable of being subject to public interest immunity. The argument for non-disclosure is likely to be that the workings of the social services department should be kept secret so people will deal with them in confidence. There appears to be less force in that argument here, because the video records a session in which James himself took part but still the council may worry that future participants may be reluctant if the videos could become evidence. In *Campbell* v *Tameside MBC* [1982] QB 1065 the Court of Appeal was presented with an application for public policy immunity concerning the records of a local education authority, but upheld their disclosure since they were necessary for the plaintiff's case. The records here concern children and the courts have frequently held such records to be protected from disclosure because there is an important public interest in keeping confidential this sensitive work. It is possible that the interests of the children rather than those of James will be paramount. However, even if the courts acknowledge on inspection that public interest immunity applies it is arguable that it is open to them to accept a waiver although there is no clear authority on this. In *Campbell* v *Tameside MBC*, Lord Denning (obiter) said there was a difference between claims affecting documents which should be kept secret on grounds for example of national security and those of lower level of confidence. Immunity should, in the latter, be capable of being waived. Thus the local authority could agree to submit the film.

In criminal cases, the balance of competing interests should be made but there is clearly a need to afford greater protection to James, as an accused, than as a party to civil proceedings. The courts must balance the public interest and the rights of the individual affected. In *R* v *Governor of Brixton Prison, ex parte Osman* [1991] 1 WLR 281 the weight to be attached to the interests of justice was very great where the documents were necessary to the defence in a criminal case. However, Lord Taylor CJ in *R* v *Keane* [1994] 1 WLR 746 at p. 751 commented in the Court of Appeal, that the right answer must result from 'performing the balancing exercise not from dispensing with it'. He said 'If the disputed material may prove the defendant's innocence or avoid a miscarriage of justice then the balance comes down resoundingly in favour of disclosing it'.

The position thus seems to be that a public interest immunity claim may be made in criminal cases. As Cross and Tapper point out (1995, p. 526) 'it can hardly be supposed that there are no means of preventing disclosure of the most vital national secrets just because they are relevant to the defence of one accused of some most trivial offence'. But as it was expressed in *ex parte Osman,* the public interest in the administration of justice will weigh very heavily in the balance if the liberty of the defendant is at stake particularly here where there is no question of national security.

QUESTION 4

Mr X is suing the Rural Retreat nursing home for negligently causing the death of his wife. He alleges that Gloria, a nursing auxiliary, administered a drug overdose. He wishes to adduce in evidence a report for the home's insurers after the death of Mrs X in which other staff gave evidence that there was lax management in the home and bottles were often mislabelled. The report was also sent to the nursing home's lawyer. Jane, Mr X's neighbour, works as a clerk for the lawyer. She took a secret photocopy of the report and sent it anonymously to Mr X. Advise on the report's admissibility.

Commentary

The specific questions here on legal professional privilege are: how far does it stretch to correspondence with third parties? what is the status of copies? if the privilege is lost can use of the document be restrained by an injunction on grounds of confidentiality?

Suggested Answer

The report contains cogent evidence of the state of affairs in the home at the time of Mrs X's death and would clearly be useful to Mr X in the litigation

However, one may argue in answering this question that the home would have been entitled to claim legal professional privilege for the report by its insurers. The House of Lords in *Waugh* v *BRB* [1980] AC 521 held that this would be so provided the report was compiled with a view to pending or contemplated litigation with the dominant purpose of obtaining legal advice. In that case the defendants were sued under the Fatal Accidents Act 1976. The plaintiff's husband had died in a railway collision. The widow asked for discovery of an internal report by the defendants submitted to the railway inspectorate and the ministry. However, the report was also intended to give details to the Railway Board's solicitor so he could give advice. There was no privilege because the intended or contemplated litigation was not on the facts 'at least the dominant purpose' of creating the document.

The fact that it was sent to the home's legal department would not confer on the report legal professional privilege which it did not already possess (otherwise every litigant could protect embarrassing documents merely by sending them to his legal representatives, as the Divisional Court held in *R* v *Peterborough JJ, ex parte Hicks* [1977] 1 WLR 1371). In *Ventouris* v *Mountain* [1991] 1 WLR 607 the Court of Appeal held that legal professional privilege could not attach to original documents which did not come into existence for the purposes of the litigation but already existed before the litigation was contemplated or commenced. Each case will turn on its facts but it appears here that the likelihood is that the insurers were anticipating legal proceedings and that is the dominant purpose for which the papers came into being.

However, the privilege extends only to the original document. The contents of a privileged document can be proved by secondary evidence, including the production of copies, following the Court of Appeal decision in *Calcraft* v *Guest* [1898] 1 QB 759. This rule was explained in *Lord Ashburton* v *Pape* [1913] 2 Ch 469 by Cozens-Hardy MR giving judgment in the Court of Appeal, as arising from the fact that the court in an action where it is sought to prove the contents of a privileged document from secondary sources is not trying the circumstances under which the document was produced. But that rule, as he pointed out, has no bearing on a case where the whole subject matter of the action is the right to retain the copy of a document which is privileged. *Ashburton* established the availability of equitable relief to restrain the use of copies of documents which were subject to a duty of confidence and possession of which had been wrongfully obtained.

It is clearly the case here that Jane the clerk is subject to a duty of confidence as against her employer. She has broken her obligation of secrecy in passing the document to Mr X. Even if the documents had been obtained without any reprehensible conduct, the home would still be entitled to an injunction against the use of the report, provided it had not already been used in Mr X's litigation. In the Court of Appeal decision in *Goddard* v *Nationwide BS* [1987] QB 670, 683 May LJ stated:

> If a litigant has in his possession copies of documents to which legal professional privilege attaches, he may nonetheless use such copies as secondary evidence in his litigation: however, if he has not yet used the documents in that way, the mere fact that he intends to do so is no answer to a claim against him by the person in whom the privilege is vested for delivery up of the copies or to restrain him from disclosing or making any use of any information contained in them.

As Nourse LJ pointed out in that case, it does not matter whether the documents were obtained innocently or by means of reprehensible conduct, because equity gives relief against all the world, including the innocent, excepting a bona fide purchaser for value without notice.

The nursing home will therefore have to act promptly and apply for the equitable remedy of an injunction if it wishes to prevent the report being put in evidence by Mr X.

QUESTION 5

Alice, the four-year-old daughter of Mrs Y is badly injured in a playground incident at Treasure Island Nursery. Mrs Y is suing the nursery. An internal report has been prepared by the Department for Education as part of its routine inspection of private nursery schools. In this report the Department indicates concern about management procedures and lack of proper vetting of staff at Treasure Island Nursery. The Department claims that the report is covered by public interest immunity because to disclose it would prejudice the conduct of future inspections in that it would deter witnesses from giving evidence. A 'mole' in the department sent a photocopy of key sections of the report to the pressure group Childwatch which is helping Mrs Y and they have offered to let her have a copy.

Advise on the admissibility of the report.

Commentary

A straightforward question about public interest immunity. Note that public interest immunity attaches to copies of documents unlike the position in relation to legal professional privilege which only extends to an original document.

Suggested Answer

Public interest immunity protects the nation or the public service against the harm which can arise by disclosure of certain documents. It is not material to the claim that the party making it is not a party to the proceedings as here. It is also irrelevant here that the report is in the form of a copy. The argument of the Department for Education is that staff and owners of nurseries would in future be less candid with their inspectors if they knew their statements were likely to be used in litigation. The Crown is not a party to the proceedings here, so should give notice that it intends to contest the production of the report and the objection can be heard either before or during the trial of the action.

The application to exclude should be supported by affidavit, usually signed by the relevant minister or a responsible official. The claim can be either on a 'class' or a 'contents' basis, saying either that the document belongs to a class of documents whose production is not in the public interest or that its production is objectionable because of its specific contents.

The claim here appears to be of the 'class' type but Lord Reid in *Conway* v *Rimmer* [1968] AC 910, indicated that courts are likely to be more sympathetic if the claim is of the 'contents' type. The court has power to inspect the documents and in a class claim is likely to do so. The courts are not obliged, since *Conway* v *Rimmer* abrogated the rule in *Duncan* v *Cammell Laird* [1942] AC 624, to accept without question the minister's certificate. Mrs Y in this case would have to show that the report was 'necessary either for disposing fairly of the cause or matter or for saving costs', which is not a difficult hurdle on the present facts: see *Air Canada* v *Secretary of State for Trade (No. 2)* [1983] 2 AC 394. In addition, the application for disclosure should not be a 'fishing expedition', though plainly that does not apply in the present case. The argument that if it became known that confidential reports might be disclosed for the purposes of private litigation, the elements of frankness and candour in their preparation might be lost, carries less weight after *Conway* v *Rimmer*. In *Science Research Council* v *Nassé* [1980] AC 1028 that reasoning was rejected by Lord Salmon. Lord Fraser saw the need to prevent disclosure as only a private interest of the individuals who prepared the documents. But the need for candour was strongly defended by Lord Wilberforce (dissenting) in *Burmah Oil Co. Ltd* v *Bank of England* [1980] AC 1090 so might still have some foundation.

Mrs Y can clearly argue that the report is relevant. She may be able to rely on waiver by the witnesses. In *Alfred Crompton Amusement Machines Ltd* v

Customs and Excise Commissioners [1974] AC 405 the documents in question were business documents submitted by third parties to the Commissioners as part of a valuation of the plaintiff's machines. In this case the balance of interests fell evenly and the House was inclined to hold in favour of the claim for public interest. However, Lord Cross thought that a person for whose benefit the objection was made could waive the immunity although this was doubted by Lord Simon in *Rogers* v *Home Secretary* [1973] AC 388. The authorities thus conflict on this point of the availability of waiver.

QUESTION 6

Jane has been the victim of an unlawful drugs raid although no charges were preferred after it. She was badly hurt in the raid. She believes the raid occurred as a result of an article she wrote after an interview with a Mr Big detailing the extent to which drug dealers were plying their wares among school children. Jane is considering suing the police, having already made a complaint to the Police Complaints Authority which it has investigated. She wonders if she will be able to obtain copies of the PCA's investigation and is worried that at the trial she may be forced to disclose the name of Mr Big since she had promised him anonymity.

Advise Jane of her legal position.

Commentary

You should not attempt this question if you are not reasonably familiar with the landmark decision in *R* v *Chief Constable of the West Midlands, ex parte Wiley* [1995] AC 274. Otherwise, there is a real danger you will be citing overruled authorities. This is an instance when it is vital to check that your textbook and lecture notes are up to date. In this case judicial review had been sought of the refusal of Chief Constables to give undertakings that material relating to complaints against the police would not be used to prepare defences to civil claims on police misconduct. The House of Lords decided that no class immunity applied to police complaints procedure documents and cases which held otherwise were overruled. It was acknowledged that in some cases a 'contents' claim might be appropriate and that there may be a 'class' claim for subgroups of documents. Subsequently, this latter view was accepted for reports of officers investigating a complaint in *Taylor* v *Anderton (Police Complaints Authority Intervening)* [1995] 1 WLR 447. The other part of the question deals with journalists' sources, and whether or not you are allowed to take a statute book into the examination, you must be reasonably familiar with the text of the Contempt of Court Act 1981, s. 10.

Suggested Answer

The House of Lords in *R* v *Chief Constable of the West Midlands, ex parte Wiley* [1995] AC 274 overruled previous authorities and decided that it was no longer necessary to impose a general class public interest immunity on documents generated in the course of an investigation by the Police Complaints Authority of a complaint against the police. What has to be decided is whether the particular documents in this case are covered by public interest immunity. This is a matter for the court hearing Jane's civil action for assault. Jane's case will not be helped by *Taylor* v *Anderton* [1995] 1 WLR 447 where the Court of Appeal held that a 'class' immunity applied to a sub-group of documents, namely reports of officers investigating a complaint. Any immunity which does attach to any of the documents is limited to the disclosure of the documents or their contents rather than the use of knowledge obtained from them. Jane may be refused sight of the documents on grounds of public interest immunity, namely that preserving the confidentiality of the reports outweighed the public interest in disclosure in that they were not necessary for fairly disposing of the case or saving costs. The important point is that it is for the court to inspect the documents and decide accordingly whether or not to admit them.

Jane is also worried that she will be forced to disclose the identity of Mr Big. The courts have been very reluctant to acknowledge privileged confidential relationships apart from that between a lawyer and client. One area of concern has been confidentiality between journalists and their sources. The attempt to assert a general journalistic immunity based on public policy, protecting for example dissemination of information by granting sources anonymity, failed in *British Steel Corporation* v *Granada Television Ltd* [1981] AC 1096. The House of Lords, recognizing the importance of protecting certain confidences while also recognizing that it had a discretion to order disclosure, ordered Granada to disclose the identity of an informant. In this case, the majority felt Granada's conduct was irresponsible in using the 'leaked' confidential reports on the national steel strike. The House agreed, with Lord Salmon dissenting, that although the courts had a wish to respect journalistic sources, no public policy immunity existed which would override the public policy of making relevant evidence available to the court. British Steel Corporation had a worthy case. Disclosure of the source of information contained in a publication is now governed by statute.

Section 10 of the Contempt of Court Act 1981 provides that:

> No court may require a person to disclose, nor is any person guilty of contempt for refusing to disclose, the source of information contained in a publication for which he is responsible, unless it be established to the satisfaction of the court that disclosure is necessary in the interests of justice or national security or for the prevention of disorder or crime.

Parliament, according to Murphy (at p. 403), 'took the most remarkable step of introducing what appears to be a new statutory privilege'.

The section will thus give Jane as a journalist a presumption against disclosure of the identity of Mr Big. The police if they wish disclosure will have to convince the court that one of the four reasons in the section applies, the two most likely being necessary either in the interests of justice or the prevention of crime. As regards the former, the majority of the House of Lords in *Secretary of State for Defence* v *Guardian Newspapers* [1985] AC 339 held it to mean technically the administration of justice in the course of legal proceedings in a court of law, tribunal or other such body. However Lord Bridge in *X* v *Morgan-Grampian (Publishers) Ltd* [1991] 1 AC 1 did not think resort to actual legal proceedings was required. In any case it will be difficult for the police to establish that they need Mr Big's identity either for their defence against Jane or to exercise another legal right. The court may however consider that the police require the identity for the prevention of crime. It will then have to balance the interests of a free press in non-disclosure of sources against the police contention. This aspect of s. 10 was considered again in *Re an Inquiry under the Company Securities (Insider Dealing) Act 1985* [1988] AC 660. Inspectors carrying out a criminal investigation contended that disclosure of the sources of a journalist's article about insider dealing was 'necessary in the interests of the prevention of . . . crime'.

Three aspects of the House of Lords ruling are relevant to Jane's concern: first, s. 10 applied to all types of proceedings, secondly, the 'prevention of crime' could refer to crime in general and thirdly, 'necessary' meant somewhere between 'indispensable' and 'expedient'. On the last point Murphy (1995 at p. 406) argues that the definition reduces the standard enacted by Parliament. If the police decide that Mr Big's identity is necessary for their general investigations into drug dealing then Jane may be ordered to disclose it.

14 Mixed Questions

INTRODUCTION

Examination questions in evidence papers frequently cover several issues. There is no way you could anticipate any particular combination of topics so the questions will be a test of your skill in identifying what specific areas of knowledge will be needed. Obviously, you will not be able to cover each area in the same depth as the single issue questions. The skill lies in identifying the relevant areas and you will lose marks if you ignore one. It is most important therefore that you spend some time in listing the various matters which raise a point of law, then specify the appropriate statute or case law and finally apply the law to the facts in the question.

QUESTION 1

Alerted by a burglar alarm, police from a nearby station arrived at a house in Meadow Way at 2.00 a.m. They find a smashed window and while two officers search the house a third searches the street for suspects. Meanwhile the owner of the house, Jack, is pursuing two figures in the street. He sees Wayne running several yards away in the street, catches up with him and grabs him. The other figure has disappeared. 'You rat,' Jack shouts, 'you've burgled my house'. Wayne says nothing but tries to shake Jack off. Wayne is arrested and cautioned. At the police station he is questioned in a series of interviews beginning at 4.00 a.m. on Friday 2 April. He is cautioned before all the interviews. Before the first interview Wayne requests access to a solicitor but this is denied by Inspector Brown on the grounds that they suspect Wayne had an accomplice who could be alerted by calling a solicitor. At the first interview, Wayne refuses to cooperate with the questioning. At the second interview Wayne is again denied a solicitor, but offers to 'tell what he knows', if the police promise to put in a good word for him to the judge. The Inspector nods his assent. Wayne then says that he was out with his friend Dan on the night in question and when making their way home Dan suggested breaking into a house. He says he had nothing to do with the burglary and just hung around outside. The second interview ends at 9.00 a.m. on Saturday 3 April. Wayne and Dan are then charged with the burglary. They plead not guilty.

Advise on evidence.

Commentary

Among the issues you must consider here are whether fleeing can constitute adverse evidence and what is the evidential value of silence in the face of questioning both by persons in authority and an ordinary citizen. You must recall both the common law rules and also the new provisions under ss. 34 and 37 of the Criminal Justice and Public Order Act 1994. In addition, you will have to deal with the possibility of breach of s. 58 of the Police and Criminal Evidence Act 1984 ('PACE') and the Codes of Practice, as revised in 1995. The Codes are very comprehensive and you will obviously not be able to remember all the details but you must touch on the main points, considering possible breaches in the period of detention and the related question of whether the offence is a serious arrestable offence. The circumstances of the obtaining of Wayne's statement, and whether it is inadmissible under ss. 76 or 78 of PACE should be considered. You must identify the various legal issues first and then in turn consider the relevant law in relation to the narrative of events. In these questions it is useful to prepare a plan for your answer to ensure your coverage is comprehensive.

Suggested Answer

The case concerns the question of whether various items of evidence are likely to be admissible for the prosecution. This essay takes each issue in turn.

Wayne is seen fleeing from the scene of the crime. Does this have evidential significance? A confession is defined in s. 82(1) of the Police and Criminal Evidence Act 1984 ('PACE'). It '... includes any statement wholly or partly adverse to the person who made it whether made to a person in authority or not and whether made in words or otherwise'. It is arguable that this definition is wide enough to include an admission by conduct. The Criminal Law Revision Committee in its 11th Report (1972, Cmnd 4991) gave as an example, a possible admission by conduct, a nod of the head. But that is clearly an express statement by conduct. It is unlikely that an implied statement by conduct such as running away will be accepted as a confession. In *Preece* v *Parry* [1983] Crim LR 170 the Divisional Court held that violent behaviour on arrest was capable of being a confession. This is generally regarded as an unusual case.

Wayne's silence in the face of accusations from Jack is more likely than his fleeing to amount to an admission. The common law rule is that a statement made in the presence of the accused cannot amount to evidence against him, except in so far as he accepts what has been said, as the House of Lords held in *R* v *Christie* [1914] AC 545. However, if in certain circumstances a reply or rebuttal would reasonably be expected, silence can be taken to be a confession. The test of admissibility of this type of silence is whether the parties are speaking on even terms: see *R* v *Mitchell* (1892) 17 Cox CC 503 and the Privy Council decision in *Parkes* v *R* (1977) 64 Cr App R 25. The court will thus have to decide first whether Jack and Wayne were speaking on even terms, which does seem likely. Thus, any direction by the judge that the silence could amount to a confession is arguably proper. The judge, however, must be careful to direct the jury to consider, first, whether the silence does indicate acceptance of what Jack said and, if so, whether guilt could reasonably be inferred from what he had accepted. It was the failure of the judge to leave these two issues to the jury and his suggestion that the defendant's silence could indicate guilt which led the Court of Appeal to quash the conviction in *R* v *Chandler* [1976] 1 WLR 585.

This common law principle is not affected by s. 34 of the Criminal Justice and Public Order Act 1994 which covers questioning under caution by a police constable. Section 34(5) of the 1994 Act provides that the section does not:

> prejudice the admissibility in evidence of the silence or other reaction of the accused in the face of anything said in his presence relating to the conduct in respect of which he is charged . . . or preclude the drawing of any inference from any such silence or other reaction of the accused which could properly be drawn apart from this section.

Under the PACE Code of Practice C paragraph 11.1, following a decision to arrest, the suspect must not be interviewed except at a police station unless the 'emergency' exceptions apply. It appears Wayne's treatment accords with this. Furthermore, Wayne should take account of paragraph 11.2A, which provides that at the beginning of an interview carried out in a police station the interviewing officer, after cautioning him, is to put to the suspect any 'significant statement or silence' which occurred before the start of the interview. Wayne should be given an opportunity to confirm or deny any pre-interview silence or statement.

Some possible procedural flaws arise in relation to Wayne's interviews at the police station. Wayne maintains silence at first and then makes a statement. It is necessary to consider the application of ss. 34 and 37 of the 1994 Act, Wayne's failure to account for his presence in the street at the initial interview may be admissible under s. 37, since the court is permitted to draw inferences, whether or not the accused gives another version of events at trial. The investigating officer must give the additional special warning set out in para. 10.5A of Code C. Section 34, on the other hand, does not allow inferences to be drawn from silence, per se, but only when the accused for his defence in later proceedings relies on evidence, which evidence could have been provided in answer form during earlier questioning. The statute in fact does not make it clear whether an earlier silence in an early interview albeit replaced by an explanation at a later one is admissible, although it would seem rather harsh to interpret the statute against the defendant in this way. The evidential value of silence which is shortly replaced by an explanation, as is the case here, must be low. We are not told what, if any other explanations Wayne puts up at trial and if his defence brings in new facts he could reasonably be expected to have mentioned during questioning up to charge, then s. 34 of the 1994 Act may apply.

Wayne's statement takes a form which is partly exculpatory and partly inculpatory. It also implicates Dan. Following the House of Lords decision in *R* v *Sharp* [1988] 1 WLR 7, such mixed statements are admissible as evidence of the facts related. However, the confession is evidence against Wayne and not Dan and the jury must be so warned, following the decision of the Court of Criminal Appeal in *R* v *Gunewardene* [1951] 2 KB 600. Confessions may also be edited. In *R* v *Silcott* [1987] Crim LR 765 at first instance, the trial judge ruled that the names of co-defendants implicated in a confession should be replaced by initials. However, in *R* v *Jefferson* (1994) 99 Cr App R 13, the Court of Appeal said it was a matter for the discretion of the trial judge whether to edit such interviews.

It is possible, however, that the whole statement itself should be excluded. Confessions may be excluded under several provisions of PACE. The grounds are oppression under s. 76(2)(a); unreliability under s. 76(2)(b), both of which operate as a rule of law; and unfairness under s. 78 which operates as the exercise of discretion. There appear to be no grounds of oppression here, but s. 76(2)(b) PACE may be appropriate. Arguably, Wayne has been induced to confess by a promise of a favour. In *R* v *Barry* (1991) 95 Cr App R 384, the promise of bail led to a confession being held potentially unreliable by the Court of Appeal. It must be shown that there is a connection between what was said or done and the confession. It is arguable that Wayne was induced to confess by the indication of favourable treatment by the Inspector. Thus the 'something said or done evidence' is the possible inducement. The 'circumstances' are arguably the absence of a solicitor with whom Wayne could discuss the offer (*R* v *Mathias* (1989) Crim LR 64). If the judge accepts this as an arguable proposition, then the burden of proof is on the prosecution to prove in a voir dire beyond reasonable doubt that the confession was not so obtained. The test is an objective one of whether any confession obtained in such circumstances would be likely to be unreliable.

Even if s. 76(2)(b) PACE is not applicable there appear to be sufficient breaches of other sections of the statute and the Code to warrant exclusion under s. 78 PACE by the exercise of the court's discretion. The circumstances in which the statement was obtained reveal a number of possible breaches of the statute and Codes of Practice.

First, Wayne has his access to a solicitor denied. Delay in obtaining legal representation is only permissible under s. 58 PACE if the offence is a serious arrestable offence. Delay is permissible for up to 36 hours if any of the conditions in s. 58 applies to justify the delay. The reason given by the police, namely fear of alerting another suspect, does appear to comply with s. 58(8)(b) PACE but the police must put up cogent evidence to justify such a fear (see *R* v *Samuel* [1988] QB 615). Burglary per se is not sufficient unless, considering the relative status of the parties, the amount taken represents either serious financial gain or loss. Further information is needed on this point. If the offence does constitute a serious arrestable offence, both the reason for and the extent of the questioning appear appropriate, as long as the delay has been authorised by a senior officer. If there are no reasonable grounds for believing that the offence is a serious arrestable offence, then there appear to be several breaches of the conditions of detention. Wayne should have been released after 24 hours or charged. Further, Wayne should have been allowed eight hours rest in any 24 hours free of questioning, with breaks for refreshment and periodic checks during the questioning.

The courts appear to take the attitude that to justify exclusion under s. 78 PACE, the breach or breaches must be 'significant and substantial', as the Court of Appeal held in *R* v *Keenan* [1990] 2 QB 54. A key issue is whether the police acted in bad faith: *R* v *Alladice* (1988) 87 Cr App R 380. In *R* v *Canale* [1990] 2 All ER 187 the Court of Appeal held that the officers had shown a cynical disregard of the Code which they had breached flagrantly. The Court held that the confession should have been excluded under s. 78 PACE. Section 76(2)(b) PACE was not appropriate since the accused had been in the Parachute Regiment and was not therefore in the position of a vulnerable defendant in the face of police questioning.

Here, there also appear to be breaches of the conditions of detention. In the absence of bad faith, the court will be concerned to look at whether the breaches were operative in leading to potential unreliability under s. 76(2)(b) PACE or unfairness to the proceedings under s. 78.

In conclusion, Wayne's silence in the face of the accusation from Jack is probably admissible. The cumulative effect of the possibly wrongful denial of legal advice, the apparent inducement and breach of the statute and Code C are together likely to lead to Wayne's initial silence at interview and his partly inculpatory statement being held inadmissible.

QUESTION 2

John is an inmate of a hostel for young stablehands employed by Harry, who trains horses. Harry has set up and owns the hostel, to provide accommodation for his staff. Ann, the residential care worker at the hostel has, unknown to

Harry, been allowing the residents to watch 'pirate' videos she has bought in a car-boot sale. A quarrel breaks out in the hostel recreation room one evening while students are watching a violent video which Ann has brought in. John, sickened by the violence, wants the video to be turned off so he can play snooker but Ann refuses. A scuffle breaks out and John is poked in the eye by Fred, another employee who is holding a snooker cue. It later becomes apparent that John has been blinded in one eye. After the incident, the snooker table is removed from the residents' lounge. At the same time Harry offered John £5,000 compensation 'without prejudice', but John rejected this as too low. Harry writes to Sally, his solicitor, after the accident and sends Fred's job application which reveals that he had been sacked from a previous post at a residential hostel after allegations of violence against the inmates. Harry also sends the snooker cue to the solicitor for 'safe keeping'. John is suing Harry as being vicariously liable for the incident and for assault. The case is set down for trial. Ann is refusing to appear as a witness.

Discuss the evidential issues involved, not the matters of substantive law.

Commentary

You are not told what the evidential issues are so you must be careful to identify the relevant ones. You are clearly warned not to discuss the matters of liability in negligence, even if you feel you could shine in that area! This is a civil case in which you would be quite justified in referring to the burden and standard of proof as a basic question of evidence. The refusal of Ann to appear prompts you to dwell on the compellability of witnesses and since there is a suggestion of criminal activity on her part, you need to bear in mind the privilege against self-incrimination on which there has been some recent case law. You also need to consider whether the removal of the snooker table after the incident is a relevant piece of evidence. Explicit questions uniquely on relevance are rare but you should not ignore a possible part question. The exchange with the lawyer raises the issue of legal professional privilege, both in relation to the correspondence and the sending of the snooker cue. As for Harry's without prejudice offer of compensation, you need to consider whether this can be disclosed in court. The approach you should adopt is to list the issues in the order in which they appear in the question and work systematically through them.

Suggested Answer

All admissible evidence must be relevant although not all relevant evidence is admissible. The removal of the snooker table is arguably not relevant to the facts in issue. To qualify for admission it should increase or diminish the probability of the existence of a fact in issue. 'What is relevant is largely a matter of common experience.' (Heydon 1991, p. 6). Does the removal of the table make it more or less probable that Harry was vicariously liable in negligence or that Fred had assaulted John? Relevance is a matter of logic not law but it may be appropriate to cite *Hart* v *Lancashire and Yorkshire Railway Co.* (1869) 21 LT 261. There, a runaway engine ran into a stationary train on a branch line injuring the plaintiff. He sued the railway company and used as evidence the fact that the company had subsequently changed the points system. On appeal, the evidence was held to be wrongly admitted since, as Bramwell B said (at p. 263):

> People do not furnish evidence against themselves simply by adopting a new plan in order to prevent the recurrence of an accident.

It is therefore likely that the removal is not legally relevant.

In this civil case John has the legal burden of proof on both suits (*Miller* v *Minister of Pensions* [1947] 2 All ER 372). There is an issue as to whether the standard of proof in these two suits of negligence and assault is the same. In *Hornal* v *Neuberger Products* [1957] 1 QB 247, CA, a case of fraudulent misrepresentation, Denning LJ said, 'The more serious the allegation the higher the degree of probability that is required'. The case law does seem to suggest that the more serious the allegation, the more cogent is the evidence required to overcome the unlikelihood of what is alleged and thus to prove it. However, the standard of proof is still the balance of probabilities. Murphy (1995, p. 109) points out that the issue has been clouded by a tendency of judges to stress that the more grave the allegation, the clearer the evidence adduced to prove it. But he stresses that the case law clearly requires the civil standard to remain. Following *Hornal* with regard to the assault charge the gravity of the issues is part of the circumstances which the court has to take into consideration in deciding as to the balance of probabilities.

Ann is reluctant to appear as a witness possibly because she is afraid that evidence of her wrongdoing, namely showing pirate videos, may be revealed. These in themselves are relevant to the suits in that they were the cause of the quarrel. Their criminal origin is not relevant. In *Blunt* v *Park Lane Hotel* [1942] 2 KB 253 Goddard LJ expressed the scope of the common law rule, that no one is bound to answer any question if the answer thereto would, in the opinion of the judge, have a tendency to expose the deponent to any criminal charge, penalty or forfeiture which the judge regards as reasonably likely to be preferred or sued for. In practice, of course it is only the exposure to possible criminal charges which is of concern. The right is referred to in the Civil Evidence Act 1968, s. 14(1)(a) which provides that if the claim is made in civil proceedings the offence must be provided for by law of any part of the UK. If the pirate videos are held to be relevant to the proceedings and counsel wish to pursue a line of questioning on this, Ann may be permitted to refuse to answer (*Rank Film Distributors Ltd* v *Video Information Centre* [1982] AC 380). If a witness is wrongly compelled to answer a question in breach of the privilege against self-incrimination, the answer will be inadmissible in subsequent proceedings against him (*R* v *Garbett* (1847) 1 Den CC 236). In *AT&T Istel* v *Tully* [1993] AC 45 Lord Templeman (at p. 53) condemned the privilege against self-incrimination in civil proceedings as archaic and unjustifiable. That case involved the disclosure of documents rather than the appearance of witnesses but it does suggest that the judiciary will not apply the privilege too readily. As Lord Griffiths said (at p. 57) the law was in need of 'radical reappraisal'. However, the House of Lords conceded that any abrogation of the privilege in such cases could only be made by statute.

There is clearly a public interest in speedy settlement of civil litigation and the law does offer some protection to communications which are aimed at achieving this. Obviously, there is a danger that an offer of settlement may be later interpreted as an admission of liability. Because of this, communications between parties, namely Harry's offer of settlement, may not be ordered to be disclosed on discovery and will not form part of the documents placed before the court, as the House of Lords held in *Rush & Tompkins Ltd* v *Greater London Council* [1989] AC 1280. The privilege is that of the parties so it only applies if Harry requests it. However, although without prejudice correspondence may not be admissible on the issue of liability, it may be admissible on other grounds such as costs, where delay or unreasonable refusal to settle may be material (see RSC Order 22 r. 14). This rule applies the proposal made by Cairns LJ in *Calderbank* v *Calderbank* [1976] Fam 93.

It is a common law rule that communications passing between lawyer and client about materials prepared for the purpose of litigation are privileged. In this question, the first aspect of legal professional privilege applies, namely, that communications between lawyer and client made in the course of seeking and giving advice within the normal scope of legal business are privileged if the client seeks the privilege. Thus, any advice that Sally gave to Harry could not be disclosed (*Minter* v *Priest* [1930] AC 558). Section 10 of the Police and Criminal Evidence Act 1984 (PACE) gives statutory recognition to legal professional privilege. However, Harry cannot claim the privilege for material objects so the snooker cue is not covered, nor can there be a claim of privilege for Fred's job application, since these did not arise in the course of his relationship with the lawyer (*R* v *King* [1983] 1 WLR 411). In that case, the court expressed doubts about the earlier decision, *Frank Truman Export Ltd* v *Commissioner of Police for the Metropolis* [1977] QB 952, where Swanwick J held that pre-existing documents which might be relevant in evidence against the plaintiff, were privileged in the hands of the plaintiff's solicitor to whom they had been delivered for his consideration in relation to likely criminal charges. The job application is likely to be highly probative and admissible as 'similar fact' evidence (*Mood Music Publishing Co. Ltd* v *de Wolfe* [1976] Ch 119).

QUESTION 3

Tanya witnessed a burglary in which the perpetrator escaped in a red car. She immediately phones the police on her mobile phone and dictates the car's registration number to PC Plod. PC Plod writes down the number in his notebook but before he can read the number back to her, the phone goes dead. Tanya also writes the number of the car down in her diary. At the scene of the accident, PC Plod finds a cigarette lighter with the initials RS engraved on it. The car is traced to Richard Smith who denies any involvement in the burglary and pleads not guilty. He alleges that the car was lent to Michelle and that Michelle had told her mother, Gertrude, that she had carried out the burglary alone. Michelle has left the country but left a video recording saying that Richard forced her to commit the burglary. Michelle has been seeing Dr Wong, a psychiatrist, who diagnosed Michelle as suffering from a form of mental disorder. One of the effects of the mental disorder is that the sufferer is unable to distinguish between fact and fantasy.

Whilst testifying in court, Tanya is unable to remember the registration number of the car and the prosecution wishes to allow her to refresh her memory from either PC Plod's notebook or her own diary.

Advise on the use of PC Plod's notebook, Tanya's diary, and the admissibility of Gertrude's testimony of her conversation with Michelle, the video recording made by Michelle and Dr Wong's testimony.

Commentary

This question requires the student to consider a number of different evidential issues. The first part requires a discussion on whether a witness can refresh his or her memory from a number of possible sources. There is also a need to consider whether this infringes the rule against hearsay. The topic of hearsay will also need to be considered in the context of the admissibility of Gertrude's testimony of her conversation with Michelle and whether it falls under any of the exceptions to the hearsay rule. The other issue relates to the admissibility of the video recording made by Michelle. It will be necessary to consider whether this is a piece of real evidence or whether it is a hearsay document. If it is the latter, the admissibility of the document under s. 23 of the Criminal Justice Act 1988 will have to be discussed. Finally, a discussion of the admissibility of expert opinion evidence will be necessary in relation to Dr Wong's testimony.

Suggested Answer

The first issue relates to the admissibility of Tanya's statement to the police. It is clear that whilst testifying in court, Tanya is unable to remember the registration number and it is therefore necessary for Tanya to be able to refresh her memory by using PC Plod's notebook or her own diary. Tanya will not be permitted to use the notebook to refresh her memory because one of the conditions for the use of such documents to refresh a witness's memory is not satisfied: *R* v *Mills* [1962] 1 WLR 1152, i.e., that the document was supervised by or read back to the witness: *R* v *Kelsey* (1981) 74 Cr App R 213. Further, the notebook itself is not admissible in evidence as it infringes the hearsay rule. This is because the notebook will be an out of court statement which is to be introduced for the purposes of proving the truth of the facts stated therein, as defined by the House of Lords in *R* v *Sharp* [1988] 1 WLR 7. In *Jones* v *Metcalfe* [1967] 1 WLR 1286, the Divisional Court refused to allow a police officer's testimony regarding the registration number of a lorry which had been told to him by an eyewitness. This was because the statement was hearsay and since the police officer had failed to read the number back to and have it verified by the witness, it could not also be used to refresh the eyewitness's memory.

It may be possible for Tanya to use her diary to refresh her memory provided the relevant conditions are satisfied. First, the document must have been made contemporaneously with the occurrence of the events about which the witness is testifying. The entry in the diary should thus have been made at the first practicable opportunity at a time when the events were still fresh in Tanya's mind. Ultimately, this is a question of fact in each case: *R* v *Langton* (1876) 2 QBD 296. In *R* v *Woodcock* [1963] Crim L R 273, a gap of 27 days between the events in issue and the making of the statement was too long. However, in *R* v *Fotheringham* [1975] Crim LR 710, a delay of 22 days was permitted. In this case, it is not clear seeing the car registration number and Tanya made a note of it in her diary. The facts seem to suggest that she did so after the telephone call to the police. This is ultimately a question of fact to be determined by asking Tanya about this.

Secondly, the diary should be handed to the defence counsel or the court so that it may be inspected and the witness cross examined on its contents. The defence counsel can request that the jury be shown the notebook if it is necessary for the determination of an issue: *R* v *Bass* [1953] 1 QB 680. Finally, the document should be the original. However, if the original has been lost, it seems that a verified or accurate copy can be used. (There is also a fourth condition, namely that the document was supervised by or read back to the witness, but that does not apply here as the entry was made by Tanya herself.)

On the facts of this case, the court will have to decide whether the entry in the diary was made sufficiently contemporaneously with the events in order for it to be within the rule. If she is allowed to refresh her memory by referring to the diary in court, the defence counsel may inspect the diary and cross examine her on the contents. Where the defence cross examines Tanya on parts which were not used to refresh her memory, then the whole diary may be put into evidence by the prosecution. However, it should be noted that the diary is only evidence of the consistency or inconsistency of Tanya's testimony and is not evidence of the facts stated therein: *R* v *Virgo* (1978) 67 Cr App R 323.

With respect to the finding of the cigarette lighter, it is submitted that this is a piece of real evidence which should be admitted into evidence for the jury to draw their own inferences. The difficulty is whether this may be inadmissible because of hearsay. It is unclear whether the identifying marks, names or initials on the item make any statement as to identity. In *R* v *Rice* [1963] 1 QB 857, the Court of Criminal Appeal allowed into evidence an airline ticket bearing the accused's name. The court rejected an argument that the airline ticket should not be admitted because it was hearsay. It was of the view that the ticket was admissible as relevant albeit circumstantial evidence to show that a person with the name of the accused had flown at the time and date stipulated on the air ticket. If *Rice* is correct then the cigarette lighter would be admissible provided that the court can be convinced that it was relevant to the facts in issue. This is supported by *R* v *Lydon* (1986) 85 Cr App R 221 where a piece of paper bearing the accused's first name, found near a gun which had been used in a robbery, was held to be admissible evidence to link the accused to the gun. Presumably, if the lighter had the appearance of just being lost, then there is a strong argument for its admission into evidence. However, if it appears that the lighter had been lost some time ago, then it is unlikely to be admitted because it may be irrelevant. The argument is that it could have been lost at the same place as the scene of the burglary sometime prior to the commission of the offence.

The next issue concerns the testimony of Gertrude as regards Michelle's conversation with her. It is likely that Gertrude will be called as a defence witness in that her evidence of what Michelle says would tend to exonerate Richard. However, her testimony may infringe the rule against hearsay: *R* v *Sharp* [1988] 1 WLR 7. This is because the purpose of adducing the evidence is to prove the truth of the facts stated therein. Although the evidence may assist the accused and may tend to exonerate him, it is inadmissible if it is hearsay and does not come within one of the exceptions to that rule. The courts have made it clear that hearsay evidence is inadmissible even though it may help the defence's case: *R* v *Turner* (1975) 61 Cr App R 67 and *Sparks* v *R* [1964] AC 964. As stated earlier, the evidence would be admissible if, however, it fell within one of the exceptions to the hearsay rule. One possibility would be to argue that it is a res gestae statement. In order for such statements to be admitted into evidence, the statement has to be made sufficiently contemporaneously with the event in question as to exclude the possibility of concoction or fabrication: *Ratten* v *R* [1972] AC 378 and *R* v *Andrews* [1987] AC 281. On the facts of the case, it is unclear when the statement was made by Michelle to her mother. If the statement was not sufficiently spontaneous as to rule out the possibility of concoction or fabrication, the statement would probably be inadmissible as a res gestae statement.

Although it may be possible to argue that the statement may be admitted to establish Michelle's state of mind and emotion, in which event it would not infringe the rule against hearsay, this is unlikely to succeed because her state of mind and emotion is not relevant here. This is similar to the facts of *R* v *Blastland* [1986] AC 41, where the House of Lords decided that what a third party said to a number of individuals, which, if true, would have exonerated the accused, was ruled inadmissible because first it was hearsay and secondly as evidence of the state of mind and emotion of the third which was irrelevant to the facts in issue.

As regards the video recording made by Michelle, the difficulty is whether the video recording is likely to be excluded because it is a hearsay statement made by a person out of court. Generally, it has been accepted by the courts that visual and audio recordings are regarded as documents for some purposes and are therefore admissible in their own right as real evidence. In *The Statue of Liberty*

[1968] 1 WLR 739, a film containing radar echoes was admitted into evidence on the basis that the film was equivalent to a photograph or series of photographs from which the court would be able to obtain the relevant information, notwithstanding that it is at least arguable that such evidence was hearsay. This case has been followed in a number of later decisions: *R* v *Minors* [1989] 1 WLR 441 and *Castle* v *Cross* [1984] 1 WLR 1372. Thus it may be possible that the court will allow the prosecution to adduce the video recording into evidence on the basis that it is a piece of real evidence. In the event that the recording is admissible into evidence, the court has to be satisfied that the evidence is relevant and is authentic.

The difficulty is that the court may rule that the recording is inadmissible on the basis that it is a hearsay statement and that unless it falls within the exceptions, it would not be admissible. It could be argued that the video recording is a document and could therefore be admissible under s. 23 of the Criminal Justice Act 1988. It would appear that in general the requirements of the section appear to be satisfied and provided the prosecution can satisfy the court that all reasonable steps have been taken to trace Michelle, the recording could be admissible under this statutory exception to the hearsay rule. It should be noted that a video recording is regarded as a document for the purposes of s. 23: para. 5 of sch. 2 of the Criminal Justice Act 1988.

With regards to the evidence of Dr Wong, it may be possible that his evidence is admissible on the basis that it relates to a matter for which the judge or jury may require assistance. The weight to be given to such evidence is a matter for the jury. It is apparent that this type of evidence is admissible because the jury would not be able to draw the appropriate inferences and form proper opinions from the facts requiring expert opinion: *Buckley* v *Rice Thomas* (1554) Plowd 118. Before an expert witness can give opinion evidence relating to any particular issue, it is for the judge to decide whether that particular witness is an expert. It is not essential that in all cases, the expert possess formal qualifications: *R* v *Silverlock* [1894] 2 QB 766.

However, expert opinion evidence is not admissible per se in all criminal trials. Where the issue is one on which the jury is able to decide and does not require the assistance of experts, no opinion evidence from experts is admissible. The restriction on the admissibility of expert evidence on matters for which the jury requires no assistance includes a restriction on expert evidence on the credibility of a witness or the accused save in exceptional circumstances: *Lowery* v *R* [1974] AC 85. Although, in *Lowery*, such evidence was admitted. The Court of Appeal in *R* v *Turner* [1975] QB 834 regarded this decision as applying only to the specific facts of the case rather than establishing any general principle. This approach appears to be correct in the light of *R* v *Rimmer* [1983] Crim LR 250, where the trial judge refused to allow the evidence of an expert on the basis that this related only to the credibility of the accused. On the facts of the present case, it could be argued that Dr Wong's evidence is relevant and admissible because it relates to an issue with which the jury may need assistance, namely Michelle's mental disorder and the effect of such an illness. The question is whether the latter falls 'within the limits of normality' referred to in *Turner* (at p. 841).

QUESTION 4

Fred is charged with the rape of Amanda, aged 18, who had been his colleague at work. They had gone out together occasionally. Fred's counsel wishes to cross examine Amanda on the basis that she had made the allegation out of malice because Fred had refused her sexual advances when they went out together. It is also alleged that Amanda had sex with someone else at the time the rape allegedly took place.

Fred wishes to give evidence on his own behalf and will say that he was in Scotland at the time. There is, however, evidence from Fred's neighbour, Jeannie, that she recalls seeing him around on the day in question.

Paul, a prosecution witness will give evidence that when he arrived at Amanda's place, a short while after the rape was alleged to have taken place, he saw someone rush out of the door. As it was already dark at the time, Paul only managed to see his face when he ran past a street light outside Amanda's house. He later identified Fred as the man at an identification parade held a week later.

Fred has a previous conviction for sexual assault on a female co-worker, five years ago.

Discuss the evidential issues.

Commentary

This is a typical evidence examination question consisting of a mixture of several different topics in one question. The issues here include the questions that can be asked in cross examination and whether if a denial is made, evidence in rebuttal is admissible. It is also necessary to consider the effect of the accused's previous conviction, i.e., whether the prosecution can introduce that into evidence either under s. 1(f)(ii) of the Criminal Evidence Act 1898 or as similar fact evidence. There is the further problem of weak identification evidence which will necessitate the giving of the *Turnbull* direction. Further, there is the issue of the falsity of the alibi. It is also important to note that a corroboration warning is no longer required although this is a sexual case.

Suggested Answer

There are a number of evidential issues to be considered here and it may be simplest just to take each one of them in turn. The first issue relates to whether Fred's counsel can cross examine Amanda on the basis that she made the allegation out of malice because Fred had previously spurned her advances. It is clear that Fred's counsel can ask the question but that if she denies it, the general rule is that since this is a collateral issue, her answer would be final: *R* v *Burke* (1858) 8 Cox CC 44. Fred's counsel can continue to cross examine her about the matter but is not allowed to bring in evidence to contradict her. However, there are exceptions to the general rule and the exception that may apply here is that of bias. In *R* v *Shaw* (1888) 16 Cox CC 503, the defence was allowed to call evidence in rebuttal of a witness's denial that he had a grudge against the accused. Thus, it is likely that in this instance, if Amanda was to deny that she made the allegation out of malice, Fred's counsel could not only cross examine her on the matter, but also call evidence to rebut her testimony on that issue.

The next evidential issue is whether Amanda can be cross examined on the basis that at the time the offence was alleged to have taken place, she was having sex with another person. As a general rule, the victim's sexual relationships with other people are generally not relevant to consent, but only to credibility. As such, whilst questions may be asked of her previous sexual relationships, her answers are final and the defence cannot call evidence to rebut her denial: *R* v *Holmes* (1871) LR 1 CCR 334. The ability of the defence to ask the victim questions of her sexual history is now restricted by s. 2 of the Sexual Offences (Amendment) Act 1976. However, in this case, the question goes not just to credibility but to the issue. As the allegation is that she was having sex with someone else at the time of the rape, if the allegation is true, then the rape cannot have taken place, which is an issue in the case and not just a collateral issue: *R* v *Funderburk* [1990] 1 WLR 587. Thus it is likely that Fred's counsel will be allowed to cross examine her on the matter and adduce evidence in rebuttal if Amanda denies the allegation.

As to Fred's alibi that he was in Scotland at the time of the offence, the difficulty is that there is evidence to prove that the alibi was false. If the prosecution was to introduce the evidence of Fred's alibi, whether Fred testifies or not, the question is whether that would infringe the rule against hearsay. If Fred did make a statement to the police that he was in Scotland at the time, then although in theory this could be a hearsay statement (*R* v *Sharp* [1988] 1 All ER 65), in reality it would not be. The reason is that the prosecution would not be seeking to establish the truth of what was stated but the falsity of it. In *Khan* v *R* [1967] 1 AC 454 statements made by two accused were allowed into evidence, not to prove the truth of the contents of the statements but the falsity which showed the accused's guilty state of mind. As such, on the facts of the present case, it is likely that the prosecution will be able to adduce this statement to prove the falsity of it.

A further issue relates to the identification of Fred by Paul. In *R* v *Turnbull* [1977] QB 224, the Court of Appeal laid down guidelines for the treatment of identification evidence where the case depends wholly or substantially on the correctness of the identification. The guidelines state, inter alia, that the judge should warn the jury of the special need for caution, before convicting the accused in reliance on the correctness of the identification evidence. The judge should draw the jury's attention to the possibility that an error was made and should invite them to examine closely the circumstances in which the observation took place. It was made clear in *R* v *Oakwell* [1978] 1 WLR 32, that the *Turnbull* guidelines are not to be interpreted inflexibly. Thus in this case, the judge will have to warn the jury that the identification evidence may be weak in that it was dark that night and Paul only had a quick glimpse of Fred's face whilst the latter was passing a street light. These factors should be drawn to the jury's attention. The judge will have to be satisfied that in the event that the identification evidence is weak, there must be other evidence to support the correctness of the identification. This will be for the judge to decide looking at all the evidence available. Furthermore, the identification parade should have been held in accordance with Code D issued under PACE 1984. If not, evidence may be excluded under s. 78 of that Act.

There is also the problem with Fred's previous conviction for sexual assault on a female co-worker five years ago. The general rule here is that the accused's previous conviction is inadmissible in evidence. The prosecution is not entitled to ask the accused any questions tending to show that he has committed or been convicted or charged with any offence other than the one with which he is being tried: s. 1(f) of the Criminal Evidence Act 1898. Such questions can be asked if he 'loses his shield' by giving evidence of his own good character, or if he or his counsel had cast imputations on the character of the witnesses or the prosecution. On the facts of the present case, there is a danger that the accused may have lost his shield and, if he is called as a witness, be open to cross examination as to whether he has a previous conviction for sexual assault. This is on the basis that his counsel's allegation of bias against Amanda is capable of amounting to an imputation against her character: *Selvey* v *DPP* [1970] AC 304 and *R* v *Bishop* [1975] QB 274. However, he will only have to disclose his previous conviction if he chooses to give evidence. If he does not give evidence, his previous conviction for sexual assault will only be admissible if it is regarded as similar fact evidence. The test as to whether such evidence is admissible is that where identification is in issue, the previous conviction or conduct must be strikingly similar to the offence with which the accused is being tried and the probative value outweighs its prejudicial effect: *DPP* v *P* [1991] 2 AC 447. In identity cases, as is the case here, the court will look for some special feature or signature, as the Court of Appeal held in *R* v *Johnson* [1995] Crim LR 53. As was held by the House of Lords in *DPP* v *Boardman* [1975] AC 421, however, such cases will be rare and there is no special category for sexual offences. Thus, unless the previous conviction is strikingly similar, the previous conviction will not be admissible into evidence.

If Fred chooses not to give evidence, it should be borne in mind that s. 35 of the Criminal Justice and Public Order Act 1994 allows the court or the jury to draw such inferences as appear proper from the accused's failure to give evidence without good cause. Thus there is a risk that the jury may draw adverse inferences from his failure to give evidence in court.

Finally, it should be noted that by virtue of s. 32 (1) of the 1994 Act, there is no longer any necessity for the judge to give the jury a corroboration warning in a case involving a sexual offence.

QUESTION 5

Jeremy, Harold and Christine are on trial for conspiracy to commit arson at a primary school. At the investigation stage they all have the same solicitor, Good & Co. Before the trial Christine changes solicitor. Jeremy pleads guilty and gives evidence for the prosecution. Christine's counsel has sought leave to produce a statement that Jeremy had made to Good & Co. which is inconsistent with evidence he gives in court and which would help Christine's defence. Christine was arrested after a tracker dog picked up her scent and traced her to a nearby park. Harold had made a confession of his responsibility for the arson in a statement to the police in which he said that Christine was not involved in setting fire to the school. Harold's confession is, however, excluded by the trial judge beforehand in a voir dire under s. 78 PACE 1984. At the trial, in giving evidence, Harold claims that he had seen Christine with a can of petrol near the school on the night of the arson. Christine's counsel wishes to question him on his statement to the police.

Advise on the admissibility of Jeremy's statement with Good & Co., the evidence of the tracker dog, and whether Christine's counsel is likely to be able to question Harold on his pre trial-statement.

Commentary

You will need to show first, an awareness of recent case law dealing with legal professional privilege when it appears to conflict with the interests of a defendant. Secondly, you will need to show that you understand how the courts deal with evidence from dogs and thirdly, an appreciation of the tricky situation arising when a defendant wishes to cross examine a co-defendant on a confession which has already been ruled inadmissible as part of the prosecution's case.

Suggested Answer

There is no general privilege attached to confidential statements made between professional people and their clients. However, the major exception to this is legal professional privilege, which covers certain types of correspondence between a lawyer and his or her client and certain communications between a lawyer and/or client and third parties. The privilege belongs to the client who can insist on non-disclosure by the lawyer or third party in question. The scope of the privilege is given in s. 10 of the Police and Criminal Evidence Act 1984 (PACE). This section, however, does not regulate its use in general but sets limits on police powers to search for and seize evidence. Jeremy can thus claim legal professional privilege for his statement to Good & Co. He may waive this if he wishes. However, if he fails to it will be impossible for Christine to challenge it successfully in the light of a recent House of Lords ruling. Christine might reasonably argue that a refusal to disclose harms her defence and in the case of *R* v *Ataou* [1988] 2 WLR 1147, that claim was heard sympathetically by the Court of Appeal. However, in *R* v *Derby Magistrates' Court, ex p B* [1995] 3 WLR 681, the House of Lords overruled *Ataou* and the earlier case of *R* v *Barton* [1972] 2 All ER 321. The House held that '. . . no exception should be allowed to the absolute nature of legal professional privilege once established'. The House also held that the privilege is the same whether it is sought by the prosecution or the defence and the 'refusal of the client to waive his privilege, for whatever reason, or for no reason, cannot be questioned or investigated by the court'. The court considered that 'if a balancing exercise was ever required in the case of legal professional privilege it was performed once and for all in the 16th century.' In that case a witness, B, who had previously been acquitted of a murder, could not be compelled to produce a confession made in the presence of his solicitor in a subsequent trial of his stepfather for the same offence. Christine is unlikely to succeed in obtaining the document.

The evidence obtained by the tracker dog is clearly relevant to increase the likelihood of Christine's connection with the arson. Discussing a case on very similar facts, Cross and Tapper (1995, p. 43) called such evidence '... a useful piece of retrospectant circumstantial evidence'. In *R* v *Pieterson and Holloway, The Times*, 11 November 1994, the Court of Appeal held that such evidence was not hearsay but in any such case an adequate foundation should be laid of the training, skills, and habits of the particular dog and its handler. It seems also that the person who gives the evidence should not express an opinion about what the dog was thinking at the material time. Finally the jury should be directed to the special need for care, given that the dog cannot be cross examined!

Evidence of Harold's confession is clearly relevant to the trial since it conflicts with his evidence in court. He had previously absolved Christine but now he is implicating her. Christine's counsel is advised to apply to present Harold's confession not as to the truth of its contents but in order to demonstrate the inconsistency of Harold's testimony and thus to undermine his credibility. In *R* v *Rowson* [1986] QB 174 the Court of Appeal held that a trial judge did not have a discretion to prevent counsel for a co-accused from cross examining the maker of an inadmissible confession. Such questioning is for the purpose of showing that the witness has made a previous inconsistent statement and thus undermining his credibility. The judge must make it clear to the jury that any evidence of the confession is not evidence of guilt. The only pre-condition is that the evidence be relevant, as the Privy Council held in *Lui-Mei Lin* v *R* (1989) 88 Cr App R 296. The right to cross examine is thus unfettered. An alternative, and perhaps better approach, however would be an application to sever the indictment. This is illustrated by *R* v *O'Boyle* (1991) 92 Cr App R 202, where a joint trial would be harmful to the defendant subject to such cross examination whereas a separate trial would not harm the co-defendant and the prosecution.

QUESTION 6

Hilda is charged with criminal damage. The prosecution case is that she painted slogans on the wall of a local factory farm which she considered was treating chickens cruelly. There had been a spate of such desecrations and police had set up watch in a neighbouring house and identified Hilda as the offender. Hilda suspects that the surveillance took place and wishes to cross examine the prosecution witness about the quality of his observation because she contests the identification. The police have searched Hilda's lodgings with a search warrant and find pots of paint identical to the colours used on the wall slogans. The police wish to call Norman, Hilda's estranged husband, as a witness. He still lives in the same house as her and had made a statement to the police that Hilda came in very late on the night in question and her hands were covered with paint. He is called at the trial for the prosecution but refuses to give any evidence. There is medical evidence to the effect that Hilda is in any case unfit to stand trial because she suffers from a mental instability and the defence are considering whether to plead this.

Advise on evidence.

Commentary

A pot-pourri of issues which means that you must have the law relating to them at your finger tips. Taking the issues in order:

Can the police be compelled to disclose the identity of the surveillance? This turns on the question of public interest immunity and the protection of informers, including how far this stretches to surveillance sites.
Is evidence arising from the search admissible? Consider whether the evidence is relevant.
Is Norman a compellable witness? What is the status of estranged spouses? Consider s. 80 PACE and appropriate case law.
If Norman does not appear as a witness, may his evidence be presented in any other form, for example under the hearsay exceptions of the Criminal Justice Act 1988, ss. 23 and 24?
What is the burden and standard of proof on the issue of Hilda's competence to testify?

Suggested Answer

The police may wish to keep the identity of the house they are using secret, either because the people who allowed them to use it have been promised confidentiality or in order not to deter other possible assistance. However, the identity of the premises may be important to Hilda's defence so she can cross examine the police witness on the quality of the identification evidence. The rule in *Marks* v *Beyfus* (1890) 25 QBD 494, allows the identity of informers to be protected as a matter of public policy. In *R* v *Rankine* [1986] QBD 861 this rule was held to apply also to the identity of persons who have allowed their property to be used as an observation post. However, if the owners do not wish to maintain secrecy, there would be no objection to identifying the premises. In any case, the prosecution must lay down a basis for the anonymity if it is required. In *R* v *Johnson* [1988] 1 WLR 1377, the Court of Appeal said it was necessary for the prosecution to satisfy the court that there was a particular need for the observation post and for anonymity before suppression would be accepted. In the event the identity in that case was not revealed. In *R* v *Brown*, *R* v *Daley* (1987) 87 Cr App Rep 52, the Court of Appeal held that the extension of the exclusionary rule to surveillance sites was intended to protect the owner or occupier, not the post *simpliciter*. Here details of an unmarked police car ought to have been revealed. It is necessary then to see whether on the facts the address is relevant information and to establish the attitude of the occupier. In view of these authorities it may be possible for Hilda to have discovery of the identity of the premises.

It is arguable that the evidence of the paint is relevant if it goes to support other identification evidence as it does here. In *R* v *Reading* [1966] 1 WLR 836 the court held that if otherwise innocent seeming articles, in that case walkie-talkie radios and imitation police uniforms, could be used for criminal purposes it is not necessary that any particular occasion on which they were used be identified. It thus appears sufficient that there is identification evidence linking Hilda to the offence to make the submission of the paint as real evidence relevant in the case.

It is assumed that Norman is a competent witness. Unless he is of defective intellect he is likely to be competent. Under the Police and Criminal Evidence Act 1984 (PACE), s. 80(5), former spouses are treated as any other witnesses. However, that only applies if the marriage has been ended by divorce or if it was voidable and has been annulled. The common law position remains that a marriage is treated as subsisting even if there has been a judicial separation, as the court held in *Moss* v *Moss* [1963] 2 QBD 799. Thus Norman is a competent witness for the prosecution by virtue of s. 80(1)(a) PACE. He is not, however, compellable since the offence in question does not fall within the categories of s. 80 (3) PACE, that is an offence that involves a violent or sexual attack on the spouse or a person under 16 years.

If he persists in refusing to testify the prosecution may need to consider whether the evidence can be adduced in any other way. His statement to the police is clearly hearsay in that the purpose of adducing it is to suggest it is true. It is arguably endorsed by him and therefore would fulfill the requirement of firsthand hearsay in s. 23 of the Criminal Justice Act 1988. However, there is difficulty in adducing it since on the facts there does not appear to be any reason for not calling him as a witness. The lack of one of the acceptable reasons listed in s. 23(2) is likely to be fatal to admissibility. Can the statement be adduced under s. 24 which admits statements received and created in the course of trade, business or profession? The Court of Apppeal held in *R* v *McGillivray* (1992) 97 Cr App R 232 that s. 23 was the appropriate section for police statements, so s. 24 is unlikely to be held to be available here. In any case, since the document was prepared for criminal proceedings, the same problem arises of giving a reason for non-appearance of the witness. It is unlikely that the additional reason that the witness could not reasonably be expected to remember the matters dealt with will apply. In fact however, the prosecution will find it impossible to evade the protection a statute affords to witnesses by using a statutory exception to the rule against hearsay. Even if the requirements of the statute were fulfilled, the court's discretion would surely militate against admissibility under s. 26. One final point on this is that the prosecution cannot use Hilda's failure to call Norman as the occasion of an adverse comment, by virtue of s. 80(8) PACE.

With regard to the possible plea of unfitness to plead, if the prosecution disagree with the contention raised by the defence, then the defence has the legal burden of proof to the civil standard, as held by the Court of Criminal Appeal in *R* v *Podola* [1960] 1 QB 325.

Selected Bibliography

Atiyah, P S, 'Res Ipsa Loquitur in England and Australia' (1972) Modern Law Review 337.

Bennion, F, 'Statutory Exemptions: A Third Knot in the Golden Thread?' (1988) Crim LR 31.

Birch, D, 'Children's Evidence' (1992) Crim LR 262.

Birch, D, 'Hunting the Snark: The Elusive Statutory Exception' (1988) Crim LR 221.

Bronitt, S, Baskerville Revisited: The Definition of Corroboration' (1991) Crim LR 31.

Choo, A and Mellors M, 'Undercover Police Operations and What the Suspect Said (or Didn't Say)' (1995) 2 Web JCLI .

Cross & Tapper on Evidence, 8th edn (London: Butterworths, 1995).

Enright, S, 'Crime Brief' (1995) NLJ 854.

Galligan, D J, 'The Right to Silence Reconsidered' (1988) Current Legal Problems 69.

Heydon, J, *Evidence Cases and Materials*, 3rd edn (London: Butterworths, 1991).

Keane, A, *The Modern Law of Evidence*, 3rd edn (London: Butterworths, 1994).

McEwan, J, *Evidence and the Adversarial Process* (Oxford: Blackwell, 1992).

Mirfield, P, 'An Ungrateful Reply' (1988) Crim LR 233.

Mirfield, P, 'The Legacy of Hunt' (1988) Crim LR 19.

Munday, R C J, 'A Sample of Lawmaking' (1995) *NLJ* 855, 895.

Munday, RCJ, 'Reflections on the Criminal Evidence Act 1898' (1985) *Cambridge LJ* 62.

Murphy, P, *Evidence*, 5th edn (London: Blackstone, 1995).

Rees, E (1994) *Counsel*, Nov/Dec 20.

Robertson, G, 'Entrapment Evidence: Manna from Heaven or Fruit of the Poisoned Tree' (1993) Crim LR 805.

Seabrooke, S, 'Closing the Credibility Gap: A new approach to s.1(f)(ii) of the Criminal Evidence Act 1898 (1987) Crim LR 238.

Sharpe, S 'Covert Police Operations and Discretionary Exclusion of Evidence' (1994) Crim LR 793.

Smith, J C 'Sections 23 and 24 of the Criminal Justice Act 1988. Some Problems' (1994) Crim LR.

Stern, Alex 'After Hunt: the Burden of Proof, Risk of Non-Persuasion and Judicial Pragmatism' (1991) MLR 570..

Tain, P, 'Non-police Station Interviews' (1995) Sol J 299.

Tapper, C., 'The Erosion of *Boardman* v *DPP*' (1995) NLJ 1223.

Temkin, J, 'Sexual History Evidence — The Ravishment of Section 2' (1993) Crim LR 3.

Tribe, L., Triangulating Hearsay (1974) Harvard Law Review, 957.

Zander, M. 'Abolition of the Right to Silence 1972-1994' in Morgan, D and Stephenson, G '*Suspicion and Silence. The Right to Silence in Criminal Investigations*' (London: Blackstone Press, 1994).

Zuckerman, A A S in Morgan and Stephenson eds (sup cit).

Zuckerman, *The Principles of Criminal Evidence* (Oxford: Clarendon Press, 1989).

Index